IRISH WILD PLANTS
MYTHS, LEGENDS & FOLKLORE

I ndil-chuimhne ar Niamh McGrath,
Anam spreagúil agus fíorchara

IRISH WILD PLANTS

MYTHS, LEGENDS & FOLKLORE

Niall Mac Coitir

Original watercolours by
Grania Langrishe

The Collins Press

FIRST PUBLISHED 2006 BY
The Collins Press
West Link Park
Doughcloyne
Wilton
Cork

British Library Cataloguing in Publication Data
MacCoitir, Niall
    Irish wild plants: myths, legends and folklore
    1. Endemic plants – Ireland 2. Plants – Ireland – Folklore
    3. Plants – Ireland – Mythology
    I. Title II. Langrishe, Grania
    398.2'6'09415

    ISBN-10: 190517201X
    ISBN-13: 978-1905172016

Printed in Malta

Cover design by Artmark

This publication has received support from the Heritage Council
under the 2006 Publications Grant Scheme.

Black and white line drawings are taken from *Sowerby's English Botany, Volumes 1
and 2*, published by George Bell & Sons, London in 1877, except sea wrack from *An
Introduction to the Study of Seaweeds*, published by George Murray, London, 1895,
and fungi from *Tableau des Pincipaux Champignons* (Paris, no date).

Contents

Minor Plants in Folklore

Introduction

A ny book about plants is faced with hard choices about what to include, or more importantly, what to exclude. In this case, the trees and shrubs already dealt with in *Irish Trees* have naturally been excluded. The decision has also been made to exclude cultivated plants, and to concentrate purely on native or naturalised wild plants. This book is not a herbal, and the reader will look in vain for herbs like parsley or rosemary. However, many herbs like mint or thyme that have wild varieties are included. This still leaves a huge number of plants to consider. As the book is about folklore, the only basis for including a plant is therefore whether or not it has any folklore. Thus, well-known and beautiful flowers like spring gentian or rockrose are not included because there is no folklore surrounding them. On the other hand, seaweed and fungi are included, along with just about all our common weeds; because like them or loathe them, they all have stories to tell. Indeed, one of the aims of this book is to encourage the reader to look anew at plants they might have dismissed before as worthless, and if it achieves that to any degree it can be considered a success.

In addition, this book is not a flora. The flowers and plants it contains are not arranged botanically, but by season and appearance. In other words, plants are placed in a seasonal order, which depends on the time of year they come to prominence in folklore. For example, shamrock comes near the beginning because it is linked to early spring through St Patrick's Day, and it is followed by primrose which is linked to both Easter and May time. Plants have also been grouped into two categories of 'major' and 'minor' plants in terms of folklore, in order to provide some focus for the reader. This differentiation is, of course, only the author's and other authors would no doubt produce a different list. Each plant description also includes a category called 'Similar Plants'. Some are botanically related, but others are included because of their similar appearance, or some other factor. So, for example, rosebay willowherb is mentioned as a similar plant to foxglove because of their physical resemblance. This may raise eyebrows among botanists, but it seems the most appropriate order for a book about folklore. It harks back to a time when plants were classified according to when they appeared in the fields and woods, what they looked like, their scent and taste, and what they were used for. None of this is to deny the importance of botany, of course, and botanical information will be included where appropriate.

The wild plants and herbs of Ireland have been bound up in our culture and folklore from the earliest times. It is only natural that an overwhelmingly rural society should be familiar with our native flora, and that a wealth of stories and local knowledge should gather around them. Wild plants appear in the ancient Irish Brehon Laws, and in the early nature poetry for which Ireland is rightly famous. Herbal medicine was important too in ancient Ireland. For instance, it was believed that there were 365 parts of the body, and that a different wild herb existed to cure the ills of each part. The folklore of our native plants has many different facets too. It varies from countless folk cures and remedies to the rich variety of local plant names, lucky plants like four-leaved shamrock and fern seeds, to love charms, and even children's games. The pages that follow should leave no doubt that until modern times, people's lives were influenced and dependant on the wild plants around them, in a way that we can barely imagine today.

For a small island, Ireland contains a wealth of different landscapes, from forest to meadow; moorland and bog to hedgerow; seashore to lakeside fen. Many different habitats are found close together in small pockets. Indeed, it is not the number of species that makes the flora of Ireland so special, (as we are relatively species poor compared to the continent) but the unique distribution of species. This means that preserving the diversity of our landscape is particularly important, whether it is by keeping old hedgerows or not draining that damp field down by the river. In that context, an all out move to intensive farming would be especially harmful, and it is heartening to see that that has been recognised by government. Many farmers have signed up to the Rural Environmental

Protection Scheme, co-funded by the European Union and the State, which pays farmers to manage their land in a sustainable way, preserving the old walls, hedgerows and meadows that shelter so many of our native plants. Hopefully this and similar measures will help to preserve our flora into the future.

However, making room for nature is not just a matter for farmers. It is also relevant to those with even a small patch of garden. It is also not just about saving pretty flowers, but about leaving room in odd corners for things to literally 'go to seed'. It should always be remembered that it is not only beautiful flowers that are of interest and worth preserving, but also those plants commonly regarded as weeds, if not outright pests. Nettles, for example, are host to the caterpillars of some of our loveliest butterflies, while teasels and thistles provide food for goldfinches and other birds. Surely there is room in all but the most urban areas for a patch of so-called waste ground to be turned over to wildlife. Such areas need not be unsightly if they are managed in a proper way.

A word should be said about the herbal cures contained in this book. Most have not been scientifically tested by modern medical standards. It may well be the case that they have no real basis; and indeed some may even be dangerous to health and well being. In other words, the cures are presented purely in terms of folklore, without any recommendation as to their medical value. The reader will try out any of them entirely at his or her own risk!

Aspects of Plant Folklore

There are few aspects of our lives that are not affected by the plants and flowers around us. Plants provide us with food, either directly through the vegetables and herbs that we eat, or indirectly, through the fodder they provide for animals. Plants also provide us with much of our clothing, be it cotton, or linen from flax, or even in earlier times cloth from nettle fibres. Plants have given us thatch to shelter ourselves and brooms to keep our houses clean, and have been the source of many other useful items like dyes and inks, gums and glues. Plants and flowers have also shaped our imaginations, providing us with potent symbols and emblems, and inspiring a wealth of stories and folklore based on their different shapes, colours, tastes and scents. There is no doubt that painters and poets through the ages would have had a hard time finding alternative sources of inspiration without the beauty of flowers and the greenery of landscapes. Most notably of all, of course, plants have provided us with medicine, without which even today a great many ailments would have no cure. Indeed, the study of plants was traditionally called herbalism, and it is in herbalism that we must first look to see how plants have shaped our lives and landscapes from the earliest times until today.

HERBS AND MEDICINE IN IRISH HISTORY
The history of herbalism in Ireland begins in the eighth-century legend of the Battle of Moytirra.[1] The story relates how Dian Cecht, the pagan Irish god of medicine, became aware of his son Miach's superior skill at healing and so killed him in a jealous rage. Out of Miach's grave grew 365 herbs, one for each of his joints and sinews, and these were gathered up by his sister Airmed, who laid them out on her cloak. She began to classify the herbs according to their different virtues, but Dian Cecht saw what she was doing and mixed up the herbs, so that to this day, all their virtues are not known. The idea that there were 365 joints and members of the body was a common

belief in early Ireland. Later during the battle, however, Dian Cecht created the *Tiopra Sláine* or Great Healing Well, by putting every herb known to grow in Ireland into a well located between Moytirra and Lough Arrow. The bodies of all the fighting men killed in the battle were put into the well, and emerged the next day alive and stronger than ever. Medicated or herbal baths are frequently mentioned in Irish tales and were apparently a major feature of healing in early Ireland.

Another example of herbs in legend occurs in the *Táin* or 'Cattle Raid of Cooley', when the warriors and childhood friends Cúchulainn and Ferdia were forced to fight each other in single combat. The fight lasted several days, and at the end of each day the two warriors shared their healing herbs equally between them, so that each might dress their wounds in the same way. This gesture was called *comraind legis* or 'equal division of healing'. In honour of this chivalrous act of generosity, the phrase appears today as the motto on the badge of the Irish Army Medical Corps.[2]

The earliest historical references to herbs in Ireland are to the *lubgort* or enclosed herb garden.[3] In ancient Ireland a prosperous farm often had a *lubgort* attached, in which both vegetables and herbs were planted. However, herb and vegetable cultivation was particularly associated with monasteries, and the *lubgortóir* or gardener was one of the seven offices of the church. All the produce of these gardens was grown to promote well being: medicinal herbs, and nourishing vegetables like *cainenn* and *imus* (probably onion and celery), which are frequently mentioned as a valued part of the diet in early Ireland. One medical law text speaks of the great service of these vegetables in nursing the sick. Another widely used edible plant was Fat Hen (*Chenopodium album*) which was known in Irish as *praiseach fiáin* or 'wild spinach'. Its leaves were extensively eaten in Ireland from pre-Norman times up until spinach proper arrived to replace it. A close relative, Good King Henry (*Chenopodium bonus henricus*) was eaten in a similar way, by boiling its leaves and eating them with butter. It has the Irish name *praiseach bhráthar* or 'monk's spinach', indicating its widespread use in monasteries. Both species still survive in the wild today, centuries after they ceased to be cultivated.

Naturally, having a medicinal herb garden implies having patients who need it, and in early Ireland such hospitals as existed were usually found attached to monasteries and convents.[4] According to legend, the first Irish hospital appeared when St Patrick enrolled St Brigid and her companions to nurse and minister to the ailing. However, the first firm date we have for a hospital is 1220, when a leper hospital was founded in Dublin on what is now Pearse Street. Throughout the Middle Ages most hospitals were leper hospitals maintained by the religious orders, though some general hospitals were also maintained by them.

Traditionally, every Irish chieftain had his own hereditary physician to serve him, and all the Gaelic septs (or clans) had hereditary medical families linked to them.[5] For instance, the O'Lees were the hereditary physicians to the O'Flahertys of west Connaught, the O'Hickeys were physicians to the O'Briens of Thomond, the O'Mearas were physicians to the Butlers of Ormond, and the O'Cassidys served the Maguires of Fermanagh. Many of the Gaelic physicians produced works in Irish and Latin that survive to this day. The most famous of these works is the 'Book of the O'Lees' which appeared in 1443. A striking feature of the manuscript is that the writing is formed into patterns resembling the astrological signs of the Zodiac (astrology was a major part of medieval herbalism). Other important works include the 'Book of the O'Shiels' from 1652 and works produced by the O'Hickeys and the O'Mearas.

The Gaelic physicians were concerned with keeping abreast of the latest medical learning, and so the books they wrote are translations of the leading European medical works of the time. These works were themselves based on Classical Greek and Roman sources like those of Avicenna, Hippocrates, Vesalius and Galen. A favourite text for translation was a medieval work by John of Gaddesden called the *Rosa Anglica*.[6] John of Gaddesden was born about 1280 and studied at Oxford, going on to became the first English court physician. The *Rosa Anglica* aimed to present a complete system of medicine and became a standard medieval text throughout Europe. It makes up the greater part of the 'Book of the O'Lees' and the work by the O'Hickeys. Some of the translations of the *Rosa Anglica* quote more extensively from other works, where the Irish translator was not happy with the text provided by Gaddesden! Another favourite text for translation was by the French physician Bernard of Gordon, whose text, the *Lilium Medicinae* appeared in the fourteenth century.

After the decline of the Gaelic order, Anglo-Irish herbalists like Threkeld and K'eogh came to the fore with works published in the eighteenth century. With Anglo-Irish dominance also came knowledge of the English herbal tradition, in particular the works of the herbalists Gerard (1597) and Culpepper (1669). The foundation of the Dublin College of Physicians in the late seventeenth century, and the start of medical training in Trinity College in the early eighteenth century marked the establishment of modern medicine in Ireland. However, even after modern medicine began to take shape, the works of herbalists like Culpepper were still widely consulted by many seeking their own cures without recourse to doctors.

In Ireland as we have seen, both Gaelic and Anglo-Irish herbalists relied almost entirely on Classical sources for their learning. This situation was true also for Europe down the centuries. European herbalists have copied each other, repeating Classical sources in particular, with the result that the herbal cures of northern Europe have been overshadowed by those of the Mediterranean. Thus northern European plants have been relatively neglected in comparison with their southern counterparts; and the herbal cures of ordinary people have been neglected in favour of the 'official' herbals. It is only in recent times that an interest in the field of 'ethnobotany' has led to any serious attempt to record properly the folk cures and remedies of Britain and Ireland. In Ireland the first attempt was Michael Moloney's *Luibhsheanchus* or 'Irish Ethnobotany' published in 1919. More recently Allen and Hatfield in their 2004 work, *Medicinal Plants in Folk Tradition* have made a comprehensive survey of the folk cures of these islands. A difficulty for the modern collector of folk cures is distinguishing between folk cures that are genuinely 'of the people', and those that have filtered down to a popular level from the herbals and other written sources. It must also be faced that the work of collecting has begun too late, and that many folk cures have simply been lost forever.

Alongside the official practioners of medicine were the unofficial, or 'folk' practioners.[7] The 'Herb Woman' or *Bean na Luibheanna* was a well-known member of every Irish community, and her knowledge of the medicinal properties of plants made her someone both respected and feared. The most famous of these was Biddy Early, who lived in County Clare in the middle of the nineteenth century. According to legend she got her powers from the fairies, but it is most likely that she actually learned her trade from her mother. As was the custom, Biddy Early never accepted payment for her cures (as that could cause the curing power to disappear) but she did accept gifts of food and alcohol. Inevitably, the fame of her alleged unnatural powers brought her into conflict with both Church and State, and she was notoriously tried for witchcraft. Luckily for her, however, she was acquited due to lack of evidence. Biddy Early naturally kept her cures a secret, but one that has been attributed to her was a poultice for treating swollen limbs. The poultice consisted of a mixture of cabbage leaves, nettles, watercress, and beaten eggwhite.

Most folk healers did not achieve the fame of Biddy Early, nor would they have wanted to. The vast majority of them only dealt with people from their locality. Along with their knowledge of herbs, these healers also knew the correct charms and prayers to say as part of the cure. Indeed, it was firmly believed by people that their healing power came as much from the charms or prayers that they uttered as any herbs they might use. Many of the charms were naturally kept secret, but others were common knowledge. For instance, a well-known cure for a severe rash involved saying the following prayer over the affected person: 'What will heal thee from the red, thirsty, shivering disease of the foreigner that kills with poisonous pain? The prayer of Mary to her Son and of Colmcille to God will'.[8] Certain kinds of people were also believed to have special curing powers, like the seventh son of a seventh son, or a son born after his father's death. In Ireland it was also believed that people with particular surnames possessed special powers.[9] For example, the blood of a Cahill could cure shingles, while the blood of a Keogh could cure ringworm. Even today, in some rural areas of Ireland, people believed to 'have the cure' are still visited by many.

At a more basic level, practically every family in rural areas had some knowledge of folk cures for common ailments like coughs and colds, sore eyes and skin complaints. These cures were used regularly and firmly believed to be effective. Some of these cures were harmless enough, like using the milk of dandelions to cure warts. Others we might find strange today. For example, a cure for burns involved smearing on a mixture of chamomile petals, unsalted butter, and fresh goose excrement on the affected area!

PLANTS IN EARLY LAW

Some plants appear in the ancient Irish Laws of Neighbourhood, which categorised trees and bushes in order of their importance.[10] Of most importance were the *Airig Fedo* or 'Nobles of the Wood', tree species like oak or ash. However, the lowest category, the *Losa Fedo* or 'Bushes of the Wood' included the following non-tree species: bracken, bog myrtle, gorse, bramble, heather, broom and gooseberry (or wild rose). Some sources also include rushes and ivy. There were harsh penalties like a fine of one milch cow for the unlawful cutting down of just one tree of the species listed as 'Nobles of the Wood'. For the 'Bushes of the Wood', however, there was no fine for cutting a single plant, but if someone unlawfully cut down a whole field of say, bracken, (an act called *earba* or extirpation) the fine was one dairt (or year-old heifer). Some texts replace the arbutus or strawberry tree with honeysuckle as one of the 'Lower Divisions of the Wood', the next highest category, but this was probably on account of arbutus' rarity, rather than any economic value attached to honeysuckle. The appearance of these plants in the Laws clearly indicates that their various uses as fuel, fodder and food were considered to be of some economic importance in early Ireland.

Medicine and the role of doctors are also regulated in the Brehon Laws, and herbs appear in these Laws too.[11] For example, according to the Laws, a physician's bag should contain various small compartments so that his medicinal herbs would not get mixed up. Special consideration was also given to medicinal herbs under the Laws. It was normally an offence to gather wild fruit and herbs on another person's land without permission. The Laws specified that a fine equal to the value of two and a half milch cows was to be levied on anyone taking wild garlic, seaweed or wild apples

from private land. However, any law-abiding person was allowed
to gather medicinal herbs no matter where they grew, so long as
they were required by an invalid. Similarly, a person engaged in an
errand of mercy such as sending for a physician, or compounding
medicines was exempt from the Law's attentions until his task was
completed. Very few herbs are mentioned by name in the Laws, and
those that are unfortunately cannot be identified. One medical law
text states that three foreign herbs must be sought if a king is
wounded in the face. These are *sraif* for healing the wound, *lungait*
for treating the colour of the wound, and *arcetlium* for the skin. *Sraif*
means sulphur and *arcetium* means orpiment, so it may be that there
was confusion with minerals on the part of the author. Another text
speaks of the cutting of three types of herb as a defence against the
'evil eye'. These are *ríglus*, the 'Royal herb' for the king, *tarblus*, the
'Bull-herb' for lords, and *aithechlus*, the 'Plebian herb' for commoners. Again there is no indication as to what these herbs might be.

Also considered important under the laws were wild plants that
provided food.[12] One text classified all fruit into two categories:
cumra meaning sweet, and *fiadain* meaning wild or bitter. Sweet
fruits included cultivated apples and plums, blackberries, bilberries, hazelnuts and strawberries. Wild or sour fruits included wild
or crab apples, sloes, acorns, haws, rosehips and rowanberries. The
suggestion is that all of these fruits were at least sometimes eaten.
Confirmation of this suggestion was found during the excavation of
an eleventh-century settlement at Winetavern Street in Dublin.
Seeds of rowan, blackerry, wild apple, sloe, rosehip and haw were
all found at the site. Wild garlic was also an important food plant in
ancient Ireland. By law every tenant had to provide a *crimfeis* or
'garlic feast' to his landlord every year before Easter, or else pay a
fine equivalent to one and a half milch cows. The 'feast' consisted of
garlic mixed in with cheese and milk.

Other plants considered of value appear in the laws.[13] As we
have seen, sufficient value was placed on seaweed to make its
removal an offence. This is reflected in the fact that the presence of
a rock which produced a good crop of seaweed was considered by
law to add the value of three cows to the adjoining land. Another
plant mentioned in the laws was woad, which was valued as a plant

because it produced a bright blue dye. This was used for dying clothes, and also for staining and tattooing the body. An eighth-century text dealing with divorce states that as part of the settlement, the woman was entitled to one-third of any woad in containers and a half of any woad which had been dried.

THEMES OF PLANT FOLKLORE

One major theme of plant folklore is the use of plants for magical protection or to provide the user with magical powers. Usually this was based on the ancient and universal idea of sympathetic magic, in other words, that like produces like, and the effect of any power can be produced by imitating it.[14] Or to put it another way, that similar things can be made to act on each other from a distance through a secret sympathy. So, for example, plants with yellow flowers were often believed to have something of the power of the sun, while red flowers had the qualities of blood and fire. Thus the yellow primrose was good at keeping away evil influences at May time, while scarlet pimpernel's blood red flowers were a sure sign that it possessed great strength and power. Similarly, plants that have an attractive scent like mint or yarrow were often used in love charms, which were a frequent magical use for plants. Most of these were based on fortune telling, with the questioner seeking to find out the identity of the person they were going to marry. It was believed that if a girl placed nine leaves of yarrow under her pillow while saying a charm, she would dream of her future husband that night. Some plants could go one step further, however, and were actually believed to have the power to make someone fall in love. For instance, the tubers of early purple orchid were widely supposed to make a powerful love potion, guaranteeing to the maker the devotion of the person who drank it.

By far the most important magical use for plants was for healing remedies and cures.[15] Plants were often believed to cure illness on the basis of sympathetic magic, or perhaps more accurately on the basis that 'fire fights fire'. So the stings of nettles have been used since ancient times as a cure for rheumatism, and the bright red stems of herb robert were used to cure cattle suffering from red water fever. It was also usually believed in folk medicine that herbal cures had to be accompanied by charms and spells to be effective. Many plants had to be plucked with a particular charm or formula of words, or plucked in a particular way. In the west of Ireland it was believed that yarrow had to be gathered with a black-handled knife to protect the gatherer from fairy influences, for example. Plants also had to be plucked at certain times of the year particularly May Eve, and St John's Eve, when the potency of herbs was thought to be greatest. In Ireland it was believed that all herbs pulled on May Eve had great power – for good if they were pulled in the name of the Blessed Trinity, and for evil if they were pulled in Satan's name. Dawn was also thought to be a powerful time of the day to collect herbs, before the dew has dried away. This was because dew was believed to have special powers, and plants that collected lots of dew like lady's mantle shared in these powers.

While the healing properties of some plants may have been based upon sympathetic magic, others, of course, had a basis in fact, for example digitalis in foxglove. Traditional medicine and herbalism was based on a mixture of these two things – the real and imagined properties of plants, without any real effort to distinguish between them or ascertain the facts. The idea of sympathetic magic lasted a long time in herbal medicine because it so often appeared to have a basis in fact. Henbane, for example, not only has an evil smell, it is also a powerful poison, while many aromatic plants have antiseptic qualities. Sometimes indeed it is hard to know which was the cause of the plant being used for cures in the first place. For example, lesser celendine was also known as pilewort because it was used to cure piles. Traditionally it was believed that this was because its knobbly roots resembled haemorrhoids. However, while this is true, it is also the case that an ointment made from the roots has earned medical respect as a excellent remedy for haemorrhoids in its own right.[16]

Ancient herbalists carried the ideas of sympathetic magic further when they linked plants and herbalism to astrology. Plants were said to be ruled by different planets and signs of the zodiac according to their perceived characteristics and healing abilities. There were several ways of determining what planet ruled a particular plant. One idea was that as different planets were believed to rule different parts of the body, if a particular plant cured an ail-ment of that part it meant that it too was ruled by the planet. For example, bilberries were considered good for complaints of the liver. The liver was ruled by Jupiter, so Jupiter ruled bilberry as well. Another idea was that if a plant shared certain characteristics with a planet then it was ruled by it. For instance, if a plant had a hot or peppery taste like hedge mustard, or was acrid like butter-cups, it was believed to be ruled by the fiery planet Mars. On the other hand, plants with soothing or aromatic qualities like lady's mantle or thyme, were usually believed to be ruled by the gentle planet Venus. These ideas formed the basis for much of medieval medicine and are to be found today in Culpeper's herbal which is still popular with many people.

In Europe, herbalism attempted to become more scientific in the sixteenth and seventeenth centuries, when it was organised on a systematic and 'rational' basis as the Doctrine of Signatures.[17] The Doctrine held that plants had characters or 'signatures' which point-ed to the diseases they could cure. It was first put forward by a writer rejoicing under the name Theophrastus Bombast von Hohenheim, better known by his Latin name, Paracelsus. In Britain and Ireland the main proponent was the scholar William Coles, who published a work in 1656 called the *Art of Simpling*. Among other things it stated that the milky juice of lettuce was a sign that it was beneficial in producing plenty of milk in nursing mothers; and the idea that because bearded lichen hung down from trees like hair, it it meant it was very useful in preventing hair loss. The Doctrine of Signatures continued to be mentioned as late as the eighteenth cen-tury, but as time went on it fell out of favour as medicine became more properly scientific. Increasingly, modern medicine was mov-ing away from herbalism and towards the scientific testing of plants to determine their real medicinal value.

Another major theme of plant folklore is the use of plants as badges or emblems.[18] Plants seem to lend themselves to this, perhaps because of their distinctive colours and shapes, and the ease of wearing them as sprigs. The most prominent Celtic examples of this are the Scottish clan plant badges. They originally arose when each clan attached a sprig of their plant onto a staff, spear or bonnet, particularly going into battle.

Thus the McGregor clan has Scots pine as their plant badge, the Robertson clan has bracken, and so on. While providing a distinguishing emblem or mark might be one reason, another more important reason seems to be that they were considered the clan's charmplant, like an amulet or talisman. The system of Scottish clan badges has been formalised, being officially recognised by the Scottish Register of All Arms and Bearings. Nothing as formalised as clan badges ever seems to have existed in Ireland, but there is evidence that sprigs of different plants were used in the same way here, at least for personalised emblems. For example, the Fianna wore sprigs of plants as they were going into battle. Diarmaid Ó Duibhne's emblem was a branch of curly topped yew, while Oscar's was a branch of red berried rowan. As for Conan, his emblem was a briar because 'he was always for quarrels and for trouble'!

It is a natural extension from personal and clan emblems to the idea of plants as national emblems. It is said that the Scottish have the thistle as an emblem because it helped to repel invaders, while the Welsh have a similar story about wearing the leek into battle against the English. In Ireland, of course, the shamrock is our national emblem because of its link with St Patrick, the patron saint. For this reason the shamrock is worn in his honour on his feast day, 17 March. Similarly, the Welsh wear the daffodil as a national emblem on 1 March, the feast day of their patron saint, St David. No doubt this is because it is in flower around this time.

Wearing emblems on a particular day to commemorate important events or people is also common. For example in Britain (and sometimes in Ireland) the poppy is worn on Remembrance Day for those who died in the First World War and subsequent wars. It is said that this custom was first inspired by the poppies that grew on the battlefields of Flanders. Poppies have been linked to battlefields since Napoleonic times, when they were said to have grown at the site of the battle of Waterloo.[19] In a similar way, Easter lilies have traditionally been worn in Ireland to commemorate the Easter Rising of 1916. In modern times a phenomenon that has grown in importance is the adoption of flowers as emblems by many charities, to promote awareness of their cause and help raise money.

Another modern use of plants as emblems that is still popular is the *Language of Flowers*.[20] This is a system whereby a particular sentiment can be communicated by the presentation of a certain kind of flower, like red roses signifying love or white lilies signifying purity. Of course, different plants and flowers have always had different meanings attached to them, but the 'Language of Flowers' was an attempt to create an organised system through which people could communicate. The language first appeared in 1818 in a book published in Paris by Charlotte de La Tour called *Le Langage des Fleurs* or 'The Language of Flowers' and most books published since then are based on it. As time moves on, so many meanings have been given to plants that any attempt to communicate using the 'Language of Flowers' is likely to lead to misunderstanding and it was never intended to be anything more than an amusing parlour game in any case. In reality the 'Language' is largely a literary creation that has little relation to folklore, but even so it has remained popular.

Plants are also widely used in children's games. It is noteworthy that the most favoured plants in these games are the very ones most despised or ignored by adults as weeds. Some of the hardiest 'weeds' like dandelions, daisies, thistles and plantains, are the plants that feature most prominantly. The daisy features in the well-known children's game which involves saying 'he loves me, he loves me not', while picking each petal in turn to test the faithfulness of a sweetheart. The fluffy seedheads of dandelions were used by children everywhere to tell the time. The number of puffs it took to blow away the seeds was the number of hours – three puffs was three o'clock, etc. Plantains were used to play 'soldiers', a game not unlike conkers where each player used the hard flowerhead of the plantain to strike at that of his opponent, hoping to knock it off and so win the game.

It is intriguing that plants have so many different names. There are a plethora of plant names, unlike animals, birds or even trees, which usually have only one or two names, at most three or four. But plant names are legion – why? One reason, of course, is that many plants are localised and so may only be known in particular areas. The people there may know the plant but find it difficult to describe to outsiders, or to recognise it under another name when outsiders describe it to them. So the local names would survive long after a standard 'book name' has been chosen. But the same diversity of names applies even to widespread and well-known plants like foxglove (fairy fingers, fairy bells, etc.) and dandelion (clock, piss the bed). It is hard to account for this, but it seems simply that there was never a pressing reason for one standard name to catch on and spread. Most names were generated by country people which probably explains why many are based on a keen eye for the plant's appearance and uses, and why many are so whimsical (Jack-go-to-bed-at-noon, Robin-run-the-hedge). Also many names given by herbalists gained general currency. Plant names in English that have 'wort' as an element (like St John's wort or mugwort) usually had a medical role. In Irish the equivalent is usually *lus* in names like *lus na fola* (yarrow).

Many plant names are based on the plant's appearance – its flowers, fruit, leaves, roots, etc. For example, bluebell is obviously named after its flowers, while dandelion is believed to be called after its leaves because it was believed they were shaped like a lion's teeth (French *dent de lion*). Sometimes it is some other notable factor which provides a name. A common name for scarlet pimpernel is 'poor man's weatherglass' because the flowers close up when rain threatens. It is not unusual for the same plant to have different names based on different parts, e.g., buttercup (flower) and crowfoot (leaves). Another common source for names are the medicinal uses of a plant, usually from the complaint they are alleged to cure. For example, marsh and hedge woundwort are so called because they were believed to have the ability to cure wounds, and eyebright got its name because it was used to soothe sore eyes. Finally, of course, plants sometimes got their names from other uses. For example, lady's bedstraw is so called because it was mixed with straw in a lady's bedchamber to provide a sweet smell – and to keep away fleas. Similarly soapwort got its name because it was used as precisely that – a soap for washing clothes.

PLANTS IN PLACE NAMES

A great many placenames in Ireland are derived from plants.[21] Not surprisingly, the most common sources for names are plants that occur widely throughout Ireland like bracken, ivy and heather.

Examples of placenames derived from bracken or fern include Coleraine (*Cúil Rathain* – nook of the ferns), County Derry; Ardrahan (*Ard Rathain* – height of the fern), County Galway; Drumraney (*Droim Raithne* – ridge of ferns), County Westmeath; and Mulraney (*Mala Raithní* – ferny brae), County Mayo. It should be noted, however, that Ferns in County Wexford comes from *Fearna* – the place of alder trees. Names with ivy include Clonenagh (*Cluain Eidhneach* – ivied pasture), County Laois; Gleneany (*Gleann Eidhneach* – ivied glen), County Donegal; and the Oweniny river in County Mayo (*Abhainn Eidhneach* – ivied river). The placename Inan in County Meath means simply *Eidhneán* – ivy. Heather provides many placenames such as Freaghmore (*Fraoch Mór* – large heathery place), County Westmeath; Freaghduff (*Fraoch Dubh* – black heathery place) County Tyrone; Ballyfree (*Baile Fraoigh* – homestead of the heather), County Wicklow; and Clonfree (*Cluain Fraoigh* – meadow of the heather), County Tipperary. The most famous heathery placename is of course Yeats' Lake Isle of Inisfree in County Sligo (*Inis Fraoigh* – the island of heather). Again not surprisingly, a number of Irish placenames derive from rushes and reeds. Thus we have Ard Lougher (*Ard Luachra* – height of the rushes), County Cavan; Loughermore (*Luachair Mhór* – big, rushy place), County Derry; Culkey (*Cuilceach* – abounding in reeds), County Fermanagh and Ballynaguilkee (*Baile na Giolcaí* – homestead of the reeds), County Waterford.

Bramble and blackberry provide another common and widespread source for placenames. Examples include Rathdrishogue (*Ráth Driseog* – fort of the brambles), County Westmeath and Derreendrislagh (*Doirín Drisleach* – brambly oak grove), County Kerry. Blackberries appear in Coolnasmear (*Cúil na Sméar* – nook of the blackberries), County Waterford and Mullaunnasmear (*Mullán na Sméar* – hillock of blackberries), County Wexford. Other plants that were valued as a food source also commonly appear in names. Thus wild garlic appears frequently in names. Examples include Cloncraff (*Cluain Chreamha* – garlic meadow), County Offaly; and Glencrew (*Gleann Creamha* – garlic glen), County Tyrone. Garlic is found mostly in woodland, and the names Crawhill, County Sligo; Crewhill, County Kildare; and Croaghill, County Galway (among others), all come from *Creamhchoill* – garlic wood. Watercress appears in names like Watergrass Hill (*Cnocán na Biolaraí* – hill of the watercress), County Cork; Askinvillar (*Easca an Bhiolair* – fen of the watercress), County Wexford; and Toberaviller (*Tobar an Bhiolair* – well of the watercress), County Wicklow. Another frequent source of placenames are those widespread plants usually thought of as weeds. For example, dock provides the names Knocknaguppoge (*Cnoc na gCopóg* – hill of the docks), County Kilkenny and Tuarnagoppogue (*Tuar na gCopóg* – pasture of the docks), County Waterford. Nettles also provide names such as Kilnantoge (*Coill Neantóg* – wood of nettles), County Offaly; and Carrownanty (*Ceathrú Neanta* – quarter of nettles), County Sligo. Many other plants and flowers appear at least a few times in Irish placenames. Thus we have names like Dunseverick (*Dún Sobhairce* – fort of the primrose), County Antrim; Cloonboo (*Cluain Bú* – meadow of blue-bells), County Galway; Pishanagh (*Piseánach* – place of vetches), County Westmeath; and Fofannybane (*Fofannaigh Bhán* – white this-tle land) in County Donegal.

Major Plants in Folklore

Mistletoe – Drualus

Viscum Album

♃ ☉ Ruled by the planet Jupiter and the Sun in traditional herbal medicine

♐ Associated with the zodiac sign Sagittarius

Mistletoe mysteriously appears in tree tops without any apparent source of nourishment. This, and its bright green leaves and luminous sticky white berries in the dead of winter, make it a powerful symbol of fertility and regeneration. It also had important medical uses and was seen as the sacred 'all-heal', with great powers to restore life and vitality.

SPECIES NAME: As above
ALTERNATIVE NAMES: (E) All-heal, Birdlime (I) *Sú Darach, Uile-íce*

FOLK BELIEFS AND CUSTOMS

Throughout Britain and the English-speaking world, mistletoe is widely used to decorate the home around Christmas time. Traditionally part of the reason was to protect the house from evil spirits, but nowadays the main reason is the well-known custom of kissing under the mistletoe.[1] This custom is also believed to originate in Britain. Many variations of the custom existed. In some places each time a boy kissed a girl he plucked a berry, and sometimes young men went about with a sprig of mistletoe in their caps. It was sometimes believed that a girl who had not been kissed would not be married in that coming year; while another belief was that if a girl had not been kissed under a mistletoe before she was married, then she would be barren all her days. In Yorkshire a girl kissed under the mistletoe would take a berry and later swallow it and prick the name of her beloved on a leaf of it. As long as the leaf remained in her clothes close to her heart, so her true love would be bound to her. In Wales if an unmarried girl placed a sprig of it under her pillow she would dream of her future husband. Sometimes it was believed that if the mistletoe was not burned after the festivities, that those who had kissed under it would be foes

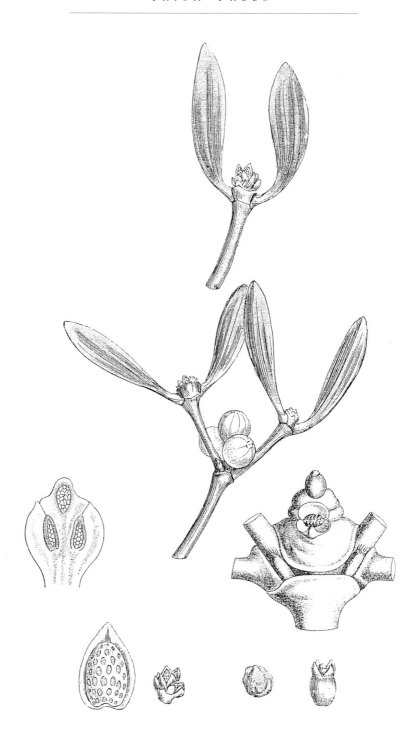

before the year was out. It was also very bad luck to take all the bunch of Christmas mistletoe. In Worcester, the mistletoe was cut on New Year's Eve by the last male domestic to enter the house, then suspended from the centre of the room. Women who were kissed under it were allowed to take a berry, and then throw it over their left shoulder for luck. Given its strong pagan associations it is not surprising that mistletoe was traditionally banned as a decoration in churches, at least until very recently.

In Ireland, even though the mistletoe is not native, it has become naturalised in parts of the country. The custom of using mistletoe as a Christmas decoration therefore became established in those areas, such as south Wicklow and near Limerick.[2] The custom of kissing under the mistletoe was only known in a few places like County Armagh, where it is also naturalised. Here it was the custom that a girl would hang a sprig over the door and kiss the first unsuspecting young man who came in. He then was obliged to buy the girl a Christmas present. On New Year's Eve in parts of Ireland, girls put holly or ivy leaves or a sprig of mistletoe under their pillow to bring dreams of their future husbands.

Apart from its powers to promote romance, the Christmas or New Year mistletoe was thought to have protective powers.[3] It was believed by many that the mistletoe must be kept in the house until it was replaced next Christmas. Usually the reason was to keep witches or evil spirits away, but sometimes the reason was to keep love in the house. In Wales the custom was to stuff the mistletoe into the fireplace for the summer. In Worcestershire the Christmas mistletoe was taken down and given to the first cow that calved after New Year's Day to bring luck to the whole dairy; while in Wales the custom was to place the mistletoe beside the cow. In Bradford the Christmas mistletoe was kept to be burned under the Shrove Tuesday pancakes. In Herefordshire the mistletoe bough was cut on New Year's Eve and hung up as the clock struck twelve to protect the house, and the previous year's one was taken down and burnt. The best mistletoe for this task was believed to come from apple trees and poplars. In many parts of Britain there was the custom of Burning the Bush – a globe of twisted hawthorn twigs and mistletoe was burnt early on New Year's Day in the first sown wheatfield to ensure its fertility for the coming year.[4]

Given its perceived powers, it is not surprising that mistletoe was involved in various customs concerning protection and fertility.[5] In England a piece of mistletoe was often hung around the neck of children as a protection against witchcraft and evil. In Devon it was believed to protect the house against lightning. However, it was also believed in Devon that if you planted mistletoe and it grew, your daughters would never marry. Mistletoe was believed to be good for divining treasure and protecting the crops of trees on which it grew, and it was said that mistletoe had the power to open all locks. Women who wished to conceive tied a sprig of it around their waists or wrists. In Brittany mistletoe is called *herbe de la croix* (herb of the cross) because it was believed that the cross on which Christ was crucified was made from it, and so it dwindled down and was degraded to a parasite.[6] Nevertheless, in Brittany it was the custom to have a sprig of laurel or mistletoe over the door of the inn.[7] The mistletoe has also been highly regarded in Wales since ancient times.[8] In early Welsh law there was a fine of 60 old pence for taking a branch of mistletoe without permission. In Wales when mistletoe was scarce Welsh farmers used to say 'no mistletoe, no luck', but if there was a fine crop of mistletoe they expected a fine crop of corn. In Wales it was also believed that a sprig of mistletoe gathered on St John's Eve, would induce dreams of omen, both good and bad, if it were placed under the pillow of the sleeper.

In Scotland mistletoe was the plant badge of the Hay clan of Errol.[9] Clan lore has it that in the neighbourhood of Errol there stood a huge oak which had a profusion of mistletoe growing on it. A sprig of the mistletoe was traditionally cut from the tree on Halloween Eve with a new dirk and then carried three times sunwise around the tree while saying a certain spell. Such a sprig was a certain charm against witchcraft and an infallible guard against harm in battle. Sprigs gathered this way were also placed in the cradle of infants to keep them from being taken by the fairies. Eventually the oak tree was destroyed and shortly afterwards the Hays were forced to sell their estates in the area. It was firmly believed by locals that the two events were connected. Indeed, it was widely held throughout Britain that death and misfortune were foretold to those who cut down a mistletoe-bearing tree.[10]

LEGENDS AND MYTHOLOGY

Mistletoe features in the description made famous by the druids. It is by the Roman naturalist Pliny and concerns the mistletoe rite of the Gaulish druids. More than any other source it has shaped (and some would say distorted) our image of the druids. Here it is in full:[11]

Here we must mention the awe felt for this plant by the Gauls. The Druids – for so their magicians are called – held nothing more sacred than the mistletoe and the tree that bears it, always supposing that tree to be the oak. But they choose groves formed of oaks for the sake of the tree alone, and they never perform any of their rites except in the presence of a branch of it; so that it seems probable that the priests themselves may derive their name from the Greek word for that tree. In fact they think that everything that grows on it has been sent from heaven and is a proof that the tree was chosen by the God himself. The mistletoe, however, is found but rarely upon the oak; and when found, is gathered with due religious ceremony, if possible on the sixth day of the moon (for it is by the moon that they measure their months and years, and also their ages of thirty years). They choose this day because the moon, though not yet in the middle of her course, has already considerable influence. They call the mistletoe by a name meaning in their language, the all-healing. Having made preparation for sacrifice and a banquet beneath the trees, they bring thither two white bulls, whose horns are bound then for the first time. Clad in a white robe, the priest ascends the tree and cuts the mistletoe with a golden sickle, and it is received by others in a white cloak. Then they kill the victims, praying that God will render this gift of his propitious to those to whom he has granted it. They believe that the mistletoe, taken in drink, imparts fecundity to barren animals, and that it is an antidote to all poisons. Such are the religious feelings that are entertained towards trifling things by many peoples.

The images in this passage have led to far-fetched ideas, like that most druids went about in white robes brandishing golden sickles. It has also fostered the untrue belief that the druids worshipped the oak virtually to the exclusion of all other trees. Nevertheless, even allowing for exaggeration, there is probably an element of truth in the description. Mistletoe indeed grows only rarely on the oak, preferring trees like apple and hawthorn; so to find it on an oak, symbol of the sky or sun god, the Celtic Jupiter, would be undoubtedly considered significant. Such mistletoe probably would be gathered with care and considered particularly potent. Elsewhere Pliny adds that if it was cut from an oak at the new moon, and without iron, and if it did not touch the ground while being cut, mistletoe would cure epilepsy, and if carried by women would make them fertile.[12] As we have seen, similar beliefs about mistletoe's powers were still held up to the present day. In addition, the Roman poet Ovid referred to the druids singing under the mistletoe; and the Celtic tribe, the Bituriges, had the surname Vivisci which probably means 'mistletoe men', implying that it was their sacred symbol.[13] There is also archaeological evidence of mistletoe's importance. In a Bronze Age burial site at Gristhorpe, near Scarborough in England, there was found an old man's skeleton in an oak coffin covered with oak branches, and with the skeleton was a bronze dagger and a large quantity of mistletoe.[14] Certainly, the Irish names *Drualus* (Druid's herb) and *Sú Darach* (Juice of the Oak), imply that the connection between the druids, the oak and mistletoe was known even in Ireland.

Mistletoe also famously appears in Norse myth in the story of the death of Baldur.[15] Baldur was the Norse god of love, the youthful god of light who was adored by all for his beauty, goodness and mercy. So much was he loved, that the myth recounts how his mother Frigg got every substance in the world to swear that it would not harm him. However, she neglected to get the mistletoe to promise, thinking it too insignificant. The god of mischief Loki found this out and out of jealousy plotted to kill Baldur. He plucked the mistletoe and fashioned its strongest stem into a spear. Loki then tricked Baldur's blind brother Hod into throwing the sharpened spear at Baldur and it pierced him through, killing him

Mistletoe – Drualus
Viscum album

Rushes – Luachra

Juncus acutiflorus   *Juncus effusus*   *Juncus inflexus*

instantly. The rest of the gods later banished Loki from Asgard in revenge for this terrible crime. Significantly the mistletoe that Loki picked was also growing on an oak tree. The myth probably derives from the idea that the otherworldly evergreen mistletoe was a symbol of the young innocent sun god Baldur, who dies and is symbolically reborn at midwinter. It follows that the mistletoe must symbolically be born out of the strength and stability of the oak, just as the youthful god Baldur is the son of Odin, father of the gods. Alternatively, the explanation put forward by the scholar Frazer was that Baldur was a deity of vegetation, the personification of the magical mistletoe-bearing oak. Whatever the truth, similar ideas no doubt applied in Celtic mythology, even if that can only be inferred from what evidence survives. It is also probably out of such ideas that in Greek myth both mistletoe and acorns were a symbol of the hero Hercules.[16]

PRACTICAL AND HERBAL USES

It has now been recognised by medicine that mistletoe produces a substance which has a relaxing effect on the nervous system.[17] This is reflected in the folk uses of mistletoe as a cure against such ailments as St Vitus' dance, epilepsy, hysteria and other nervous disorders, and heart palpitations. Although the bulk of folk cures in these islands naturally come from the south of England where mistletoe is most common, it has been recorded in Ireland as a cure for soothing the nerves in Cavan and Meath, and in Limerick and Cork for palliating epilepsy and hysteria. Mistletoe also contains a resin called Viscin, which by fermentation becomes a sticky resinous mass that can be successfully used as a birdlime.[18] Birdlime is any substance that traps birds by sticking them to their perch when they land, so that they cannot then escape by flying away. Mistletoe gives its name to the *Viscaceae*, the mistletoe family.

Rushes – Luachra

Juncus

♄   Ruled by the planet Saturn in traditional herbal medicine

♒   Associated with the zodiac sign Aquarius

*R*ushes were traditionally used for thatching, and for strewing on the *floor to keep rooms fresh. This made them symbols of hospitality, shelter and protection. The St Brigid's Cross made in honour of the saint at her festival was usually made of rushes. Rushes grow near water and in wet places, and this linked them in folklore to the purity and cleanliness of water and holy wells.*

SPECIES NAMES:
Soft Rush – *Geataire – Juncus effusus*
ALTERNATIVE NAMES: (I) *Fidheog, Geaftaire, Luachair Ghallda*
Hard rush – *Luachair Chrua – Juncus inflexus*
Compact rush – *Luachair Dhlúth – Juncus conglomeratus*
Sharp-flowered rush – *Fiastalach – Juncus acutiflorus*
Common club-rush – *Bogshifín – Scirpus lacustris*
ALTERNATIVE NAME: (E) Bulrush

ALTERNATIVE NAMES FOR RUSHES: (E) Rash (US), Rusheen (FB), Snel (TC). (I) *Blíneach, Bruadna, Feag, Feagh, Féith, Feodhg, Feog, Fiag, Fig, Fiog, Leaglaidh, Sifín, Simhean*

FOLK BELIEFS AND CUSTOMS
Rushes in Ireland are closely associated with the festival of St Brigid on 1 February. The main reason for this was the universal custom of making the *cros Bríde* or *bogha Bríde,* the St Brigid's cross, out of straw or rushes.[1] The crosses were hung up in houses, and often in the byre and stable as well to honour the saint and gain her protection. The straw crosses were usually a diamond or lozenge shape bound around a cross of twigs, and were the most common type in Connaught and Munster. The rush crosses were made by doubling

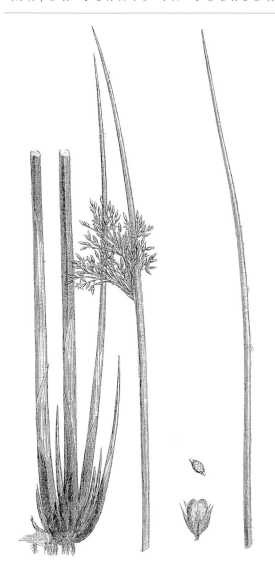

rushes over each other to form a centre square of overlapping rushes, with four projecting bunches tied at the ends in a rough point. It
was the most common type of cross in Ulster and Leinster and was
adopted by Radio Telefís Eireann (Irish radio and television service)
as its logo for many years. A variation of the rush cross, where the
cross had only three legs, also traditionally existed in parts of Ulster.

The making of the crosses was usually accompanied by some

ceremony. In some places the cross was sprinkled with holy water, and then hung above or close to the entrance door with an appropriate prayer such as 'May the blessing of God, Father, Son and Holy Spirit be on this cross and on the place where it hangs and on everyone who looks at it'. In other places, especially Connaught and Ulster, the custom was more elaborate. One of the family, a girl representing St Brigid, left the house and returned carrying a bundle of fresh rushes in her hands. She knocked on the door three times, calling out that the occupants should get down on their knees to pay homage to St Brigid and let her enter the house. The third time she was answered with 'O tar isteach, tá céad fáilte romhat' (Oh come in, you are a hundred times welcome). The girl then came in and put the rushes on the table which had been laid for supper. The dishes holding the food for the supper were then brought in and placed on top of the rushes. Alternatively, in places the rushes were placed under the table. At this point grace was said and the supper eaten, and then afterwards there was a prayer of thanksgiving. It was usually only then that the rushes were taken and plaited into crosses of varying thickness. In some places, however, the crosses were made before the supper and the supper things placed upon them. When they were completed the crosses were sprinkled with holy water and hung around the house on the roof and the walls. Sometimes the old cross was removed when the new one was put up, but more usually the old crosses were left in position, growing in number over the years. It was considered important that the rushes for the crosses should be fresh and green, and should have been pulled, not cut.

St Brigid's crosses were believed to have great powers of protection against fire, storm and lightning, and against illness and infectious diseases. It was also believed that evil spirits could not enter the house where it hung near the door. The residue of the material left behind after the crosses were made was also considered important. In parts of Donegal, Tyrone and Antrim, the cross was neatly arranged near the hearth and covered with a white cloth to make a bed for the saint when she visited the house. In some houses the residue was made into rushlights that were then lit in honour of the saint. In general the leftover straw or rushes was believed to have curative powers. Strands of it were tied about an aching head or a sore limb during the night, and then burnt the next morning to bring about a quick cure. A wisp of it might also be put under the pillow or mattress to ward off disease. In parts of Donegal, fishermen wove the material into a little ribbon which they wore at sea to gain the saint's protection.

Rushes were also involved in other customs surrounding the festival of St Brigid.[2] For example, there was a widespread custom of welcoming the saint into the household on St Brigid's Eve by spreading a bundle of straw or fresh rushes on the threshold, so that the saint might kneel to bless the house, or else wipe her feet before entering. Another custom involved a virgin selected from the community to go door to door on St Brigid's Day, with St Brigid's crosses in her apron. She went to the houses of the district and knelt on a rush mat which had been laid on each doorstep for her. In addition rushes could be used for marriage divination on St Brigid's Eve night. The boys would make an imitation spinning wheel out of a few rushes woven together, while the girls would weave the rushes into an imitation ladder. They then went to bed and slept with them under their pillow. Doing this meant that their future partners would be climbing a ladder or spinning a wheel on the first occasion they were seen. This could also be done on Halloween night which was the more usual time for divination of all kinds. A custom that has now fallen into disuse was the wearing of crosses on St Patrick's Day, and rushes were sometimes used for making these.

A similar St Brigid's Eve custom to those in Ireland took place in the Isle of Man.[3] A bunch of green rushes was gathered and the gatherer stood with them at the threshold of the house. He or she said a short verse to invite St Brigid to come and lodge with the household that night, and the rushes were then strewn on the floor by way of a carpet or bed for the saint. Also on the Isle of Man an offering of green rushes was made to Mannanán, the Celtic god of the sea and protector of the island, on Midsummer Eve.[4] Green rushes were commonly strewn on the floor in Ireland and Britain to keep down dirt and provide a sense of comfort.[5] In ancient Ireland garments were strewn under the feet of kings, but rushes under those of a lower degree. In Irish-speaking parts of Ireland the infrequent and unexpected caller was greeted with the phrase:

dá mbeadh soipín luachra againn chuirfimís fáth chosaibh é (if we had a handful of rushes we would strew them under your feet). In parts of England, particularly Cumbria, churches were traditionally strewn with rushes, and a ceremony to carry in the rushes was held once a year in the summer.

Rushes were often linked to the fairies and other supernatural beings in folklore.[6] In Ireland green rushes were believed to have the power to break the fairy spell on milk vessels. If the fairy wind passed by, it was said that you should throw a green rush after it and say 'God speed you' to avert harm. It was also believed that a person could see the fairies by twisting a green rush into a loop and looking through it. There was a high price for gaining this power, however, as it meant that you would never be able to look through that eye again! Throughout Britain, rushes were said to have special healing and protective powers, and it was said to be lucky to find one with a green top. In Wales it was said that the fairies liked to dance on the top of rushes. In Scotland it was believed that a supernatural hag called the *Cailleach bheur* hid in lochs and among rushes, and that the fairy waterhorse called a kelpie, which often appeared in human form, could be spotted by a tell-tale fragment of rush or cleavers in his hair.

LEGENDS AND MYTHOLOGY

A traditional story explains the link between St Brigid and the crosses made on her feast day.[7] The story goes that St Brigid was passing an old shed when she heard a moaning cry from within. Entering the shed she found a dying man. The saint tried in vain to tell the man before his death about Our Lord, but he wouldn't listen. In the end she went out, and taking some rushes made them into a cross. She returned to the man, and when he saw the cross he understood and was moved to sorrow. He then made his confession and received the last sacrament. Ever since then the rush cross has been associated with St Brigid.

Rushes were traditionally laid down on the floors of a house to keep rooms fresh and provide a welcoming atmosphere for guests, and this practice appears in several celtic tales.[8] For example, in the tale the 'Cattle Raid of Cooley', the envoy of Queen

Maedhbh is welcomed by a feast, and the laying down of fresh rushes in the hall before him. In the same tale Maine Morgor is welcomed to his wedding by his future father-in-law laying down green-leaved birch branches and fresh green rushes in the house. Similarly, in the tale about the boyhood deeds of Cúchulainn, when King Conchubar enters the house of the smith Culain there is a welcome for him, and fresh rushes laid down. In the British tale of Owein, King Arthur holds court while sitting in the middle of his chamber on a pile of green rushes. Beds of rushes to give rest to the weary and comfort to the sick also appear in various tales.[9] During their elopement Diarmaid makes a bed of soft rushes for Gráinne to sleep on. In the 'Cattle Raid of Cooley', the warriors Cúchulainn and Ferdia fight each other by day, and rest to heal their wounds on beds of green rushes by night. When he journeys to the Land Under Wave, Diarmaid finds that the king's daughter is gravely ill, and that the only thing that gives her comfort is sleeping on a bed of green rushes.

Considering that they grow in watery places, it is hardly surprising that rushes appear in association with holy and healing wells in many tales.[10] For example, a tale from the *Metrical Dindshenchus* (or folklore of places), tells of the one-eyed king Eochaid, who was so famed for his generosity that it was said he would never say no to any request. Hearing this, a poet called Ferchertne maliciously asked the king for his only eye, and true to his reputation, the king gave it to him without hesitation. The now blind Eochaid then set out with a guide to search for healing water, until he reached a particular bed of rushes. He plucked out a clump of the rushes and a clear spring immediately appeared out of the ground. Eochaid bathed his head in the water, and as a reward for his generosity he was granted not one, but two new eyes. In the Tripartite Life of St Patrick, on a visit to Clonmacnoise, the saint told a leper who was living there to pull out a particular bundle of rushes by the roots. The leper did so and a well of clean water sprang forth from that spot. St Patrick declared that it was the well of St Kieran who was yet to come. Similarly, in the life of Brigid the saint cured a leper by asking him to bring to her a clump of rushes from his home. When he did so a well sprang out of the spot, and after bathing in it the leper was cured. The healing powers of the well could also extend to the rushes themselves. One folktale tells of how the juice from nine rushes growing beside a holy well could cure a person afflicted from standing on the enchanted *féar gorta* or hungry grass.[11]

PRACTICAL AND HERBAL USES

In Ireland rushes were used for making candles, thatch for houses and corn stacks, matting for human dwellings, hats, toys and ropes.[12] Rushlight candles were made by peeling the rushes when green and then soaking them in some inflammable substance, traditionally tallow or lard. Rush toys were usually dolls and toy cages and other such 'fancies'. Rushes were also traditionally used for bedding. The many uses of rushes earned them a place in the Old Irish Brehon Laws, as some sources include rushes as a 'bush of the wood' in the Brehon Laws concerning trees and shrubs.[13] Rushes do not feature much in folk medicine, but the hard rush (*Juncus inflexus*) was used in parts of Ulster for curing jaundice, and in various parts of Ireland rushes were burnt and the ashes used for cures.[14] For example, in Offaly and Waterford the ash was used to cure ringworm, and in Westmeath it was mixed with lard and made into an ointment for curing shingles. It was also believed in Ireland that a green rush tied around the neck cured a person suffering from a 'crick'.[15] Rushes give their name to the rush family, the *Juncaceae*. The club-rush belongs to the sedge family, the *Cyperaceae*.

SIMILAR PLANTS:

Bulrush – *Coigeal na mBan Sí* – *Typha latifolia* [16]
ALTERNATIVE NAMES: (E) Great Cat's-tail, Great Reed-mace, The Fairies' Cighaul (Fin). (I) *Biorrach, Bocaifín, Bodán Dubh, Bog-luachair, Boigiún Slaite, Boigrín, Curchas, Eachlasca Ban Sí* (?), *Eireaball Cait, Féith Fiáin, Fiag Fiáin*

In Ireland bulrush was considered a fairy plant as its Irish name indicates: *coigeal na mban sí* or 'fairy woman's spindle'. In Scotland it was believed that if a bulrush was gathered at midsummer midnight and then wrapped in a shroud, that it would guarantee freedom from every ailment for the rest of the person's life. In Scotland bulrush is also the badge of the Innes and Mackay clans. Bulrushes were traditionally used to make mats and baskets. Bulrush gives its name to the bulrush family, the *Typhaceae*.

Common Reed – *Giolcach* – *Phragmites australis* [17]
ALTERNATIVE NAMES: (I) *Biorrach, Biorrach Laighean, Biorrach Lachan, Crúiscearnach, Cuilc, Curchas, Gáinne, Lachán, Sifín, Simhean*
In Scotland the reed was considered to be cursed because it carried the sponge dipped in vinegar which was given to Our Lord on the cross. Reed is generally considered to be the best material of all for thatching, and was also used for making mats. Common Reed is a member of the grass family, the *Poaceae* or *Gramineae*.

Common Sedge – *Cíb Dhubh* – *Carex nigra* [18]
ALTERNATIVE NAMES: (E) Black Sedge, Reed-grass (I) *Seasc-fhéar, Seisc, Seasclach*
In Ireland sedge was used to make lights in the same way as rushes, and it was also used for thatching and rope making. Common Sedge gives its name to the sedge family, the *Cyperaceae*.

Shamrock / Clover – Seamair/Seamróg

Trifolium

☿ Ruled by the planet Mercury in traditional herbal medicine

♊ Associated with the zodiac sign Gemini

*S*hamrock is the seamair óg, *the young, fresh, green shoots of clover or trefoil when they first appear in the spring. The rich, clover-covered meadows of Ireland have always been a symbol of the fertile 'Emerald Isle'; while through its link to St Patrick, Ireland's patron saint, the shamrock has become the main emblem of Ireland.*

SPECIES NAMES:
Lesser Trefoil – *Seamair Bhuí* – *Trifolium dubium*
ALTERNATIVE NAMES: (E) Lesser Clover, Lesser Yellow Trefoil
White Clover – *Seamair Bhán* – *Trifolium repens*
Black Medick – *Dúmheidic* – *Medicago lupulina*
Red Clover – *Seamair Dhearg* – *Trifolium pratense*
ALTERNATIVE NAMES: (E) Broad Clover, Honeysuckle (Don), Purple Trefoil (I) *Seamair Chapaill*

ALTERNATIVE NAMES FOR CLOVER: (E) Meelough (FB), Milagh (FB). (I) *Clóbhar, Milseog* (for the flower) (Ant), *Seabhar, Seimle, Seimre, Simearóg* (Muns), *Siomair*

FOLK BELIEFS AND CUSTOMS
The shamrock is associated with Ireland. It features in our tourist literature, on our national airline, and in the logos of many Irish companies. It adorns countless objects from clothes to tea towels to jewellery. The best-known Irish custom is the 'wearing of the green' on 17 March, St Patrick's Day, when Irish people the world over sport a sprig of shamrock to honour the nation's patron saint and show they are Irish. However, for a symbol that is so well known, its origins are somewhat mysterious. In fact, nowhere is the shamrock mentioned in Patrick's own writings, or in any of the early biographies of his

life. The first mention of wearing the shamrock on St Patrick's Day occurs as late as 1681 when English traveller Thomas Dinely made the following note in his journal: 'The 17th day of March yeerly is St Patrick's, an immoveable feast when the Irish of all stations and condicions wore crosses in their hats, some of pins, some of green ribbon, and the vulgar superstitiously wear shamroges, 3-leaved grass, which they likewise eat (they say) to cause a sweet breath.'[1] The mention of crosses is a reference to a now extinct custom of wearing homemade decorated crosses on St Patrick's Day.

The next major reference to shamrock and St Patrick's Day occurs in 1726 in a botanical work by the Reverend Dr Caleb Threkeld, who identified the shamrock as white clover (*trifolium repens*) and had this to say: 'This plant is worn by the people in their hats on the seventeenth day of March yearly, which is St Patrick's Day, it being a current tradition that, by this three-leaved grass, he emblematically set forth to show them the mystery of the Holy Trinity. However that may be, when they wet their *semar-oge*, they often commit excess in liquor, which is not a right keeping of a day to the Lord, error generally leading to debauchery.' Hard as it may be to imagine, this is the first written reference anywhere to the legend of St Patrick using the shamrock to teach the mystery of the Holy Trinity. Threkeld's comments are also famous because of his acerbic remarks on the custom of 'wetting the shamrock'. Part of the St Patrick's Day festivities was to have a drink to honour the saint called the *Pota Pádraig* or 'St Patrick's Pot',[2] and at some stage the idea took hold that the shamrock which had been worn that day should be dipped or drowned in the drink. The earliest reference seems to be in lines written by an English poet John Taylor, who wrote in 1630 of 'Hibernian kernes' feasting 'with shamroges steeved in usquebagh' (whiskey).[3] In Kildare the custom of the 'drowning of the shamrock' was described as follows: 'At the end of the day the shamrock which has been worn in the coat or the hat is removed and put into the final glass of grog or tumbler of punch; and when the health has been drunk or the toast honoured, the shamrock should be picked out from the bottom of the glass and thrown over the left shoulder.'[4]

In Ireland, the four-leaved shamrock, or *seamróg na gCeithre*

gCluas, was very lucky in folklore because of its rarity.[5] The possessor of such a shamrock was believed to gain a host of supernatural
powers. Whoever had it would have luck in gambling and racing,
could not be cheated in a bargain or deceived, and witchcraft would
have no power over him. Whatever he undertook would prosper,
and through the power of the shamrock achieve wondrous things.
It also enlightened the brain and made the possessor see and know
truth. However, to keep these powers, the possessor must carry it
always about their person, must never give it away, or even show it
to another. It was also believed to grant to its possessor the power
of second sight. The four-leaved shamrock was believed to grow
where an ass had foaled three times or where a mare dropped her
first foal, or else where a cow or mare had been born.

The truth-seeing powers of the four-leaved shamrock feature in
a well-known folktale.[6] The story tells of a farmer who, unknown to
himself, had a four-leaved shamrock in the hay he was carrying on
his back. A large crowd had gathered at a particular spot on his way
home, and he stopped to see what they were looking at. The crowd
was marvelling at the impossible sight of a cockerel hauling a huge
log of wood behind it as it walked, but the farmer was unable to see
this. He could only see a wisp of straw trailing behind the bird. The
circus man who had organised the illusion overheard him telling
this to another member of the crowd, and whispering to the farmer,
he immediately offered to buy the bundle of hay. At first the farmer
refused, but in the end the circus man offered him seven times the
value of the hay and he accepted. As soon as he handed over the
bundle to the circus man the farmer saw the huge log of wood just
like everyone else! He then realised too late that his bundle must
have contained a four-leaved shamrock, which had given him the
power to see through the illusion.

The four- (or five-) leaved shamrock was also considered to be
very lucky in the Scottish Highlands, and was believed to be a great
charm against evil spells.[7] If its powers were to work, the shamrock
must be found by accident and without seeking. It was believed to
grow from the pale sponge-like substance coughed up by a foal
after birth, and people buried this in the ground, believing that the
lucky shamrock would grow from it. A traditional Scots Gaelic

verse sums up the virtues of the shamrock:

Thou shamrock of foliage,
Thou shamrock entwining,
Thou shamrock of the prayer,
Thou shamrock of my love.

Thou shamrock of my sorrow,
Plant of Patrick of the virtues,
Thou shamrock of the Son of Mary,
Journey's end of the peoples.

Thou shamrock of grace,
Of joy, of the tombs,
It were my wish in death,
Thou shouldst grow on my grave.

Outside Ireland and Gaelic Scotland, the four-leaved clover had the same powers as the four-leaved shamrock.[8] Finding one meant lifelong riches, or at the very least that a good thing would follow. In Somerset finding one meant that you would meet your true love. In Sussex it was said that the first leaf was for fame, the second for wealth, the third for a faithful lover, and the fourth for glorious health; while an Essex rhyme stated that 'If you find a four-leaved clover, all your troubles will be over'. In Northumberland it was said that possessing a four-leaved clover allowed a person to see the fairies. In Cornwall it was said that an ointment could be made with a four-leaved clover that rendered Fairyland visible, and the user invisible. In Wales it was believed that a four-leaved clover found in May was a good charm against witchcraft. In Wales it was also given as an emblem of good luck, and if worn on the person or placed under the pillow, induced cheerfulness and lightheartedness. In Norfolk it was believed that they only grew where a foal had dropped her first foal. A British tradition states that the four-leaved clover was supposed to be lucky because Eve took one with her when she left Paradise.

Other unusual numbers of leaves could also be lucky.[9] To find a five-leaved clover was especially lucky, as it meant that you would become extremely wealthy. In Cambridgeshire it was believed that, if a two-leaved clover was put in your shoe the first eligible young person you met would be your true love, or at the least they would share the same name as your true love. However, the ordinary three-leaved shamrock or clover was also believed to have special powers.[10] In the Glens of Antrim it was believed that rubbing a mixture of clover and whiskey into the eyes would lift the 'fairy blindness' caused by malignant spirits. On Rathlin Island it used to be said that pounded shamrock rubbed across the eyes would allow sight of a particular fairy island which was believed to lie between Rathlin and the Antrim mainland. Shamrock and clover could also keep away evil influences. In one folktale a healer called Foranen O'Fergus used a mixture of clover, mountain heather, whiskey and shamrock to try to drive out an evil spirit which had gripped a man in a fever; while in another tale, holding on to a shamrock saved a musician called Garrett Barry from being attacked by an evil spirit. In Britain, the leaves of red clover were worn to ward off witches and warlocks and bring good luck. However, in Cornwall to have a pot of shamrock growing in the house was considered to be most unlucky. Finally, the notion that cattle particularly enjoy grazing in fields of clover led to the phrase that someone was 'in clover' when they were doing well in life.

But which plant is the 'real' shamrock – in other words, what is the botanical species of plant that Irish people identify as the shamrock? Two separate surveys almost a century apart looked into this question and came up with very similar answers. The two surveys employed much the same methods, in that they both asked people from all over Ireland to send them a specimen of what they considered to be shamrock. The specimens were then potted up and allowed to flower, so they could be correctly identified botanically. The first survey was done in 1893 by the naturalist Nathaniel Colgan, and the second in 1988 by botanist Charles Nelson. The results of both surveys are compared by Nelson in his study *Shamrock: Botany and History of an Irish Myth* with the following table:[11]

Botanical Name	English Name	% of samples (1893)	(1988)
Trifolium dubium	Lesser Trefoil	51	46
Trifolium repens	White Clover	34	35
Trifolium pratense	Red Clover	6	4
Medicago lupulina	Black Medick	6	7
Oxalis acetosella	Wood Sorrel	-	3

The results show that very little change occurred between the two surveys, and that for the vast majority of people shamrock is one of two species – lesser trefoil (*Trifolium dubium*) or white clover (*Trifolium repens*). However, a breakdown of the 1988 results by county reveals the intriguing fact that different parts of the country disagree in their choice. While lesser trefoil reigns supreme over most of the country, the favoured choice in Connaught and Donegal is white clover. The north Midlands is a kind of 'transition zone' with both kinds favoured in roughly equal amounts. Could it be that Connaught and Donegal are more traditional and favour white clover as the older form of shamrock, while the rest of the country changed its preference to the greener, more delicate lesser trefoil as the shamrock gained in stature as the national emblem? The choice of wood sorrel (*Oxalis acetosella*) by some reflects the efforts of some Victorians to promote it as the real shamrock, thankfully without much success.

Of course, discussing which species of clover is shamrock will upset those who are adamant that shamrock is not clover, and that it is unique to Ireland. Some even hold that it will not grow anywhere but in Ireland, and will wither and die if transplanted elsewhere. This is botanically untrue. Shamrock is indeed young clover or trefoil (there is no difference between the two), and the species can be found growing wild all over the world. But in myth it is another story. Nowhere else in the world is young clover given its own name, and venerated as somehow representing the soul of a country. In that sense the shamrock that grows in Ireland is indeed unique.

Given its place in the national mythology, it is no surprise to find that shamrock or clover appears in such placenames as Knocknashamroge (*Cnoc na Seamróg* – hill of the shamrock), County

Wicklow, Coolshamrogue (*Cúil Seamróg* – nook of the shamrock), County Clare, and Lugnashammer (*Log na Seamar* – hollow of the clover) County Roscommon.[12]

LEGENDS AND MYTHOLOGY

Clover appears as a symbol of the prosperity and fertility of the land in early Irish myth.[13] The *Metrical Dindshenchus* (or folklore of places) mentions flowering clover several times in this context. One story tells of how Tailtiú cleared rough land until it became a 'plain blossoming with clover'. Tailtiú died from her labours, and a fair was held every year in August at the spot (Teltown, County Meath) to commemorate her. Elsewhere a poem makes the boast that because the reign of the king Cairpre will be just, the bogland of Raigne 'will be overspread with clover flowers'. This is a version of the ancient idea that the rule of a good king will literally cause the land to blossom. A similar image is used to tell of the hero Dedad bearing home his bride to Temair Luachra in County Kerry, where 'the flowering clover was beneath their feet'. The *Lebor Gabála* or Book of Invasions tells of the Firbolgs, one of the early inhabitants of Ireland. According to legend, before their arrival in Ireland they were in servitude to the Greeks, forced to carry bags of clay onto bare rocks to make them fertile. In time, as a result of their efforts, the rocks became 'plains under clover flowers'. Another story tells of how St Brigid decided to stay in the curragh in County Kildare because when 'she saw before her the delightful plain covered in clover blossom, she determined to offer it to the Lord'. These Irish references are echoed in the famous description of the maiden Olwen in the Welsh tale *How Culhwch won Olwen*. Olwen is described as so beautiful 'that anyone who saw her would fall deeply in love', and wherever she went four white trefoils sprang up behind her, giving her her name which means 'white track'.[14]

Generally the word used for the clover flower in these stories is *scoth-shemrach* from *semair* meaning clover. There is no reference anywhere to the *seamróg* or shamrock as such. In his work on the shamrock, Nelson traces its early history and shows that there is no sign of the word *seamróg* or shamrock in either Irish or English until 1571, when the first reference appears in the work of Edmond

Campion. In the draft of his never-published 'Boke of the Histories of Irelande', Campion gives a description of the habits of the Irish which includes the line: 'Shamrotes, watercresses, rootes, and other hearbes they feed upon.' The spelling 'shamrotes' is of no significance, as spelling varied a great deal at that time. Campion's work was used as the basis of a later piece published in 1577 by Richard Stanihurst which wrongfully changed the meaning of the line to: 'Watercresses, which they terme shamrocks, rootes and other herbes they feed upon.' This false identification with watercress later caused endless confusion as to the true identity of shamrock. Also in 1571, a herbal in Latin was published called *Stirpium Adversaria Nova* which claimed that the Irish ate meadow trefoil (or Clover) ground into cakes and loaves and kneaded with butter. The authors claimed to get their information from 'certain gentlemen of our acquaintance' who had served for several years with the English army in Ireland. Although it does not mention the word shamrock, it is not hard to see a connection with the ideas expressed by Campion. In fact in 1597 John Gerard published a herbal in London which includes the meadow trefoil, identified by him as white and red clover and with the words 'which are called in Irish Shamrockes'.

From these sources a whole tradition grew up in English literature that the Irish subsisted on shamrock, along with watercress and other wild herbs. Stanihurst's words in particular were very influential, and were repeated in various forms over the next century. It is significant that all these authors got their information at best from second-hand sources, as there is no real evidence that the Irish ever ate shamrock or clover as food. There is no reason why they should, as the plant has no nutritional value for humans. The most likely explanation is that the source of the story is the custom of eating a sprig of shamrock after 'drowning' it on St Patrick's Day; and that this was blown out of all proportion as the story was repeated. We have already seen Dinely's 1681 description of how some Irish ate shamrock on St Patrick's Day 'to sweeten the breath'. Whether it was for this reason, or for luck, or because the shamrock was 'steeved in usquebagh' as Taylor put it in 1631, that was probably the extent of shamrock consumption. It might be argued these authors make no mention of St Patrick's Day, but the very use of the word shamrock or *seamair óg* denotes a springtime custom, when clover is young. It is not as improbable as it sounds that Protestant English visitors, totally ignorant of the ways of the Roman Catholic Irish, might have heard stories of the Irish eating a plant called shamrock, and missed the connection with St Patrick's Day. Up until the seventeenth century it was not a national holiday but primarily a Roman Catholic religious feast day, even if some used it as an excuse for merry-making. The fact is that shamrock has always been bound with St Patrick's Day, and it exists outside of it only as a symbol. Even today shamrock is only worn on 17 March. After that date interest in the real plant declines and it becomes 'mere' clover again as it grows older.

Central to the identity of shamrock is the legend of St Patrick using it to explain the mystery of the Holy Trinity to the Irish.[15] The most widespread version states that St Patrick preached his sermon at Tara on Easter Sunday after his dramatic contest with the druids. Trying without success to explain the concept of the three divine persons in one, St Patrick saw the trefoil growing on the green sod beneath his feet. Taking it up in his hand, he pointed out that just as the triple leaf sprang from the one stem, so each person was distinct, yet part of the one God. The Irish immediately understood what he meant, and allowed themselves to be baptised. Other versions claim that St Patrick preached his sermon in Wicklow, at Cashel, and in various places in Ulster and Leinster. There is no written evidence of the existence of this legend before its first recording by Threkeld in 1726. Nowhere in Patrick's own writings, or in the early biographies of his life written a few centuries later, is there any reference to the saint using the shamrock to teach the lesson of the Holy Trinity. So how did the legend come about? For a start, there is no other substantial reason to link St Patrick with the shamrock, so it is surely safe to assume that the legend goes back at least as far as the first record in 1681 of shamrock being worn on 17 March. In all probability we could also go back at a stretch to 1571 and the first mention of shamrock in the work of Edmond Campion. However, given the lack of evidence before that, we cannot go further back with any confidence. It must be accepted therefore that the likely origin of the legend is not any earlier than the sixteenth century.

Despite the lack of firm evidence, there have been many attempts to find an earlier origin.[16] It has been pointed out that trefoils appear on tiles in medieval Irish churches, and trefoil-like marks appear on Irish coins minted between 1399 and 1413, and later in the reigns of Kings Henry VI and Edward IV. Trefoils also appear on medieval Irish icons, including the shrine of St Patrick's tooth, and indeed in the *Book of Kells* itself trefoils are to be found on almost every decorated page. There are two main problems with accepting these facts as evidence of linking St Patrick with the shamrock, however. The first is that the trefoil was a common design motif throughout Europe in the Middle Ages, so its appearance cannot be linked to St Patrick. The second, and more damning fact is that none of the representations of St Patrick show him holding a shamrock until a coin minted in about 1674. Prior to this, images of St Patrick usually show him holding a crozier or a cross only. In fact it has been argued that images of St Patrick holding a 'Tau Cross', which was a medieval symbol of the Holy Trinity, is what led to the shamrock legend in the first place. Despite all this, it cannot be denied that the shamrock or clover is indeed an ancient symbol of Ireland's green pastures. All that happened was that a national symbol was linked to the national saint in a creative act of storytelling.

The custom of wearing the shamrock on Patrick's feast day was at first most likely not as a symbol of national pride. The shamrock's significance in the beginning was probably as much as a symbol of the coming of Christianity to Ireland as it was a badge of Irishness. The development of the shamrock as a national emblem came later with the development of a modern sense of nationalism in the eighteenth century. According to Nelson it began in the latter half of that century when rival armed groups began to use the symbol of shamrock on their regalia. On one side were the Loyalist Volunteers formed in the 1770's who pledged to protect the status quo; and on the other side were the United Irishmen, formed in 1791 with the aim of bringing about Ireland's independence as a republic. The United Irishmen adopted green as the colour of their uniforms and of revolution, in imitation of the shamrock, and thus cemented green's place as Ireland's national colour. Yet despite this, shamrock continued to be worn on St Patrick's Day and began to be used in official British emblems alongside the rose and thistle (and occasionally the leek). Both sides were anxious to claim the shamrock as a symbol of their claims to being true representatives of Ireland.

The shamrock continued its march to ubiquity throughout the nineteenth century, and began to be the subject of many sentimental songs and poems. The best known must be Thomas Moore's 'Oh the Shamrock', which appeared in 1812. The chorus contained the immortal lines:

Oh the shamrock, the green, immortal shamrock!
Chosen leaf
Of Bard and Chief,
Old Erin's native shamrock.

Shamrocks began to appear in ornamentation of all kinds from stone carvings in churches and on headstones, to glassware, costumes and book covers. The shamrock attained the status as a universal symbol of Irishness that it still retains today. There has been a downside to this fame, however, because in many respects the constant use of the shamrock has made it somewhat unreal and divorced from its origins. It would be a great pity to forget that it is in essence the *seamair óg*, the young clover, symbol of prosperity and good fortune, and the ancient emblem of Ireland's rich green pastures.

PRACTICAL AND HERBAL USES

Clover's most valuable asset is as a pastureland plant because of the ability of its roots to fix nitrogen in the soil, thus enriching it; and for this reason it is often sown by farmers along with grass. Clover had little use in folk medicine in Ireland or elsewhere in Europe. However, white clover has been recorded as a cure for coughs in Kerry, and liver ailments in Cavan.[17] Red clover features more widely, with records of its use as a cough remedy from Cavan, Wicklow, Clare and Kerry.[18] The leaves of red clover were also used for bee stings in Offaly, while an infusion of the flowers was drunk as a cure for cancer in Wicklow and Meath. In Scotland, children used to suck red clover to get the taste of the honey it contains.[19] Clovers and trefoils are members of the pea family, the *Fabaceae*.

SIMILAR PLANTS

Wood Sorrel– *Seamsóg – Oxalis acetosella*

ALTERNATIVE NAMES: (E) Alleluiah, Cuckoo Clover (Ulst), Cuckoo Meat, Cuckoo Sorrel, God-Almighty's-bread-and-cheese, God's Bread, Lujula, Protestant's Shamrock (Dub), Sheep's Sorrel, Sourock. (I) *Bia Éanáin, Bileog na nÉan, Samhadh Coille, Sealbhóg Fiodha, Seamair Choille, Seamair Ghéar, Seamróg Ghéar, Seamsán, Siomsán.*

Wood sorrel was eaten in ancient Ireland and appears in some Irish legends.[20] It appears, for instance, in the legend *Buile Suibhne* or 'Sweeney Astray'. Sweeney was a County Antrim king who fled from society to live in the wild, and wood sorrel is mentioned several times as one of the plants he depended on for his survival. The leaves were also traditionally eaten throughout Europe in a green sauce as a flavouring for food.[21] In modern times, however, it has only been eaten by children, who relish its sharp taste on hot days.[22] The names 'Alleluiah', 'God's bread' and so on, reflect the fact that it flowers around Easter, and so is said to partake in the rejoicing of that time.[23] In 1830 the London botanist James Bicheno put forward the notion that wood sorrel was the true shamrock, on the grounds that it could be eaten, that it had a prettier trefoil leaf and that it flowered in March around St Patrick's Day.[24] The only point of any substance in these arguments is the fact that wood sorrel was sometimes eaten, but the idea that it might be the true shamrock does not hold because there is no evidence. Before Bicheno's intervention no one had even mentioned wood sorrel as a candidate for shamrock, and the folk tradition was emphatic that it was (and is) young clover of some kind. Despite the lack of evidence, it was favoured by some writers in the nineteenth century as the shamrock, probably because it was seen as more 'refined' than the humble clover. Even today shamrock is sometimes depicted as wood sorrel, despite all the evidence that it is an imposter! In Irish folk medicine wood sorrel was used to cure diarrhoea in Counties Mayo and Wicklow, as a blood tonic in County Cavan, and as a cure for palsy in County Limerick.[25] Wood sorrel gives its name to the wood sorrel family, the *Oxalidaceae*.

Primrose – Sabhaircín

Primula vulgaris

♀ Ruled by the planet Venus in traditional herbal medicine

♉ Associated with the zodiac sign Taurus

*P*rimrose, with its pale yellow flowers which appear in early spring, is a symbol of the vitality and strength of the season, and was traditionally considered a powerful source of protection of the home and farm against evil influences. It is also a symbol of otherworldly beauty and love.

SPECIES NAME: As above

ALTERNATIVE NAMES: (E) Boneo-block, Bonnyboblock (Ker), Mayflower, Summer (Fin, Ulst). (I) *Bainne Bó Bleacht(áin)*, *Béacán*, *Buíocán* (*Bó Bleacht*) (Muns), *Padhacán* (Wfd), *Péacán* (*Buí*), *Peidhceán*, *Peidhreacán*, *Sabharcán*, *Sadharclann*, *Samhaircín*, *Seibhirín*, *Seimhirín*, *Sobhaircín*, *Sobharcán*, *Sobhrach*, *Soibhircín*

FOLK BELIEFS AND CUSTOMS

Throughout these islands the primrose was considered a harbringer of spring and early summer. In Scotland on St Brigid's Eve (31 January) a sheaf of oats was fashioned in the likeness of a woman, dressed in female attire and decorated with crystals and early flowers like snowdrops and primroses.[1] The *brideog*, as it was called, was then carried in procession to mark the feast. In England primroses were an emblem especially associated with Easter, and bunches were picked as presents for parents and decoration for churches.[2] In Ireland the primrose was particularly linked to May Eve, when it was widely used to protect against the fairies and evil influences.[3] The custom was that primrose, along with other yellow flowers, should be gathered by children before dusk on May Eve, or at the latest before dawn on May Day. The children then made 'posies' or small bouquets of flowers, which they hung in the house or over the door, or laid on the doorsteps and windowsills. Sometimes loose

flowers were strewn on the thresholds of the front and back doors, and on the floors of the house and byre. Flowers could also be strewn on the roofs, and in and around the nearest well. Bunches of primroses were also tied to the cows' tails to keep evil spirits from harming them; and primrose was rubbed on cows' udders to increase milk yield and prevent barrenness. Similar customs prevailed in the Isle of Man where primroses were gathered on May Eve to put around the doors of the house.[4] In Ireland primroses were also used to decorate the May altar dedicated to the Blessed Virgin Mary.[5]

In many places primrose flowers were associated with poultry keeping.[6] In Counties Cork and Limerick it was believed to be unlucky to bring primroses into the house if eggs were being hatched. In England it was believed that the number of flowers that were brought into the house would portend the number of chickens or geese that would hatch. Accordingly, never less than thirteen flowers should be brought in to ensure a good hatching. This was because thirteen was the traditional number of a clutch of eggs placed under a hen in spring. A development of this idea was the belief that any primroses given as a gift should be a very full bunch or misfortune would ensue, but when used in abundance, primrose flowers were good protection against evil spirits.[7] In England it was also sometimes believed that primroses were directly linked to the health and well being of humans.[8] In the village of Cockfield in Suffolk it is still said that no primroses grow, nor would they grow if planted there. The story goes that the village was depopulated during the plague, and the flowers died along with the people. In Cheshire it was believed that a primrose blossoming in winter was an omen of death, while in Lincolnshire bringing a single primrose into the house meant a death in the family. In Wales it was believed that primrose was unlucky if it bloomed in June.[9]

The phrase 'the primrose path' has come to mean a path to love and pleasure, even if often a rather uncertain and illusory one.[10] It seems that the phrase first appeared in *Hamlet*: 'Whilst like a puft and recklesse Libertine / Himselfe the Primrose path of dalliance treads.' In English folklore primroses are frequently associated with courtship, and they appear in many traditional songs like the following:

And when we rose from the green mossy bank
In the meadows we wandered away;
I placed my love on a primrosey bank
And I picked her a handful of May.

LEGENDS AND MYTHOLOGY

Primrose features as a symbol of otherworldy beauty in Celtic myth.[11] In the story 'The Wooing of Étaín' Mider tries to persuade Étaín to come with him to fairyland with the words: 'hair is like the blooming primrose there; smooth bodies are the colour of snow.' In the tale the 'Cattle Raid of Cooley' the warrior Nera enters a fairy mound at Samhain (or Halloween). It is summer in fairyland, so he returns from the mound carrying flowers of summer with him as proof of his stay. The flowers he brings are wild garlic, primrose and golden fern. In Welsh myth the beautiful maiden Blodeuedd was made by enchantment out of flowers, to be the wife of Lleu Skilful Hand. The flowers used to create her included primrose.

PRACTICAL AND HERBAL USES

In traditional herbal medicine an infusion of primrose flowers were considered a good remedy for nervous disorders and for promoting relaxation, while in Ireland they had a variety of uses in folk medicine.[12] In County Cork a tea made of primrose was considered a good cure for insomnia, while in County Dublin toothache could be cured by rubbing the affected tooth with a leaf for two minutes. In Ireland a salve made of primrose and other herbs was also used as a cure for burns. In County Westmeath the salve was made of primrose flowers and pig's lard, while in County Wicklow it was believed that putting a primrose leaf to the burn would be enough. In Ireland primrose was also widely used to cure jaundice. For example, in County Cavan a mixture of the juice of boiled primrose flowers and milk was drunk every morning as a cure for jaundice. In Kildare boiled primrose was also used as a cure for tuberculosis. Coughs in horses were cured using crushed primrose roots strained in breast milk or whey of goat's milk, and put into the horse's nose frequently. Primrose gives its name to the primrose family, the *Primulaceae*.

SIMILAR PLANTS:

Cowslip – *Bainne Bó Bleachtáin* – *Primula veris*
ALTERNATIVE NAMES: (E) Herb Peter, Keys-of-heaven, Paigle, Palsywort (Wex), Peter's Keys, St Peter's Wort. (I) *Bainne Bó Báine, Lusra na Múiseán, Múiseán, Péacán (Buí), Seibhirín.*

Cowslip seems to have been regarded in Irish folklore in much the same way as primrose. In Ireland cowslips were rubbed on the cow's udders on May Day to protect the milk.[13] The names 'Peter's keys' and 'St. Peter's wort' derive from a story in European folklore that the cowslip blossomed from the saint's keys when he accidently dropped them to earth.[14] This is probably a later reworking of the notion in Norse mythology that the flowers were dedicated to the goddess Freya, who was known as the 'Key Virgin'.[15] The stories are based on the idea that the pendulous flowers are reminiscent of a bunch of keys. In the Scottish Highlands the flowers of cowslip were boiled and an ointment made from them as a cosmetic, and for removing blemishes of the skin such as spots, wrinkles and freckles.[16] In Irish folk medicine the main use for cowslip has been as a remedy for insomnia, while a tea made from cowslip was also used to strengthen the nerves and provide relief from giddiness, hallucinations and ghostly presences.[17] In Counties Limerick and Wexford cowslip was used as a cure for palsy, hence the Wexford name 'palsywort', which reflects the use given to cowslip in traditional herbal medicine.[18] Cowslip is a member of the primrose family, the *Primulaceae*.

Marsh Marigold – Lus Buí Bealtaine

Caltha palustris

♂ Ruled by the planet Mars in traditional herbal medicine

♈ Associated with the zodiac sign Aries

*M*arsh Marigold, with its bright golden flowers, is a symbol of May and the return of summer, and was used on May Eve as a powerful protection against evil influences.

SPECIES NAME: As above

ALTERNATIVE NAMES: (E) Kingcup, May-flower, Plubisheen (Fin). (I) *Bearnán Bealtaine, Pleibistín (Buí) (Cght), Plobairsín, Plobaistín, Riasc-bhláth Órga*

FOLK BELIEFS AND CUSTOMS

In Ireland the marsh marigold, like the primrose, was particularly linked to May Eve, when it was widely used to protect against the fairies and evil influences. If anything it was more prominent in the folk customs surrounding the day, and was known simply as May-flower in many parts of the country. The most common names for it in Irish also mean 'the shrub of Bealtaine'. Marsh marigold, along with other yellow flowers, was gathered by children before dusk on May Eve, or at the latest before dawn on May Day.[1] Bouquets of the flowers were then made and hung in the house or over the door, or laid on doorsteps and windowsills. Alternatively the loose flowers were strewn on the threshold, and on the floors of the house and farm buildings. The flowers could also be strewn on the roofs, and in and around the nearest well. In the Isle of Man marsh marigold was used as a charm against fairies and witches, and it was considered essential that it should flower by May Eve so it could provide its protection for the festival.[2] It was also used in England in May Day festivals, and in the same way as in Ireland, was strewn before cottage doors and made into garlands.[3]

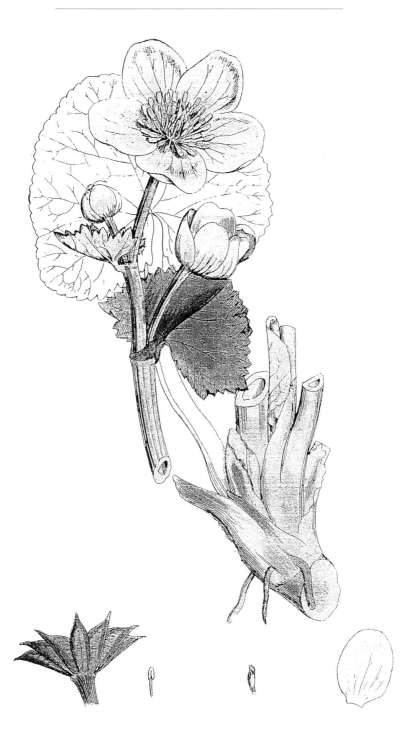

In Ireland the marsh marigold was the chief ornament of the garlands and other floral decorations surrounding the festival.[4] Dancing and games traditionally took place around the May bush on May Eve, with the girls decked out with wreaths of daisies and garlands of May flowers and buttercups. In some parts of Ireland a hoop wreathed with rowan and marsh marigold was carried by villagers on May Day. The hoop had two balls covered with silver and gold paper suspended from it. Marsh marigold could also be used to protect against fairies and other malign influences throughout May.[5] In Ireland garlands of marsh marigold were made to protect the cattle and their produce from the evil influence of fairies and witches; and marsh marigold was rubbed into the udders of newly calved cows to protect the milk. In the Scottish Highlands a hoop made of milkwort, butterwort, dandelion and marigold was bound with a triple cord of lint and placed under the milk vessels to prevent witches spiriting away the substance of the milk.

Marsh marigold gets its name from its use in church festivals in England in the Middle Ages, when it was one of the flowers devoted to the Virgin Mary, hence 'Mary Gold'.[6] The origin of the alternative name 'kingcup' comes from the word 'cop' meaning button or stud, and refers to the gold buttons that English kings used to wear.[7] Shakespeare refers several times to the flower: 'Winking Marybuds begin to ope their golden eyes.'[8]

PRACTICAL AND HERBAL USES

An infusion of the flowers of marsh marigold was traditionally used as a herbal remedy to cure fits, but the use of marsh marigold was generally limited as all parts of it are strongly irritant.[9] However, in County Meath the flowers were boiled into a soup and used for heart ailments, while in County Roscommon the leaves were used in a hot poultice to relieve boils.[10] Marsh marigold is a member of the buttercup family, the *Ranunculaceae*.

SIMILAR PLANTS:

Lesser Celandine – *Grán Arcáin* – *Ranunculus ficaria* [11]

ALTERNATIVE NAMES: (E) (Lesser) Figwort, Pilewort. (I) *Aonscoth, Lus na gCnapán*

Lesser celandine closely resembles marsh marigold, except that it is slightly smaller and grows in drier woodland. In the Scottish Highlands it was believed to have magical properties for protecting the milk, and was placed under the milk boyne and over the byre door to ensure milk in the cows. Lesser celandine got this reputation on account of its butter coloured flowers and its roots, which were said to resemble the teats of a cow. The names 'figwort' and 'pile-wort' also refer to the shape of the roots which were said to resembles 'figges' or piles (haemorrhoids), and because of this the roots were considered in traditional herbal medicine to be a remedy for piles. Lesser celandine is not related botanically to greater celandine (*Chelidonium majus*), but shares the name purely because the flowers were believed to be very similar. Lesser celandine is a member of the buttercup family, the *Ranunculaceae*.

Creeping Jenny – *Lus an Dá Phingin* – *Lysimachia nummularia*[12]
ALTERNATIVE NAMES: (E) Herb Twopence, Moneywort, String-of-sovereigns (Ulst)
The names 'herb twopence' and 'moneywort' refer to the rounded leaves running in pairs up the stems, which look like coins. Creeping Jenny was used in traditional medicine against wounds and bloodflow. Creeping Jenny is a member of the primrose family, the *Primulaceae*.

Nettle – neantóg

Urtica

♂   Ruled by the planet Mars in traditional herbal medicine

♏   Associated with the zodiac sign Scorpio

The nettle, with its harsh stinging leaves and stems, and habit of grow-ing near ruins and deserted places, is a symbol of desolation and aban-donment. However, its nutritious leaves and many herbal uses also make it a well-respected plant. In addition, nettle was traditionally highly regarded as a source for making cloth.

Species names:
Common Nettle – *Neantóg* – *Urtica dioica*
Small Nettle – *Neantóg Bheag* – *Urtica urens*

Alternative names for nettle: (E) Cool Faugh (Ulster), Stingers (Dub), Stinging Nettle. (I) *Cál Faiche, Coll Faiche, Cúl Fáich, Cúl Faiche, Cúl Fáidh* (all Ulst), *Neannta*

Folk Beliefs and Customs
In southern parts of County Cork, May Eve (30 April) was known as 'Nettlemas Night' when boys would parade the streets with large bunches of nettles, stinging their playmates and occasionally unfor-tunate passersby who got too close. Girls would join in too, usually stinging their lovers or boys whom they held in affection. It may be that this custom arose from the belief that nettle stings were good for rheumatism and inflamed joints.[1] Similar customs were found in Devon and Cornwall, where 1 May (or 2) was known as 'Stinging Nettle Day'.[2] Nettle was considered to be good for purifying the blood, and it was widely believed in Ireland that taking three meals of nettles in May guarded against illness for the rest of the year.[3] In west Galway the man of the house would go out on the night of May Eve and gather a handful of nettles. The nettles were pressed and everyone in the house would drink a mouthful of the juice to

'keep a good fire' in them for the rest of the year.[4] Nettles were also used as food in England, and a folk belief there held that they should not be gathered after May Day, because on that day the devil gathered the nettles to make his shirt.[5] This belief was actually good sense, because as the plant develops the leaves become course and unsuitable for eating. Nettle's use as food is reflected in the Ulster Irish name *Cúl Faiche* which means 'field cabbage'. It was also said in Ireland that nettle was one of the three plants that kept a lot of people from starving during the great famine – the others being charlock and carrageen.[6]

Nettle is famous, of course, for its stinging hairs, and the origin of the phrase 'to grasp the nettle' arises from the idea that if a nettle is firmly grasped it will not sting. A traditional rhyme put it as follows:[7]

If you gently grasp a nettle,
It will sting you for your pains.
Grasp it tightly like a rod of metal,
And it soft as silk remains.

However, an alternative explanation from England holds that the phrase comes from the belief that a person could be cured of a dangerous fever if a relative were to take hold of a nettle and pull it up by the roots, at the same time repeating the name of the sufferer and his or her parents.[8] In England country children would play a trick on town children by telling them that 'nettles don't sting this month', grasping the nettle firmly to prove the point. The unsuspecting 'townie' would gingerly touch the nettle and thus be stung.[9] In County Galway it was believed that the nettle was once the finest flower in the Garden of Eden, but the serpent hid under it after it tempted Eve, and so it became poisonous, stinging anyone who touched it.[10] In Achill in County Mayo, when a person was grumpy they were traditionally told 'You pissed on nettles this morning'.[11]

The name nettle is said to come from the Anglo-Saxon word for needle, and to refer either to its stinging needles, or to its role as the plant that provided thread for early cloth makers.[12] The universally acknowledged folk cure for nettle stings was to rub them with a dock leaf.

Nettle's habit of growing in disturbed soil and on rubbish heaps means that it is often found growing near human settlements, particularly when they have been abandoned and there is nothing to check its growth. This trait features in an Irish folktale which tells of how a clump of nettles aided a priest in curing a very ill woman. The clump of nettles grew in the heart of a mountain area in the place where a church once stood. When the church was in use, a consecrated host had fallen from the lips of the woman at mass and into a crack in the floor. Later on the church fell into ruins, but the nettles that grew there still guarded the host from harm. Using the clump of nettles as a guide to pinpoint its location, the priest and a boy working together were able to rescue the host, and when it was given to the woman she was completely cured of her illness.[13] In Ireland it was widely believed that nettle and comfrey growing together was a sign that there had once been a monastery at that spot.[14] Less benignly, it was believed in the Scottish Highlands that nettles grew out of the bodies of dead men, while in Denmark nettles were supposed to grow from the shedding of innocent blood.[15] In Denmark nettles also marked the dwelling places of elves and nettle stings were a protection against sorcery. Nettles also prevented the milk from being affected by house trolls and witches. In England it was believed that carrying some nettle about the person gave protection from lightning.[16]

LEGENDS AND MYTHOLOGY

Nettle's habit of growing in abandoned settlements made it a symbol of desolation, and it appears several times this way in legend.[17] For example, when the children of Lir return as swans to their home after many hundreds of years in exile, they find it empty 'with nothing in it but green hillocks and thickets of nettles, without a house, without a fire, without a hearthstone'. Similarly when Oisín, the last of the Fianna, returns to the site of their great hall at Almhuin in Leinster, he finds it deserted except for weeds and nettles. In ancient Ireland the Law of Adamnán forbade combatants to kill women and children. Anyone who broke this law, as well as facing the usual penalties for murder (usually heavy fines), would be cursed so that their heirs would be 'elder and nettle and corncrake' i.e. they would face ruin.

Nettle's use as food also appears in legend.[18] A famous story about the life of St Colmcille tells of how the saint saw an old woman cutting nettles, and asked her why she was bothering to do such a thing. The woman replied that nettle pottage was enough for her to live on. Inspired by her example of a humble life, Colmcille resolved to live only on nettle pottage from then on. However, his servant was concerned for Colmcille's health as a result and so devised a clever strategy. Whenever the servant mixed the saint's pottage, he made sure to use a hollow pipe for the task, so he could secretly pour meat juice down into it. Over time Colmcille's good appearance was remarked upon, and the saint became suspicious. He asked his servant what was in the pottage, and the servant replied: 'Nothing but nettles, unless something comes from the iron of the pot, or from the stick used to stir it.' Colmcille was satisfied with this answer, and the canny servant kept his conscience clear! Nettles also appear in the 'Life of St Brigid', in a tale which tells of how the saint was confronted with entertaining a large number of guests from an empty larder. The saint solved the problem by miraculously changing nettles into butter and the bark of trees into delicious food.

Nettles also appear in Welsh myth in a poem about the beautiful maiden Blodeuedd. She was made by enchantment out of flowers to be the wife of Lleu Skilful Hand, and nettle flowers are mentioned as among those used to create her.[19] This may be a comment that Blodeuedd's nature had a sting to it, as she later betrayed her husband for her lover Goronwy! The eighth-century text 'Cormac's Glossary' refers to nettle's stinging qualities when it rather implausibly gives the origin of the name *nenaid* or nettle as *Teine faid* – 'fire heat'.[20]

PRACTICAL AND HERBAL USES

Nettle traditionally had, and still has, a great many uses.[21] Nettle fibres have been used since ancient times to make a cloth which is both fine and strong, and in Ireland nettle has been used to make cloth since at least the Bronze Age. Its use goes back that far in Europe too, and nettle cloth has been found in a Danish Bronze Age burial site, wrapped around cremated bones. The juice of nettles was also used in Ireland and elsewhere to make a green dye. It was also an important food in Ireland since the earliest times, and a porridge called *brachán neantóg* was made in ancient Ireland out of a mixture of nettle and oatmeal. The young green tops are still eaten as 'greens' and believed to clean the blood and increase mothers' milk.[22] Nettle also had many medical uses.[23] Its use as a spring tonic to cleanse the blood meant it was considered a cure for rashes, pimples, boils and other skin complaints, and in Ireland nettle tea was drunk to help clear measles rash. Nettle stings were also considered good for rheumatism, paralysed limbs, circulatory problems and even epilepsy. It was traditionally believed that the crushed leaves applied to wounds stopped bleeding, or if pounded with salt they were useful for the bites of mad dogs. The famous folk herbalist Biddy Early had a cure for swollen limbs which was a poultice made from cabbage leaves, nettles and watercress bound up with egg-white.

Nettle gives its name to the nettle family, the *Urticaceae*.

SIMILAR PLANTS

Pellitory-of-the-Wall – *Feabhraíd* – *Parietaria judaica* [24]
ALTERNATIVE NAMES: (E) Billy Beatie. (I) *Lus an Bhalla, Miontas Caisil*
Pellitory-of-the-wall gets its name from the fact that it is usually found growing on old damp walls, though the name is a tautology as 'pellitory' itself derives from the Latin *paries*, meaning a wall. In traditional medicine it was valued as a diuretic and used to alleviate dropsy and gravel complaints. Pellitory-of-the-wall is a member of the nettle family, the *Urticaceae*.

Red Dead-Nettle – *Caochneantóg Dhearg* – *Lamium purpureum*[25]
ALTERNATIVE NAMES: (E) Blind-nettle, Daynettle (US), Red Archangel, Stinking Archangel. (I) *Marbhneantóg, Neantóg Chaoch, Neantóg Dhearg*

White Dead-Nettle – *Teanga Mhín* – *Lamium albu*[26]
ALTERNATIVE NAMES: (E) Blind-nettle, Daynettle (US), White Archangel. (I) *Marbhneantóg, Neantóg Chaoch*
Despite their name and similar appearance, dead-nettles are not related to the true nettle. The name 'archangel' derives from the fact

that they are said to first flower around the feast of St Michael the Archangel – 8 May. In Irish folk medicine a decoction of the roots of red dead-nettle was used in County Meath to bring out the rash in measles, and in County Kerry an infusion was drunk for headaches. Doubt exists as to whether white dead-nettle is native to Britain and Ireland, or whether it was introduced. For example, in County Dublin its distribution closely coincides with the known sites of early Norman settlement. Dead-nettles give their name to the dead-nettle family, the *Lamiaceae*.

Marsh Woundwort – *Cabhsadán* – *Stachys palustris*
ALTERNATIVE NAMES: (E) All-heal, Clown's All-heal, Clown's Woundwort, Keanadha-hassog (Don), Roughweed (Ulster), Sheep's Brisken. (I) *Duilleog na Saor, Lusra Saor*

Hedge Woundwort – *Créachtlus* – *Stachys sylvatica*
ALTERNATIVE NAMES: (I) *Créachtlus an Fháil*
As their name suggests the woundworts were used in traditional medicine for treating wounds.[27] In Irish folk medicine woundworts were used for that purpose in Counties Wicklow and Galway, and the leaves were used to dress sores in County Westmeath. Woundworts are members of the dead-nettle family, the *Lamiaceae*.

Watercress – Biolar

Nasturtium officinale

☽ Ruled by the Moon in traditional herbal medicine

Watercress, with its peppery tasting, nutritious leaves, was tradition-ally an important food in Ireland, and was valued for its cleansing and purifying properties. It was considered an important salad plant for combating scurvy, and for promoting general health and wellbeing.

SPECIES NAME: As above
ALTERNATIVE NAMES: (E) Bilders, St Patrick's Cabbage (Longford), Tongue-grass, Water-grass (Cork, Dublin, Longford, Ulster). (I) *Biolar Uisce, Biolrán, Biorar, Durlus*

FOLK BELIEFS AND CUSTOMS
Watercress was believed, in both Ireland and Scotland, to have the power to steal the goodness from milk when used in a charm.[1] An Irish folk tale tells of how a farmer caught an old woman at a spring well, cutting the tops of watercress with a pair of scissors, mutter-ing the names of certain persons who had cows, and the words *is liomsa leath do chodasa* – 'half your portion is mine'. Seeing her, the farmer cried out and rushed towards her and the old woman imme-diately fled. The old woman had intended to steal half the goodness of the milk from the peoples' cows, and each sprig of watercress stood for a person who was to be robbed. Watercress was occasion-ally believed to have beneficial mental and emotional effects along with its physical benefits.[2] In County Tyrone a sprig of watercress was put into the hand of a newborn child to protect it from depres-sion. In Devon in England it was believed that eating watercress increased a person's intelligence, and a 'simple' person was described as someone who 'never ate his watercress'. In County Cork it was said that on the night of the feast of Little Christmas (6 January) watercress was turned into silk, and water into wine.[3]

Watercress was thought by some writers to be the true identity of shamrock. However, this was based on a confusion on the part of

some early commentators about references to shamrock being eaten in Ireland (see the section on shamrock). All the evidence is clear that young clover or trefoil is the 'true' shamrock. However, watercress was linked to St Patrick in County Longford where it was known as St Patrick's cabbage 'as it needed no dressing'.[4]

LEGENDS AND MYTHOLOGY

Watercress features as a valued food in several ancient Irish legends.[5] In the story 'The Cattle Raid of Cooley', the hero Cúchulainn greets his rival Fergus as a guest and offers him a handful of watercress, seaweed and brooklime to eat. It is also mentioned as one of the traditional foods of the hero Fionn Mac Cumhaill and his band of warriors, the Fianna. However, the most significant appearance of watercress is in the legend *Buile Suibhne* or 'Sweeney Astray', as the main food source of the eponymous Sweeney. *Suibhne Geilt* or 'Mad Sweeney' was a County Antrim king cursed by St Ronán for his aggression, who lost his wits as a result and fled from society. Sweeney made his way to Gleann Bolcáin, a glen variously located in County Antrim or County Kerry according to myth. It was said that all the madmen and lunatics of Ireland would gather there, seeking solace and healing in its beauty and peace. There they would drink from wells and streams and eat the watercress that grew around them, and so sought after was the watercress that the madmen used to fight each other for the pick of the crop. As well as Gleann Bolcáin, Sweeney stayed in a number of locations around Ireland, living near a well in each place and eating the watercress that grew nearby. For example, beside a well in Ros Comáin he was about to take some of the watercress when a local woman picked it first. Sweeney was distraught and remonstrated with her: 'O woman sad is it that you should take my watercress from me ... For kine I have my watercress, my water is my mead'. Although it does not say so directly, there is a strong implication in the story that the watercress is not just a source of physical nourishment, but also a source of healing for Sweeney's distressed condition. The legend includes many lays or poems of Sweeney, and watercress features in most of them:

Watercress I pluck,
Food in a fair bunch,
Four round handfuls
Of fair Gleann Bolcáin.

Watercress also appears in some legends as a source of magical powers.[6] In the Life of St Mochua the saint blessed two sprigs of watercress for a barren woman, who at once conceived both a son and a daughter. In one story about the Fianna, a druid army is made by enchantment from stalks of grass and the tops of the watercress to help the Fianna defeat their enemies. Watercress' habit of growing near wells and streams links it to water in Irish myth.[7] In one Irish legend the three cupbearers of the king of Tara are described as each having a cup of water in front of him, with a bunch of watercress in each cup. The eighth-century text 'Cormac's Glossary' gives the origin of the Irish name for watercress or *biolar* as 'the hair of the well' from *bir*, 'a well or stream' and *hor*, 'hair'.

PRACTICAL AND HERBAL USES

In ancient Ireland watercress was regularly collected from the wild and eaten raw or cooked in a soup or broth,[8] and it continues to be eaten to the present day. Watercress was sold about the streets of Dublin as a salad plant to purge the blood in spring, and was considered good to protect against scurvy.[9] In Ireland generally watercress was considered as a purifying tonic and a remedy for colds, coughs and chest complaints, and eating watercress was also said to cure rheumatism.[10] Watercress was also used for a variety of cures in different parts of Ireland.[11] In County Kerry watercress was used to alleviate women's ailments, and was made into a poultice to ease labour pains. In County Mayo watercress was rubbed on the skin to remove rashes and other skin blemishes, while in County Longford, it was said to be good for heart disease. The famous folk herbalist Biddy Early had a cure for swollen limbs which was a poultice made from cabbage leaves, watercress and nettles bound up with eggwhite.[12] Watercress is a member of the cabbage family, the *Brassicaceae* (or *Cruciferae*).

SIMILAR PLANTS

Cuckooflower – *Biolar Gréagáin* – *Cardamine pratensis*[13]
ALTERNATIVE NAMES: (E) Lady's-smock, Milking Maids (Donegal). (I)
*Glasair Léana, Gleorán, Gleorann, Glórán, Lasair Léana, Léine Mhuire,
Lus na mBan, Seilín Cuaiche*

Cuckooflower gets its name from the fact that it flowers in late spring
and early summer, when the cuckoo 'begins to sing her pleasant note'.
The name 'lady's-smock' is said to have arisen because the flowers
first appear around 25 March or Lady Day. Cuckooflower appears in
some old Irish legends. In the legend *Suibhne Geilt* or 'Mad Sweeney',
Sweeney is a king who has been driven mad by a curse and taken to
living in the wilds. Cuckooflower is one of the wild flowers whose
beauty he praises. An old Irish poem in praise of a glen called Gleann
Ghualainn mentions cuckooflower as one of the flowers that grew
there at the time of the Fianna, the legendary warriors of Ireland. In
traditional herbal medicine the flowering tops of cuckooflower were
believed to be good for nervous afflictions, such as hysteria, epilepsy
and St Vitus' dance. Cuckooflower is a member of the cabbage family,
the *Brassicaceae* (or *Cruciferae*).

Garlic Mustard – *Bóchoinneal* – *Alliaria petiolata*[14]
ALTERNATIVE NAMES: (E) Jack-by-the-hedge, Sauce Alone, Stinking
Hedge Mustard. (I) *Amharag, Gairealach Coilm, Gáirleog Choille,
Garbhlach Coilm*

In England garlic mustard, as its name indicates, was sometimes
used in cooking as an alternative to garlic. It was also used there in
folk medicine for sore throats and gums and for mouth ulcers.
Garlic Mustard is a member of the cabbage family, the *Brassicaceae*
(or *Cruciferae*).

Hedge Mustard – *Lus an Óir* – *Sisymbrium officinale*[15]
ALTERNATIVE NAMES: (E) Scrambling Rocket, Wild Rocket. (I)
Taithigín Taibhseach

In traditional medicine hedge mustard was valued as a cure for coughs, chest complaints and hoarseness. An infusion of it was said to inhance the vocal performance of singers when taken as a gargle. Hedge Mustard is a member of the cabbage family, the *Brassicaceae* (or *Cruciferae*).

Bluebell – Coinnle Corra

Hyacinthoides non-scripta

♍ Associated with the zodiac sign Virgo

The blubell is an iconic image of the Irish countryside, with its delicate, deep-blue flowers carpeting our wild woods in late spring and early summer. It appears in Irish myth as a symbol of beauty, and is linked to the hyacinth of Classical myth, which was a flower of grief and mourning.

SPECIES NAME: As above

ALTERNATIVE NAMES: (E) Blue Rocket, Bummack (Donegal), Bummuck (Donegal), Crowpicker (Donegal), Crowtoes, Cuckoo's-boots, Harebell (Ulster), Wild Hyacinth. (I) *Bú* (*Muc*), *Búgha* (*Muc*), *Ceann Chorach* (Aran Is), *Cloigín Gorm*, *Fuath Muice*, *Lus na gCoinnle gCorrach*, *Lus na gCoinnle Gorm*

FOLK BELIEFS AND CUSTOMS

A long-established custom in Ireland is the picking of bluebells in spring and early summer when they appear in our woodlands. Although research has shown that picking the flowers does not do any lasting harm, trampling on the leaves while collecting the flowers does damage the plant's ability to manufacture food and thus replenish itself.[1] As it is hard to see how one can be accomplished without causing the other, the best course of action is to leave the flowers where they are so that everyone can enjoy them! Although bluebells are also widely gathered in England, in parts of the country like Devon, Staffordshire and Yorkshire it was considered unlucky to bring the flowers indoors.[2] Bluebell appears in the placenames Cloonboo (*Cluain Bú* – meadow of bluebells); County Galway; and Coolbooa (*Cúil Bú* – nook of bluebells), County Waterford.[3]

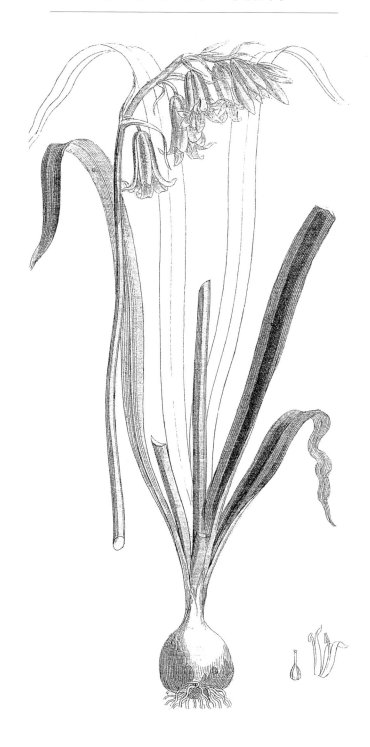

LEGENDS AND MYTHOLOGY

Bluebell appears in several places in Irish legends as a symbol of beauty.[4] In the tale 'The Destruction of Da Derga's Hostel', the beautiful maiden Étaín is described as having eyes of hyacinth blue. Later in the same tale the hero Conall Cernach is described as having 'as blue as hyacinth one eye, as black as a beetle's back the other', while another warrior is said to have 'eyes blue grey and brighter than hyacinth'. In the tale 'The Colloquy of the Ancients', St Patrick is approached at one point by a handsome youth with cheeks as red as a bullfinch (*corcair chaille*) and eyes as blue as hyacinth (*bugha*), who helps the saint by offering him the use of his chariot.

Our native bluebell was identified by botanists as related to the hyacinth mentioned by the ancients as a flower of grief and mourning.[5] In Classical myth Hyacinthus was a charming youth loved by both the sun god Apollo and Zephyrus, god of the west wind. Hyacinthus, however, preferred Apollo over Zephyrus, which enraged Zephyrus and caused him to seek revenge. So when Hyacinthus was playing quoits one day with Apollo, Zephyrus blew one of the quoits out of its proper course, and it struck Hyacinthus and killed him. Stricken with grief, Apollo caused a purple flower to rise up out of Hyacinthus' blood, which bore his name forever after. On the flower was inscribed the Greek letters AI, so that Apollo's cry of woe would be remembered for eternity. When botanists examined our own bluebell they found no similar markings on it, and so described it as a hyacinth that was *non-scripta* – 'not written on'.

PRACTICAL AND HERBAL USES

Bluebell is noted for the gummy sap of its bulbs, which made it useful as a substitute for starch. It was also used as a glue for purposes like bookbinding and setting the tail feathers on arrows.[6] Bluebell was little used in folk medicine. However, it has been boiled for throat ailments in County Cavan, and applied to whitlows in County Monaghan, and in County Donegal the juice was drunk as a cure for coughs.[7] A story from the Glenties in County Donegal states that Fionn and his men were put asleep with a mixture of bluebell and tormentil by Gráinne before she and Diarmaid eloped.[8] Bluebell is a member of the lily family, the *Liliaceae*.

SIMILAR PLANTS

Harebell – *Méaracán Gorm* – *Campanula rotundifolia* [9]

ALTERNATIVE NAMES: (E) Bluebell, Bluebottle, Fairy Bells, Hairbell, Lady's-thimble (Ulster), Witch's-thimble. (I) *Corrach na Cuaiche, Méaracán Púca*

Although it is also widely known as bluebell, harebell is not related to *Hyacinthoides non-scripta*. In Ireland and Britain harebell was considered a fairy plant, which was not to be picked. In Scotland harebell is the badge of the Ramsey clan. In European folklore harebell is dedicated to St Dominic. Harebell is a member of the bellflower family, the *Campanulaceae*.

Common Milkwort – *Lus an Bhainne* – *Polygala vulgaris* [10]

Heath Milkwort – *Na Deirfiúiríní* – *Polygala serpyllifolia*

ALTERNATIVE NAMES FOR MILKWORT: (E) Fairy Soap (Donegal), Four Sisters (from the different colours of the flower) (I) *Glúineach, Lus na Seacht mBua*

Looking like a miniature bluebell among the grass, milkwort is easy to miss if you are not looking out for it. Throughout Europe milkwort was traditionally carried in processions in Rogation week (the week before Ascension Day, when Christ ascended into heaven), when the bounds were beaten and the crops blessed. In Donegal it was believed that the fairies made a lather from the roots and leaves, hence the name 'fairy soap'. In traditional medicine milkwort was recommended to nursing mothers for promoting the flow of milk after childbirth. Milkwort gives its name to the milkwort family, the *Polygalaceae*.

Ramsons – *Creamh* – *Allium ursinum*

ALTERNATIVE NAMES: (E) Ramps, Wild Garlic. (I) *Cneamh, Féarán, Gáirleog Fiáin*

Ramsons or wild garlic appears in many Irish woodlands in springtime as a flowering carpet instead of bluebell. In Irish folklore ramsons was a metaphor for sharpness or bitterness: *Chomh searbh le creamh* – 'as bitter as wild garlic' – was a Donegal saying.[11] Nevertheless, cloves of ramsons were sometimes planted in the thatch over the door in Irish cottages for good luck.[12] Ramsons is mentioned in some old Irish legends and poems.[13] It appears, for instance, in the legend *Buile Suibhne* or 'Sweeney Astray'. Sweeney was a County Antrim king who fled from society to live in the wild, and ramsons is mentioned several times as one of the plants he depended on for his survival. It also appears in a poem in praise of the Hill of Howth in north County Dublin: 'the peak bright-knolled beyond all hills ... full of wild garlic and trees'. Ramsons or wild garlic was considered an important food in early Ireland, and along with watercress and wild sorrel was regularly collected from the wild and then eaten raw, or cooked in a broth or soup.[14] Indeed in the Old Irish Brehon laws there was a fine of the value of two and a half milch cows for taking wild garlic, seaweed or wild apples from private land without permission. In more recent times, in nineteenth-century Ireland ramsons was often used to flavour butter instead of salt.[15] In Irish folk medicine wild garlic was highly valued as a preventative of infection, as well as a cure for coughs, cold and flu.[16] It was also believed in many parts of Ireland to clear the blood of impurities, and wounds of infection, and to cure toothache.[17] Ramsons is a member of the lily family, the *Liliaceae*.

Yellow Iris – Feileastram

Iris pseudacorus

  ☽   Ruled by the Moon in traditional herbal medicine

  ♋   Associated with the zodiac sign Cancer

The yellow iris or flag, with its dramatic and showy flowers appearing along waterways in early summer, is one of the best- known flowers of the Irish landscape. In Irish myth it was a symbol of beauty, while in the Classical world it was associated with purity, faith and wisdom.

SPECIES NAME: As above

ALTERNATIVE NAMES: (E) Flag, Flagger, Flaggon, Leavers, Marsh-flag, Saggon, Shellistring, Seggen (Ulster, US), Sword Lily, Water-flag, Water-lily (Donegal), Wild Iris, Yellow Flag. (I) *Alartram* (Clare), *Alastram, Curchas, Duileastram, Eileastar, Eileastram, Feileastar, Ga Gáinne, Seileastram* (Connaught), *Seilistring, Siolastar* (Ulster), *Siolastrach, Sléibhtrach, Soileastar, Soileastrach.*

FOLK BELIEFS AND CUSTOMS

In south-west County Cork the long leaves of yellow iris or 'flag- gers' were placed on the doorsteps and windowsills on May Eve, or used to decorate the dresser, even though yellow iris does not come into flower in the area until late May or early June.[1] On Cape Clear Island in County Cork, bunches of the 'flaggers' were also put in the fishing boats for luck.[2] The leaves of yellow iris could also be used to decorate May bushes.[3] In many parts of Ireland the feast of Corpus Christi was known as *Diardaoin Álainn na mBínsí Breátha* (lovely Thursday of the fine benches), when the custom was to spread fresh rushes and wild iris leaves on benches outside the house doors, where the old people sat telling stories to the young on the day.[4] In County Wexford bunches of yellow iris were hung out- side every door on the day of the feast. In Ireland it was said that if a fairy changeling was banished into water such as a river, lake or

bog, that it would turn into a bunch of yellow iris or fern.[5]

Yellow iris also appears in customs in other European countries.[6] In France yellow iris was a plant especially associated with St John's Eve. In the Channel Island of Guernsey the yellow iris was a favourite plant for strewing in front of a bride on her way to her wedding ceremony. In Shetland children used to make boats out of the leaves of yellow iris by selecting a large leaf and making a small lengthwise slit about halfway along its length. The tip of the leaf was then bent over and pushed through the slit to make both a sail and keel. The 'seggie boats' were then launched on the nearest water and could cover short distances. In Shetland it was also believed that anyone who bit into a yellow iris would develop a speech impediment such as a stammer.

Yellow iris appears in placenames such as Lisatilister (*Lios an tSeileastair* – fort of the yellow iris), County Monaghan; Bunnafollistran (*Bun na bhFeileastram* – bottom of the yellow iris), County Mayo; and as just itself in Allistragh (*Aileastrach*) County Armagh, and Ellistrim (*Eileastraim*), County Galway.[7]

LEGENDS AND MYTHOLOGY

Yellow iris appears several times in Irish myth as a symbol of beauty.[8] In the legend 'Midhir and Étaín' the beautiful maiden Étaín is described as having hair 'like yellow flags in summer, or like red gold after it is rubbed'. Later in the same tale, Midhir attempts to persuade Étaín to come with him to fairyland where there are 'beautiful people without blemish; their hair is of the colour of the flag-flower, their fair bodies are as white as snow'. An early Irish poem attributed to the Gaelic hero Fionn MacCumhaill in praise of the beauties of May time mentions the golden flag-flower among the delights of the season.

In the ancient world the iris stood as a symbol of power and majesty.[9] Iris was the Roman goddess of the rainbow and the flower was named after her on account of the beauty and variety of its colours. She was the attendant of the Roman goddess Juno, goddess of marriage and childbirth. The Romans also used the iris in purification ceremonies, and it was the origin of the sceptre. In ancient Egypt it was placed on the brow of the sphinx and the three leaves of its blossoms symbolised faith, wisdom and valour. The yellow iris was the origin of the *fleur-de-lys*, the heraldic emblem of the kings of France.[10] The legend goes that the sixth-century Frankish king Clovis, who was a pagan, was induced to pray for victory to the god of his Christian wife Clothilde because he was faced with defeat in battle. He was victorious over his enemies, and in gratitude converted to Christianity. As a token of this he replaced the three toads on his banner with three irises, the iris being the Virgin

Mary's flower. Six hundred years later it was adopted by Louis VII of France as his heraldic bearings in his crusade against the saracens; and it is said the name *fleur-de-lys* is a corruption of the name *Fleur de Louis*. However, another explanation has it that the name refers to the river Lys, where the yellow iris was said to grow abundantly.

PRACTICAL AND HERBAL USES

In Ireland the leaves of yellow iris were used for bedding and thatching, and the root could be used to make a black dye.[11] In parts of Ireland like west Galway and Cork, the dried leaves of yellow iris were used until recently as bedding for livestock, and dried leaves have been found from medieval Dublin which had been used as bedding for people. In Fingal in north County Dublin the leaves were also saved like hay to provide food for cattle and horses.[12] In traditional herbal medicine yellow iris was used as a cure for diarrhoea, and as a cathartic.[13] In Ireland and Scotland yellow iris was used to cure toothache, with a piece of the rhizome being held against the affected tooth.[14] In northern Scotland the rhizomes of yellow iris were also used to cure colds and sore throats, the juice being poured or snorted up the nose.[15] In parts of Ireland the flowers of yellow iris were boiled and strained and the water drunk as a cure for jaundice.[16] Yellow iris is a member of the iris family, the *Iridaceae*.

SIMILAR PLANTS

Stinking Iris – *Glóiriam* – *Iris foetidissima*[17]
ALTERNATIVE NAMES: (E) Gladding-root, Gladum
Stinking iris does not quite deserve its name, as the smell is said to be something like raw beef, and only noticeable if the leaves are crushed. In England stinking iris was employed as a purgative, while in Ireland it was applied to fresh wounds, or used to treat mumps or a swollen throat by tying the heated leaves around the neck. It was esteemed in County Tyrone as a cure for dropsy. Stinking iris is a member of the iris family, the *Iridaceae*.

Sweet Flag – *Feileastram Cumhra* – *Acorus calamus*[18]
ALTERNATIVE NAMES: (E) Sweet Sedge
Sweet flag gets its name from its pungent scent which resembles

orange peel. On account of this it was often strewn on the floors of churches and in houses to freshen the atmosphere. It was used in traditional medicine for bruises, rheumatism and chest complaints in children, and to aid digestion. Sweet flag is a member of the arum family, the *Araceae*.

Bog-myrtle – Raideog

Myrica gale

☿   Ruled by the planet Mercury in traditional herbal medicine

Bog-myrtle, with its resinous, fragrant leaves and flowers, was considered to be a blessed plant in folklore. It was also valued for its many uses, which included being used to repel insects, flavour beer and provide a yellow dye.

SPECIES NAME: As above

ALTERNATIVE NAMES: (E) Bog Gaul, Bog Sally, Dutch Myrtle, Dwarf Sallow, Gale, Gowan (Ulster), Sweet Gale, Sweet Willow, Wild Sumac. (I) *Cam-shaileog, Raid, Raidleog, Reileog, Rideog, Roid(eog), Roidleog, Roilleog* (Munster), *Roithleog, Ruideog, Rudóg, Truideogach*

FOLK BELIEFS AND CUSTOMS

Although bog-myrtle is unremarkable in appearance it emits a resinous, balsamic fragrance, especially when in flower. In fact, the scent from large colonies of bog-myrtle is strong enough to travel hundreds of metres.[1] This pleasant aspect of bog-myrtle meant that it was widely regarded as a blessed plant in Irish folklore.[2] For example, bog-myrtle was used in some parts of Ireland as palm on Palm Sunday, when Jesus' entry into Jerusalem is commemorated. In Achill in County Mayo bog-myrtle also provided the ashes that were used on Ash Wednesday, the first day of Lent. In Scotland bog-myrtle is the badge of the Campbell clan, and was also considered to be a blessed plant.[3] In the Scottish Highlands it was picked in the name of the Trinity to bring good luck and to protect from harm, and was often picked while saying the following verse:

> I am plucking thee,
> Thou gracious red myrtle,
> In the name of the Father of virtues,
> In name of the Son whom I love,
> In name of God's eternal spirit.

For virtue of good man,
For virtue of good span,
For virtue of good woman,
For virtue of good life,
For virtue of good step.

Despite its positive aspects, bog-myrtle was seen in some ways as unlucky in Irish folklore.[4] It was said that bog-myrtle was once a large tree, but it was used to make Our Lord's cross and so was cursed thereafter, becoming small and stunted. A similar story states that bog-myrtle was cursed because it was supposed to have been used to scourge Our Lord. Whatever the reason for bog-myrtle's curse, it was considered bad luck to strike cattle with it. In Ireland it was also believed that walking over bog-myrtle would bring bad luck.

LEGENDS AND MYTHOLOGY

In the *Lebor Gabála*, or 'Book of Invasions of Ireland', the first brewer in Ireland was named Malaliach and he was said to be the first person in Ireland to make *lind ratha* or 'fern ale'.[5] The Old Irish word for bog-myrtle (*rait*) is very close to that for fern (*raith*), so it is possible that bog-myrtle is in fact the proper translation. The evidence is ambiguous, however, because although there is no record of either ferns or bog-myrtle being used to make ale in Ireland, both plants have been used for that purpose elsewhere. In Norway the fronds of both male fern and bracken were used to make beer, while the branches of bog-myrtle were used to flavour beer in France, Wales and England (especially Yorkshire).[6]

Bog-myrtle was sufficiently useful to earn a place in the Old Irish Brehon Laws on trees and shrubs as one of the 'bushes of the wood', probably on account of its use as a dye.[7] This meant that the unlawful clearing of a whole field of bog-myrtle was subject to a fine of one *dairt* (or year-old heifer) under the laws. Bog-myrtle was also linked by some medieval scholars with the ancient Irish Ogham alphabet.[8] Each letter of the alphabet was named after a different native tree or shrub, and the letter *Gétal* (which had a sound like *Gw*) was said by some authorities to be named after bog-myrtle.

PRACTICAL AND HERBAL USES

Bog-myrtle was widely used to flavour and strengthen beer.[9] The medieval English herbalist Gerard stated that bog-myrtle gave a headiness to beer or ale, which was then 'fit to make a man quickly drunke'. In Yorkshire until recently, the branches were put into beer as a substitute for hops, and the result known as 'Gale beer' was considered very good for quenching thirst. Similarly, in France and Wales the flowers of bog-myrtle were put into barrels of beer to strengthen it. In Ireland and Scotland bog-myrtle was gathered for fuel, and was noted for the fragrance the smoke gave throughout the house.[10] Throughout Britain and Ireland the dried leaves of bog-myrtle were placed in linen presses to scent clothes and keep moths away, and in Scotland and west Cork it was put into beds to repel fleas.[11] An infusion of the tops of its branches was used for tanning and for making a yellow dye.[12] The fruits of bog-myrtle were also widely used to flavour soups and stews.[13] Bog-myrtle was generally not much used for medical purposes, but in County Donegal it was taken for kidney troubles, and for sore throats in County Kildare.[14] Bog-myrtle gives its name to the bog-myrtle family, the *Myricaceae*.

Meadowsweet – Airgead luachra

Filipendula ulmaria

♃   Ruled by the planet Jupiter in traditional herbal medicine

♓   Associated with the zodiac sign Pisces

*M*eadowsweet, with its sweet-smelling flowers, was valued for its use in flavouring beer, and for strewing with rushes on the floor of rooms to keep them fresh and pleasant smelling. It was also considered a useful herbal plant for a variety of ailments.

SPECIES NAME: As above
ALTERNATIVE NAMES: (E) Bridewort, Queen-of-the-meadow (Ulster).
(I) *Crios Conchulainn, Cubhar Léana* (Louth), *Lus Cneas*

FOLK BELIEFS AND CUSTOMS
It was believed by some that the scent of meadowsweet was perilous, because it could cause people to fall into a deep and possibly fatal sleep.[1] Perhaps for this reason it was believed in parts of England that it was unlucky to bring meadowsweet flowers indoors.[2] On the other hand, in west County Galway it was believed that if a person was pining or wasting away because of fairy influence, that putting some meadowsweet under their bed ensured they would be cured by morning.[3] Meadowsweet is unusual among plants in that, although the flowers have a sweet scent, the leaves have a different, sharper and more bitter smell. This fact was the reason for the cynical Yorkshire name of 'Courtship and Matrimony'.[4]

LEGENDS AND MYTHOLOGY
In the Welsh myth 'Math Son of Mathonwy' the beautiful maiden Blodeuedd was made by enchantment out of flowers to be the wife

of Lleu Skilful Hand. The flowers used to create her included those of oak, broom and meadowsweet.[5] In Irish myth Áine, the land goddess of Munster, was supposed to have given meadowsweet its scent.[6] Meadowsweet was also known in Irish by the name *Crios Conchulainn* or 'Cúchulainn's Belt', but the reason for this is not clear. Meadowsweet, along with watermint and vervain, was considered to be one of the three most sacred herbs of the druids.[7]

PRACTICAL AND HERBAL USES

Contrary to popular belief, the name meadowsweet has nothing to do with meadows. It comes from the Anglo-Saxon *meodu-swete* which means 'mead-sweetener'; and indeed meadowsweet has been used to flavour mead, beer, wine and other drinks since early times.[8] Despite the negative folk beliefs associated with it, the leaves and flowers of meadowsweet were also widely used alongside rushes to carpet the floors of houses and keep them fresh and smelling pleasant.[9] Indeed, it is said that Queen Elizabeth I would have nothing but meadowsweet mingled with the rushes on her bedroom floor. According to the herbalist Gerard 'the smell thereof makes the heart merrie and joyful and delighteth the senses'. Perhaps this is where the Irish name *Airgead Luachra* or 'Silver Rushes' comes from. In Ireland meadowsweet was used to scour milk vessels and was mixed with copperas (Ferrous sulphate) to give a black dye.[10] Meadowsweet was also used to cure a variety of ailments. According to the herbalist K'eogh a powder made from the roots was effective in preventing diarrhoea and dysentry, and an infusion of the flowers was good for curing fevers.[11] In fact meadowsweet was widely used in Ireland and Britain to cure fevers, colds, sore throats and other pains, and there is a medical basis for this as it contains salicylate, which has a similar effect to aspirin.[12] Meadowsweet was also used for complaints as diverse as dropsy and kidney trouble in Counties Cavan and Sligo, and as a tonic for nerves in County Westmeath. Meadowsweet is a member of the rose family, the *Rosaceae*.

SIMILAR PLANTS

Lady's Bedstraw – *Boladh Cnis* – *Galium verum*[13]

ALTERNATIVE NAMES: (E) Cheese Rennet, Yellow Bedstraw. (I) *Mada Fraoigh, Rú Mhuire*

Like meadowsweet, lady's bedstraw was used to freshen homes with its aromatic flowers, but it was mainly used in bedding for this purpose, on account of its astringency, which also helped to repel fleas. According to an old European legend, lady's bedstraw was in the manger in Bethlehem with Jesus along with bracken. Bracken refused to acknowledge the child and so lost its flower, but lady's bedstraw welcomed Him and so burst into flowers, their previous white colour changing to gold. The name 'cheese rennet' derives from the fact that it was also extensively used to curdle milk for making cheese. In County Westmeath lady's bedstraw was used to cure fits in dogs. Lady's bedstraw is a member of the bedstraw family, the *Rubiaceae*.

Woodruff – *Lus Moileas* – *Galium odoratum*[14]

ALTERNATIVE NAMES: (E) Hayplant (Ulst), Woodroof. (I) *Lus Molach*

Like meadowsweet, woodruff was used to freshen homes with its aromatic flowers and leaves, and was traditionally strewn on floors, stuffed into beds and placed among the linen. The sweet aroma is said to be like that of newly mown hay – hence the name 'hayplant'. The leaves of woodruff were dried and used to make a tea against colds and fevers in the Scottish Highlands. Woodruff is a member of the bedstraw family, the *Rubiaceae*.

Scarlet pimpernel – Falcaire Fiáin

Anagallis arvensis

☉   Ruled by the Sun in traditional herbal medicine

♌   Associated with the zodiac sign Leo

The scarlet pimpernel, with its blood-red flowers, was seen as a source of magical energy and life. It was also an important herb used for a wide variety of complaints in traditional medicine, particularly to dispel sadness and to counteract venomous bites.

SPECIES NAME: As above
ALTERNATIVE NAMES: (E) Male Pimpernel, Poor Man's Weatherglass, The Blessed Herb. (I) *Falcaire Fuar, Glanrosc* (Cork), *Luibh na Muc, Rinnrosc, Ruinnrosc, Sailín Cuach* (Galway), *Seamair Mhuire*

ALTERNATIVE NAMES FOR THE BLUE-FLOWERED FORM OF SCARLET PIMPERNEL ARE: (E) Black Melilot, Female Pimpernel. (I) *Seamair na Mumhan, Seamair Mhuire*

FOLK BELIEFS AND CUSTOMS
In Ireland scarlet pimpernel was widely known as *Seamair Mhuire* ('Virgin Mary's Shamrock'), and was believed to possess special powers.[1] The person who possessed it was said to have second sight and hearing and to be able to understand the speech of birds and animals. One folktale relates how a man with some in his possession was able to understand what two dogs were saying to each other! Scarlet pimpernel was also said to grow at the spot where a mare had been born, and to have the ability to move against the current if it was in a river or stream. A well-known folktale features the truth-seeing powers of the scarlet pimpernel. The story tells of a farmer who, unknown to himself, had a sprig of *Seamir Mhuire* in the hay he was carrying on his back. A large crowd had gathered at a particular spot on his way home, and he stopped to see what they

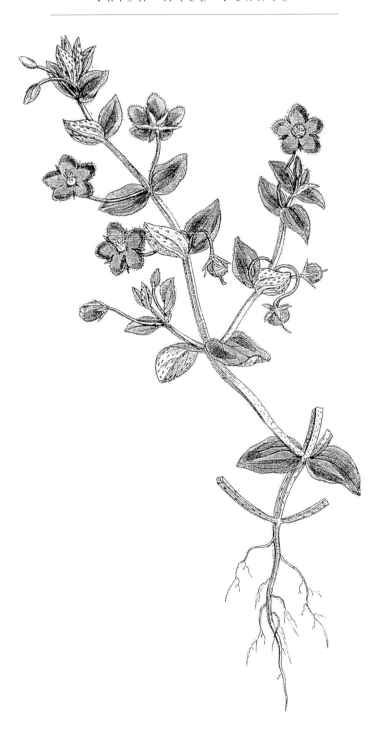

Shamrock/Clover – Seamróg
Trifolium dubium
Trifolium repens

Primrose – Sabhaircín
Primula vulgaris

Marsh Marigold (Kingcup) – Lus Buí Bealtaine
Caltha palustris

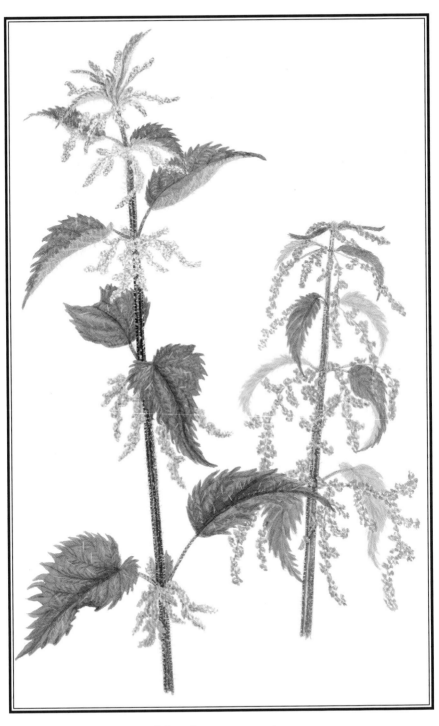

Nettle – Neantóg
Urtica dioica

Watercress – Biolar
Nasturtium officinale

Bluebell – Coinnle Corra
Hyacinthoides non-scripta

Yellow Flag – Feileastram
Iris pseudacorus

Bog-myrtle – Raideog
Myrica gale

were looking at. The crowd was marvelling at the impossible sight of a cockerel hauling a huge log of wood behind it as it walked, but the farmer was unable to see this. He could only see a wisp of straw trailing behind the bird. The circus man who had organised the illusion overheard him telling this to another member of the crowd, and whispering to the farmer, he immediately bought the bundle of hay from him for a generous price. As soon as he handed over the bundle to the circus man the farmer saw the huge log of wood just like everyone else! He then realised too late that his bundle must have contained some *Seamair Mhuire*, which had given him the power to see through the illusion. The same story is told about the four-leaved shamrock, which was considered in folklore to have many of the same powers as scarlet pimpernel. Belief in scarlet pimpernel's powers was not unique to Ireland. In medieval England scarlet pimpernel was believed to be good for preventing witchcraft.[2]

Scarlet pimpernel is noted for the fact that its flowers open early in the morning and close up again about three o'clock in the afternoon.[3] The flowers also close in damp or humid weather, or when rain is on its way. For this reason it has been given such names as 'Poor Man's Weatherglass' and 'Shepherd's Clock'. In Scotland it was known as the 'Reaper's Weather Gauge'. The Irish name *Falcaire* also means a reaper or workman, and probably expresses a similar idea. In the same way, when the flowers were seen to be fully open it was taken as an indication of fine weather. A variety of scarlet pimpernel sometimes occurs with bright blue flowers, and it was thought by medieval herbalists that this was the female form of the plant, while the more usual form with red flowers was thought to be the male.[4]

LEGENDS AND MYTHOLOGY

An English legend from Devon explains why scarlet pimpernel has such vivid scarlet flowers.[5] The story goes that when England was still a pagan country, some Christian Irish came to Devon and Cornwall and settled there. They began to convert the locals, but nevertheless faced persecution for their beliefs. A young Christian girl called Urith was captured by pagans, and because she refused to renounce her faith she was put to death by having her head cut off. At the spot where her blood stained the corn, there sprang up a blood-red flower, which was the first scarlet pimpernel. Indeed, not only was the flower scarlet, but the underside of the leaves were spotted with scarlet as well in token of Urith. For this reason, in Devon the scarlet pimpernel is still said to be called 'Urith's Blood'.

PRACTICAL AND HERBAL USES

Scarlet pimpernel was very well thought of in traditional herbal medicine.[6] As an old rhyme put it: 'No heart can think, no tongue can tell/The virtues of the pimpernel.' It was thought to be a remedy for the bites of mad dogs and serpents, to be good for liver complaints, and to have the ability to dispel sadness. Indeed, the Latin name for scarlet pimpernel, *Anagallis*, derives from the Greek word 'to laugh'. Scarlet pimpernel was also used as a cosmetic for removing freckles, and as a remedy for diseases of the eye. In Ireland scarlet pimpernel was used as a cure for jaundice, dropsy, inflammation of the kidneys and toothache.[7] In Cork scarlet pimpernel was used for eye complaints, and it was also used in parts of Ulster for chronic or muscular rheumatism.[8] Scarlet pimpernel is a member of the primrose family, the *Primulaceae*.

SIMILAR PLANTS

Common Chickweed – *Fliodh* – *Stellaria media* [9]

ALTERNATIVE NAMES: (E) Chickenweed (US), Tongue-grass. (I) *Flig* (Waterford), *Flíoch* (Galway, Clare), *Fuilig* (Kerry, Cork), *Luibh na bhFranncach*, *Luibh na Triucha*, *Seamair Mhuire*

To the casual observer, common chickweed is a low-growing plant looking a lot like scarlet pimpernel except for its small white flowers. The main use for chickweed has usually been as a food for hens and other poultry – hence its name. However, it was also eaten by people in various times of shortage. For example, it was said to be one of the plants that sustained the townsfolk during the siege of Derry in 1690. Chickweed was also one of the plants that were eaten in Ireland in famine times to stave off starvation. An ancient remedy called Diancecht's porridge after the Irish god of healing, was used in Ireland to cure fourteen different disorders of the stomach. It involved a brew of hazel buds, dandelions, chickweed, wood sorrel and oatmeal. The porridge was also used to relieve colds, phlegm, sore throats and worms. In Irish folk medicine chickweed was very popular as a hot poultice for treating sprains, mumps and other forms of inflammation. It was also used in some parts of Ireland to cure sores and cuts. Common chickweed is a member of the pink family, the *Caryophyllaceae*.

Common Mouse-ear – *Cluas Luchóige* – *Cerastium fontanum*
ALTERNATIVE NAMES: (E) Upright Cudweed. (I) *Liathlus Beag, Lochall Caol, Luibh na Triucha, Lus Mí, Lus na Míol, Seamair Mhuire*
Common mouse-ear is a low-growing plant that is easy for the casual observer to believe is a kind of pimpernel. The name 'mouse-ear' derives from the shape of the leaves. It is often confused in conversation with mouse-ear hawkweed (*Hieracium pilosella*), and the Irish name *luibh na triucha* or 'whooping cough herb' is probably a translation based on this confusion, as *hieracium* was used in folk medicine to cure that ailment. Common mouse-ear, however, does not seem to have had any role in folk medicine in Britain or Ireland. Common mouse-ear is a member of the pink family, the *Caryophyllaceae*.

Foxglove – Lus Mór

Digitalis purpurea

♀ Ruled by the planet Venus in traditional herbal medicine

♉ Associated with the zodiac sign Taurus

Foxglove contains the powerful drug digitalis, which affects the heartbeat. This made foxglove a mysterious fairy plant, both feared and respected. Foxglove's unusual and striking purple and white flowers also made it a symbol of otherworldly beauty.

SPECIES NAME: As above

ALTERNATIVE NAMES: (E) Blob, Cottagers, Dead Man's Fingers (Ulster), Dead Man's Thimbles, Fairy Bells, Fairy Cap, Fairy Fingers, Fairy Gloves, Fairy Thimble, Fairy Thimmles (US), Fairy Weed, Fox-and-leaves, Foxe's Thumbs, Foxy, Harebell, Lady's-fingers, Lady's-glove, Sheegie-thimbles (Donegal), Shilly-thimbles (Donegal), Thimbles. (I) *Creaics* (Galway), *Féirín Sí* (Galway), *Lus Mór Baineann, Lus na mBan Sí, Maide Méaracán, Méaracán an Diabhail, Méaracán Daoine Marbh, Méaracán Dearg, Méaracán na mBan Sí, Méaracán Púca, Méaracán Sí, Méiríní Dearg, Méiríní Púca, Méiríní Madra Rua, Méiríní Sí, Sian Sléibhe, Sídhean Sléibhe, Síodhan Sléibhe*

FOLK BELIEFS AND CUSTOMS

In Irish folk belief a child who was wasting away for no apparent reason was thought to be under fairy influence or the 'fairy stroke', and foxglove was traditionally believed to be a powerful herb to counteract this.[1] This belief no doubt derived from the powerful, if dangerous, effects of digitalis in reviving the weak. One such remedy for the 'fairy stroke' was the juice of twelve leaves of foxglove taken daily. Another from County Leitrim was to give the child three drops of foxglove on the tongue and three in each ear. The child was then placed on a shovel at the door of the house and swung out the door three times saying, 'if you're a fairy away with

you'. If the child was a fairy 'changeling' put in place of the real child, then it would die, if not then it would begin to recover. Similarly, in Wales it was believed that a fairy changeling could be got rid of by bathing the infant in a solution of foxglove.[2] In Scotland too, foxglove was credited with great ability to break the fairy power over a child.[3] In Ireland it was believed that foxglove would also work for adults who were under the fairy spell. Such a person should be given a drink made from the leaves of foxglove. If they were not entirely under the fairy spell they would drink it and get sick and so be 'brought back'. If they were too far gone under the fairy enchantment, they would know what it was and refuse to drink it.[4] An amulet of foxglove could also cure the delirious urge to keep travelling which gripped a person who had stepped on the fairy grass, the 'stray sod' or *fód seachrán*.[5]

St John's Eve (23 June) was considered the best time in Ireland to collect foxglove for medicinal purposes, as this was considered the time when herbs usually had their greatest strength.[6] This was some-times extended to the season between St John's Eve and 'Old St John's Day' (29 June or 4 July). For example, an eighteenth-century herbal work recommended 'foxglove and figwort gathered between the two feasts of St John, boiled in the water of three boundaries' as a cure for a child who got fits or spasms while asleep. However, it was also believed that if the wind changed while you were cutting the foxglove, that you would lose your mind.[7] Strangely it was also believed that it was perfectly safe to cut foxglove if you were being paid to do it, but if you were cutting it for your own purposes then the fairies might be annoyed. One tale tells of a woman stopped from cutting foxglove by an enchanted voice which called out: 'Don't cut that if you're not paid, or you'll be sorry.'

In parts of Ireland it was said that the foxglove would nod its flowers or bend its head if one of the fairy host was passing by, as a mark of respect.[8] In Wales it was believed that foxgloves were one of the places where the fairies hid.[9] In the south of Scotland foxglove was one of the plants favoured by witches, along with hemlock and nightshade.[10] In parts of England it was considered unlucky to bring foxglove indoors, because it gave witches or the devil access to the house.[11] Similarly, an Irish folk belief held that it was bad luck to bring foxglove into the house on May Day.[12] In English folklore the mottlings on the blossoms were said to mark where the elves had left their fingers, and one legend ran that the marks on the fox-glove were also a warning sign of the baleful juices contained in the plant.[13] More innocently, the thimble-like flowers of foxglove have always been a favourite with children, who delight in putting them on their fingers. A favourite children's game throughout Britain and Ireland was inflating the flowers of foxglove and then bursting them with a pop, while another was trapping bees in the flowers to hear their enraged buzzing.[14]

Authorities differ as to the origin of the name foxglove.[15] Some hold that it is as it appears – the 'foxe's glove'– because the Anglo-Saxon name *foxes glofa* appears as early as 1,000 AD, and the name appears in Norwegian as *Revbielde* ('Foxbells'). A Norse legend also tells that that the fairies gave these blossoms to the fox so that he might put them on his toes to prowl among the hen roosts. However, a widespread alternative view is that the name foxglove comes from 'folk's glove', or glove of the fairies, and the number of names for foxglove involving fairies (Fairy Thimble, Fairy Finger etc) is cited as proof of this. The theory has also been put forward that the 'glove' part of the name may come from Anglo-Saxon *gliew* – a musical instrument with many small bells. In Irish things are sim-pler, as *Lus Mór* simply means 'great herb', and the next most popu-lar name *Méaracán* means 'thimble', the same as the Latin *Digitalis*.

Foxglove appears in such placenames as Carrickatane (*Carraig an tSiain* – rock of the foxglove), County Tyrone; Lugateane (*Log an tSiain* – hollow of the foxglove), County Roscommon; Cloonameragaun (*Cluain na Méaragán* – meadow of the foxglove) County Galway; and Gortnamearacaun (*Gort na Méaracán* – field of the foxglove), County Clare.[16]

LEGENDS AND MYTHOLOGY

In Celtic mythology foxglove appears as a symbol of otherworld beauty.[17] In the story 'The Wooing of Étaín' Mider tries to persuade Étaín to come with him to fairyland with the words: 'A delight to the eye the number of our hosts, the colour of foxglove on every cheek.' In another tale, a description of Étaín's own beauty includes the words: 'as tender and even and red as foxglove her clear, lovely cheeks.' Similarly, in the story 'The Exile of the Sons of Uisliu' it is said of the great beauty Deirdre of the Sorrows that: 'Foxglove her purple pink cheeks, the colour of snow her flawless teeth.' The same image appears in Welsh myth when the maiden Olwen is described as having cheeks 'redder than the reddest foxgloves'. In Welsh legend too the fairy woman of the lake of Lyn-y-Fan had a 'mouth on her red as the reddest foxglove'. However, it is not only women who had such beautiful cheeks. The warrior Conall Cernach is described in one tale as having one cheek as bright as snow, and the other as speckled red as the foxglove; while in another tale the young men in the retinue of the prince Maine Morgor had 'cheeks like the flowers of the woods in May, or like the foxglove of the mountains'. Finally, foxglove's fairy aspect is emphasised in another story, when the interior of a fairy fort is described as being decorated with curtains the colour of foxglove, hanging on rods of copper.

PRACTICAL AND HERBAL USES

Foxglove is famous for containing digitalis, a powerful drug that effects the heart. Digitalis works by slowing the pulse rate and making it regular, but it also has the effect of dramatically raising blood pressure.[18] This potentially dangerous power of digitalis led to differing reactions to foxglove in folk medicine.[19] In Ireland it was declared by some that foxglove should never be used internally, while others swore by it as a tonic. Some people believed that putting a bit of foxglove into everything they drank would ensure a long life. Although foxglove was used in some parts of Ireland for heart trouble, the most common use by far was to make a tea or broth out of it as a cure for colds, sore throats and fevers. Foxglove was also widely used in Ireland as a salve for skin complaints, wounds, lumps and swellings and burns. Foxglove has diuretic properties and so was sometimes used in folk medicine for complaints such as dropsy or gravel. In Ireland the poisonous properties of foxglove meant that it was also used for banishing fleas.[20] In Ireland foxglove was considered the king of Irish herbs, as figwort was the queen.[21] Foxglove is a member of the figwort family, the *Scrophulariaceae*.

SIMILAR PLANTS

Common Figwort – *Donnlus* – *Scrophularia nodosa*
Water Figwort – *Donnlus Uisce* – *Scrophularia auriculata*
ALTERNATIVE NAMES: (E) Water Betony. (I) *Samhadh Corraigh, Samhadh Feárna*

ALTERNATIVE NAMES FOR FIGWORT: (E) Brownwort, Great Figwort, Kernelwort, Knotted Figwort, Queen-of-herbs, Rose Noble, Stinking Roger, Throatwort. (I) *Batram, Dúnlus, Farach Dubh, Fearadh, Fothram, Lus na gCnapán, Taithigín Taibhseach*

In Irish folklore figwort was considered the queen of Irish herbs, as foxglove was the king. It was considered a powerful herb, regarded with respect and not a little fear, because it was thought to be a fairy herb.[22] Its Irish name *fothrom* is supposed to come from *faoi trom* or 'under elder', because it was said to derive some of its powers from growing under the elder, a witch's and fairy tree. For this reason care had to be taken in the manner in which it was to be collected for use. One story tells of a clever (if heartless) healer who tied one end of a string to a dog's neck and the other end to the figwort, and then went some distance away and called the dog. The dog ran towards the man, uprooting the figwort as he did so, and but then fell down dead due to the figwort's power.[23] Mostly though, the care was more in the time and manner of collection. An Irish eighteenth-century herbal work recommended 'foxglove and figwort gathered between the two feasts of St John (29 June or 4 July), boiled in the water of three boundaries' as a cure for a child who got fits or spasms while asleep. In Ireland the roots, leaves and berries of figwort were usually boiled and the liquid drunk to remove impurities of the blood and as a cure for bronchial ailments, sore throats, coughs and consumption.[24] The leaves were also used as a poultice to cure sprains and other swellings in Counties Donegal, Derry and Leitrim, to cure burns in Counties Leitrim and Mayo, and for cuts and wounds, also in County Mayo.[25] In traditional medicine figwort was used to cure 'figs' or piles, hence the name 'figwort'.[26] Figwort gives its name to the figwort family, the *Scrophulariaceae*.

Rosebay Willowherb – *Lus na Tine* – *Epilobium angustifolium*[27]
ALTERNATIVE NAMES: (E) Blooming Sally, Fireweed (I) *Saileacháin*
Rosebay willowherb is a striking plant, with its tall spires of purple flowers. It was relatively uncommon until recent centuries, when the growth of railways, industrial waste ground, and the felling of woodlands, allowed it to spread exponentially. It is also one of the first plants to colonise open ground after there has been a fire – hence the name 'fireweed'. Willowherb gives its name to the willowherb family, the *Onagraceae*.

Purple-Loosestrife – *Créachtach* – *Lythrum salicaria*[28]
ALTERNATIVE NAMES: (E) Brian Braw, Foxtail, Longpurples, Purplegrass, Sally, Spiked Willowherb, Stray-by-the-lough, Willowstrife. (I) *Cró Dearg, Crólus, Eireaball Caitín, Lus na Síochána*
Despite its Irish name *créachtach*, which means 'wound-herb', purple-loosestrife does not seem to have ever been used for healing wounds in Ireland. It was used instead to cure diarrhoea and dysentry. The Irish name is perhaps due to a confusion with yellow loosestrife (*Lysimachia vulgaris*), which was traditionally valued in herbal medicine as a cure for wounds. In Ireland purple-loosestrife was considered a weed by farmers because it spread so much. Purple-loosestrife gives its name to the loosestrife family, the *Lythraceae*.

Honeysuckle – Féithleann

Lonicera periclymenum

♂ *Ruled by the planet Mars in traditional herbal medicine*

♏ *Associated with the zodiac sign Scorpio*

Honeysuckle, with its bright flowers and sweet perfume, is a symbol of beauty and summertime. However, the wood of honeysuckle, although it begins life soft and flexible, becomes very hard as it matures, with the ability to choke off the growth of any other wood by binding it tightly in its grip. This has made it a symbol in Irish legend of strength and slow, inexorable power.

SPECIES NAMES: As above

ALTERNATIVE NAMES: (E) Irish Vine, Woodbine. (I) *Bainne Gamhna, Cas Fá Chrann, Duilleabhar Féarána, Feath, Féith, Féithleog (Fá Chrann), Iashlat, Luibh Féarána, Lus na Meala, Mil Ghabhair, Táith-fhéithleann, Tromán na hAbhna*

FOLK BELIEFS AND CUSTOMS

In folklore honeysuckle was believed to protect against harmful influences and witchcraft.[1] In Ireland honeysuckle was believed to have a power against bad spirits, and it was used in a drink to cure the effects of the evil eye. In the north east of Scotland on May Day, farmers put pieces of honeysuckle and rowan over the doors of the cowhouses to prevent the goodness of the milk being stolen by witchcraft. A variation on this in the Hebrides was to make a wreath of ivy, honeysuckle and rowan to place over the lintel of the cowhouse and under the vessels in the milk house, to safeguard the cows and their milk from witchcraft, the evil eye and murrain. In Moray in the Scottish Highlands, withes of honeysuckle were cut down at the waxing of the March moon, twisted into wreaths, and preserved until the following March, when children sick of fever and consumptives were made to pass through them three times as

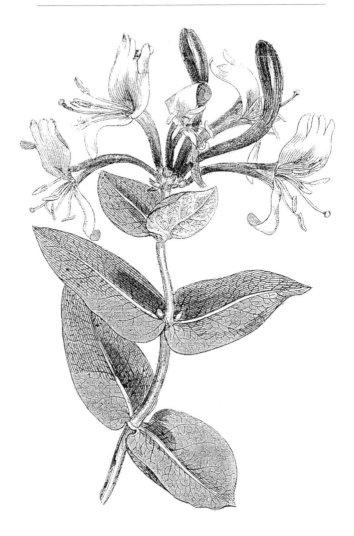

a means of cure. In the Isle of Man honeysuckle was considered good 'to keep milk from stinginess and butter from blackness'. It was also used there to keep animals from enchantment.

But honeysuckle's powers could also be used for witchcraft. A British ballad tells of how a witch uses various means to prevent the birth of a lady's child, including planting a 'bush o' woodbine' between her bower and the lady's. Fortunately a good house goblin tells the lady's husband of the enchantment and once the binding, restricting influence of the honeysuckle is removed, the birth proceeds normally.[2] Honeysuckle or woodbine is noted for the toughness of its wood, and it has the ability to choke off the growth of any tree it wraps itself around. In Ireland this trait led to the old saying that anything that was hard to break was *chomh righin leis an táith-fhéithleann,* 'as tough as the honeysuckle'.[3]

In England honeysuckle has romantic associations. If it is brought into the house a wedding will follow, and if its flowers are placed in a girl's bedroom it will bring her dreams of love.[4] However, in many places throughout Britain and Ireland it was considered bad luck to bring honeysuckle indoors. In Cheshire it was believed that honeysuckle should never be cut because it would prevent a second crop of hay, while in Dyfed in Wales it was believed that bringing honeysuckle indoors would be the cause of a sore throat. The two ideas are not mutually exclusive, however, because in the fen country of England honeysuckle was banned from entering the house due to the fear that it might give young girls erotic dreams![6] Honeysuckle is mentioned by Shakespeare in a romantic context: 'Sleep thou, and I will wind thee in my arms. / So doth the woodbine – the sweet honeysuckle / gently entwist.'[7]

The flowers of honeysuckle are full of nectar, and a favourite pastime of children was to suck them for the sweet taste, and this trait gave honeysuckle its name.[8] Some local names in England have a similar theme, such as 'Sweet Suckle' in Somerset or 'Sucklings' in East Anglia.[9] In Irish the name *Bainne Gamhna* or literally 'Calve's Milk' refers to the same idea of something sweet for suckling. The name appears in a well-known old Irish song: *Samhradh, samhradh, bainne na ngamhna, / Thugamar féin an samhradh linn, / Samhradh buí na nóiníní glégeal, / Thugamar féin an samhradh linn* – 'Summer, summer, the honeysuckle, / we brought the summer with us. / Golden summer of bright daisies, / we brought the summer with us.' The name is usually just translated literally, but it is clear from the context that honeysuckle is what is meant. The song was traditionally sung at May time as part of the festivities, when there was singing and dancing, and the making of garlands of flowers. Honeysuckle appears in the placenames Aghnaveiloge (*Achadh na bhFéithleog* – field of honeysuckle), County Longford, and Stranafeley (*Srath na Féithle* – river bottom of honeysuckle), County Fermanagh.[10]

LEGENDS AND MYTHOLOGY

Honeysuckle or woodbine's ability to choke off any other wood made it an image of power and strength in Celtic legend.[11] Honeysuckle features prominently in a tale called 'The Death of King Fergus'. At one point in the story Iubhdan, the king of the Leprechauns calls on King Fergus, and observes a servant throwing a piece of honeysuckle twisted around a length of wood into the fire. Iubhdan is shocked that the servant does not realise that this will bring ill fortune, and so recites a poem about the properties of various woods to educate him. It begins with a description of honeysuckle's own powers as 'the king of woods':

> O servant to King Fergus, make sure the fire's good,
> On land or on sea, do not burn the king of woods.
> High king of Irish woods, that no army can hold,
> It is no weak service tough trees to enfold.
> But burn the weak woodbine and warning cries will sound
> Of danger at spear point, or strong waves to drown.

The implication is that the burning of the woodbine in some way foreshadows or contributes to King Fergus' death later in the tale. In fact the Irish word *féithleann* could itself be used to mean a chief. In the tale *Táin Bó Cúailnge* or 'The Cattle Raid of Cooley', Cúchulainn is goaded into continuing to fight his enemy Ferdia by being told that Ferdia has: 'bested you as a woodbine binds trees'. Later, when Cúchulainn has turned the tables on Ferdia, he himself uses the same image. He tells Ferdia to stand aside or 'I will entwine you as a woodbine binds trees'. It is not the gentle embrace of love that is meant here, but the crushing of an enemy in an iron grip. Something similar may be at play in the mention of honeysuckle in the early Welsh poem the '*Cad Godeu*' or 'Battle of the Trees'. The poem imagines letters in the form of trees and shrubs going to an enchanted war of words and poetry, and speaks of : 'The wild rose and the woodbine, and the ivy intertwined.'

Honeysuckle's themes of love and strength come together in the tale of the love between the youth Baile Mac Buain and the princess Aillinn.[12] Their love is ill-fated and they both die of broken hearts and are buried separately. A yew tree grows from Baile's grave and an apple tree from Aillin's, and after seven years poets make writing tablets out of each of them. It so happens that the poets later attend the feast of Tara at the same time, and the high king Cormac MacArt is taken with their poems. He asks to see the two tablets, and as soon as he takes them into his hands, they spring together and become entwined like honeysuckle around a branch. So tightly are they intertwined that no one could part them. Honeysuckle also appears as an image of beauty in an eighth-century poem about the hermit Marbán. Marbán eulogises his simple life in a hut in the woods close to the beauty of nature, and describes how the honeysuckle grows over his door.[13]

Despite its lack of any major economic uses, honeysuckle was sufficiently well regarded to replace the rather rare arbutus or strawberry tree as a 'lower division of the wood' in some versions of the Old Irish Brehon Laws on trees and shrubs.[14] Honeysuckle was also prominent enough to be linked by some medieval scholars with the ancient Irish Ogham alphabet.[15] Each letter of the alphabet was named after a different native tree or shrub, and the letters *Gort* (G) and *Uilen* (UI) were both said by some authorities to be named after honeysuckle.

PRACTICAL AND HERBAL USES

In traditional herbal medicine the flowers of honeysuckle have been used to make a syrup to cure diseases of the respiratory organs and asthma, and a decoction of the leaves has been used for diseases of the liver and spleen.[16] In folk medicine in both Britain and Ireland honeysuckle was used for a variety of cures.[17] The most common cure was to employ the leaves and flowers for gargles and lotions for inflammations of the mouth, especially for thrush. The bark of honeysuckle was used in Counties Leitrim and Cavan as a cure for jaundice, and in Counties Wicklow and Cork honeysuckle was used as a cure for consumption or whooping cough. According to K'eogh the powdered leaves of honeysuckle were considered in Ireland to be very effective in preventing fevers. In Ireland people would also eat honeysuckle as a cure for toothache. Beekeepers used to smear their hives with honeysuckle flowers so that the bees would regard them as their homes and return to them.[18] The leaves of honeysuckle were traditionally said to be the favourite food of goats, hence the Latin name of the honeysuckle family comes from *Capri folium* 'goats' leaf'. Honeysuckle gives its name to the honeysuckle family, the *Caprifoliaceae*.

SIMILAR PLANTS
Traveller's Joy – *Gabhrán* – *Clematis vitalba*[19]
ALTERNATIVE NAMES: (E) Lady's-bower, Old Man's Beard, Virgin's-bower

As its Latin name suggest, traveller's joy is a wild clematis that has become naturalised in Ireland. It was said to have sheltered the Holy Family on their flight into Egypt by springing up in a bower around the Virgin Mary whenever she stopped to rest, hence the names 'Lady's Bower' and 'Virgin's Bower'. The name 'Old Man's Beard' refers to the fluffy seedheads which resemble white whiskers. In many parts of Europe, the dry stems were smoked like tobacco. Traveller's joy is a member of the buttercup family, the *Ranunculaceae*.

St John's Wort – Beathnua

Hypericum

☉   Ruled by the Sun in traditional herbal medicine

♌   Associated with the zodiac sign Leo

*S*t *John's wort, with its bright yellow flowers and red sap, was linked in European folklore to the feast of St John and midsummer, and was believed to provide powerful protection against evil influences. It was also one of the most important herbs in European medicine, and was used to cure a wide range of ailments, including melancholia and nervous depression.*

SPECIES NAMES:
Perforate St John's Wort – *Lus na Maighdine Muire – Hypericum perforatum*
Imperforate St John's Wort – *Beathnua Gan Smál – Hypericum maculatum*
Square-Stalked St John's Wort – *Beathnua Fireann – Hypericum tetrapterum*
Slender St John's Wort – *Beathnua Baineann – Hypericum pulchrum*
Irish St John's Wort – *Beathnua Gaelach – Hypericum canadense*

ALTERNATIVE NAMES FOR ST JOHN'S WORT: (E) Aaron's Beard, Rose-of-Sharon, St Peter's Wort (Square-Stalked), Touch-and-heal (Ulster). (I) *Allas Muire, Luibh Eoin Bhaiste, Lus Cholm Cille*

FOLK BELIEFS AND CUSTOMS
In Ireland St John's wort was considered an important medicinal herb, which also had strong powers of protection against harmful influences.[1] It was believed, for example, to have the power to expel demons, and even to possess it guaranteed abundance. It was given to children on St John's Eve to avert sickness, and worn on the body to ward off evil influences. It was also believed that some sailors had the 'evil eye', and that decline was in store for people or

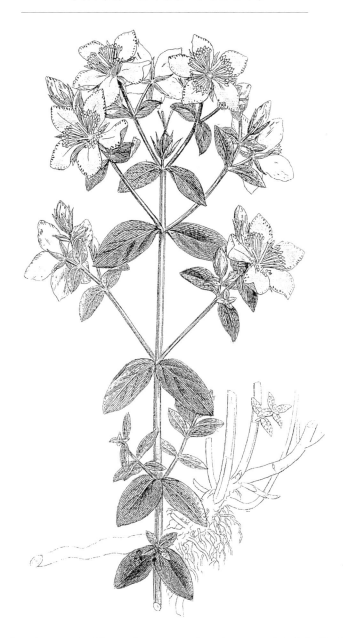

animals who saw it. The only cure against it was a drink boiled up from the juice of Marsh St John's wort. St John's wort was considered one of the seven Irish herbs that nothing natural or supernatural could injure. The others were vervain, speedwell, eyebright, mallow, yarrow and self heal. To be fully effective, they had to be pulled at noon on a bright day near the full moon. However, if they were collected on May Eve and Satan invoked, the same seven herbs could do great harm. St John's wort was also hung up outside the house and placed in windows on St John's Eve to protect the inhabitants from harm. In Ireland St John's wort was associated in folk belief with the Blessed Virgin and St Colmcille, as well as St John.[2]

The feast of St John's Eve (23 June), which was held by Irish people to be midsummer, was the time of year considered to be the best for gathering St John's wort for medicinal purposes; although many extended that to the season between St John's Eve and 'Old St John's Day' (29 June or 4 July).[3] Throughout Europe, and especially France, St John's wort was one of the main herbs associated with the feast of St John. It was picked before sunrise on the day and then its powers were strengthened by smoking it over the bonfires that were lit to mark the festival. Other herbs were strengthened in the same way, and it was considered that the herbs of St John were the most effective herbs to possess. In French the phrase: *avoir toutes les herbes de la St-Jean* – 'to have all the herbs of St John' – meant to be ready for anything.

St John's wort was also highly regarded in the Scottish Highlands as a powerful medicinal and magical herb.[4] It was believed to ward off second sight, witchcraft, enchantment, the evil eye, and even death. Being in possession of some ensured peace and plenty in the home, increase and prosperity of livestock, and growth and fruition in the field. In Scotland St John's wort was carried about by the people, secreted under the left armpit in the bodices of women and in the vests of men, as a charm against witchcraft and enchantment. However, it was only effective if the plant was accidently found, and was especially effective when found in the fold among the flocks, where it would augur peace and prosperity to the herds throughout the year. According to Scots Gaelic lore it was especially revered by St Colmcille (or Columba), because it was dedicated to his favourite evangelist St John. When children found it they would say a rhyme: 'St Columba's wort, unsought, unasked, and please God I won't die tonight.' When it was picked the following verse was often said:[5]

Arm-pit package of Columba, kindly
Unsought by me, unlooked for!
I shall not be lifted away in my sleep
And I shall not be thrust upon iron.

Better the reward of it under my arm
Than a crowd of calving kine;
Better the reward of its virtues
Than a herd of white cattle.

In England too, St John's wort was considered an important and powerful herb.[6] It was believed that the devil could not approach within nine paces of anyone who carried it; and if it was gathered on a Friday and worn around the neck, it could drive away evil spirits and help against melancholia. In England it was also believed that if a woman thought that she was possessed by the devil and all Christian prayers had failed, then all she had to do was place some leaves of St John's wort on her bosom and strew them throughout the home. St John's wort was widely brought into English homes on midsummer's eve to decorate the house and protect it, especially from fire and lightning. The flowers were tied into bunches and hung in the windows. In north Wales it was put over the doors to purify the house and drive away evil spirits. In Wales it was also believed that St John's wort gathered at noon of St John's Day was good as a cure for many complaints, and that if the roots were dug at midnight on St John's Eve, they were good for driving the devil and witches away.[7] In the Isle of Man it was said that if a person trod on St John's wort after nightfall on St John's Eve, a fairy horse would rise up out of the ground and carry the person on a fairy ride until dawn.[8]

St John's wort was also used for divination or fortune telling.[9] In England girls would pluck a piece of St John's wort on midsummer eve to test their chances of matrimony. If it appeared still fresh the following morning their chances of marriage were good. St John's wort was also used as a love charm in Europe by village girls to gauge the feelings of local youths. The plant was twisted around the finger, and if it bled red sap the loved one was true, but if it bled colourless sap there was no hope. Similarly, it was thought in Ireland that if a person saw you with St John's wort in your hand they would fall in love with you. In Wales St John's wort was used in a rather macabre ritual to foretell life expectancy. A piece of the plant was gathered for each person in the house and hung on one of the rafters. In the morning those whose pieces had withered most were expected to die soonest.

LEGENDS AND MYTHOLOGY

The Latin name for St John's wort, *hypericum*, was originally given by the Greeks to a plant which was placed above religious figures with the purpose of warding off evil spirits. The name meant 'over an apparition', a reference to the belief that it was so obnoxious to evil spirits that a whiff of it would cause them to fly away.[10] A Scottish folktale explains the origin of the Scots Gaelic name for St John's wort: *Achlasan Chalm Cille* or 'St Colmcille's parcel'.[11] The story tells of how St Colmcille came upon a shepherd boy who was weeping copiously. When questioned, the boy revealed that he was in dread of the evil spirits that would come during the night to harm him and his flocks. Hearing this, the saint bent down and picked a sprig of St John's wort and put it under the boy's armpit. He told him then to sleep peacefully because no harm would come to him or his flocks. The reason for the emphasis in Scottish folklore on placing St John's wort under the armpit is not known, but perhaps it is to have the plant near to the heart.

PRACTICAL AND HERBAL USES

St John's wort is best known nowadays for its effectiveness against depression, but it was also considered useful in traditional medicine against a range of other ailments. Amongst other things, herbalists recommended it for pulmonary complaints, bladder troubles, dysentery, diarrhoea and jaundice, as well as the expected 'hysteria' and nervous depression.[12] The main use in folk medicine for St John's wort in Britain and Ireland, however, has been to staunch bleeding from cuts and scratches.[13] In Ireland it was also used in places boiled in milk as a cure for diarrhoea.[14] Despite this, it is difficult to believe that St John's wort's elevated status in folklore has nothing to do with its powers as an anti-depressant. In fact, it was indeed used in County Waterford to dispel 'an airy fit' or melancholia and other forms of insanity.[15] In Ireland St John's wort was also used as a remedy for sore eyes, and for a blast in cow's udders.[16] St John's wort gives its name to the St John's wort family, the *Clusiaceae*.

SIMILAR PLANTS

Tutsan – *Meas Torc Allta* – *Hypericum androsaemum* [17]
ALTERNATIVE NAMES: (E) Park Leaves, Touch-and-heal (Leitrim). (I) *Meas Torc Allaidh, Úll an Mhadra Rua*
The Irish name *meas torc allaidh* – 'fruit of wild pig' – is said to derive from the strong swine-like smell of the bruised plant. Despite this, the smell of the dried leaves was said to expel ghosts, evil spirits and impure carnal desires. In ancient Greece it was associated with chastity, and women who wished to remain chaste put it under their beds. In traditional medicine tutsan aquired its name from *toutsaine* – 'all-heal' – on account of its supposed virtues. In Ireland and Britain the pounded leaves were mixed with lard to produce an ointment for dressing cuts and wounds. Tutsan is a member of the St John's wort family, the *Clusiaceae*.

Yellow Loosestrife – *Breallán Léana* – *Lysimachia vulgaris* [18]
ALTERNATIVE NAMES: (E) Yellow Baywort, Yellow Willowherb. (I) *Lus na Síochána Buí, Seamair Mhuire*
Yellow loosestrife has star-like flowers similar to St John's wort, but it is in fact unrelated. The name loosestrife derives from the Greek *lusimachion*, meaning 'ending strife', because it was believed by the Greeks to end strife between horses and oxen yoked to the same plough. Alternatively it is said to be named after King Lysimachus of Sicily, who first discovered its medicinal properties and introduced them to his people. Yellow loosestrife was much

valued in traditional medicine as a treatment for wounds, and for staunching bleeding. Yellow loosestrife is a member of the primrose family, the *Primulaceae*.

Bog Asphodel – *Sciollam na Móna* – *Narthecium ossifragum* 19
ALTERNATIVE NAMES: (E) Cruppany Grass (Donegal), Far-fia (Donegal), Glashurlana (Donegal)
Bog-asphodel has yellow star-like flowers similar to St John's wort, but it is unrelated. The name 'cruppany grass' derives from the traditional belief among farmers that bog asphodel gave their sheep foot-rot or 'cruppany'. In England bog asphodel was traditionally known as 'bone-breaker' for the same reason. Bog asphodel is a member of the lily family, the *Liliaceae*.

Mugwort – Mongach Meisce

Artemisia vulgaris

♀   Ruled by the planet Venus in traditional herbal medicine

*M*ugwort was considered one of the most important herbs in traditional European medicine, especially for female complaints and nervous
afflictions. This gave it the reputation as a powerful, magical plant effective
in protecting against all harmful influences.

SPECIES NAME: As above

ALTERNATIVE NAMES: (E) Muggert, Muggurth. (I) *Bogúird, Buachalán
Bán, Buachalán Liath, Buachalán Ná hEascarann, Buafanán, Liathlus
(Mór), Lus an tSeanduine, Mugard, Mugúird*

FOLK BELIEFS AND CUSTOMS

Mugwort was traditionally believed to have strong powers of protection against evil.[1] It was known in Europe as the *Mater Herbarum*
or Mother of Herbs, and throughout Europe it was one of the main
herbs associated with the festival of St John's Eve (23 June). It was
picked on the morning of that day and its powers were then purified and strengthened by smoking it over the bonfires that were lit
to mark the festival. Afterwards it was made into garlands and
hung over doors and windows to keep away all evil powers. In
Germany people wore chaplets of mugwort and vervain for good
luck at the St John's Eve celebrations. As people left the festivities
they would take off the chaplet and throw it into the bonfire saying:
'May all my ill-luck depart and be burnt up with these.' In parts of
Bohemia people wore mugwort in a crown or girdle while the midsummer fire was burning, as a protection against ghosts, witches
and sickness. A wreath of mugwort was also supposed in Bohemia
to prevent sore eyes. In Prussia on midsummer eve, pieces of mugwort and burrs were stuck on the gates or hedges that cattle passed
through as a preservative against witchcraft.

   In Ireland mugwort was held over the St John's bonfires in

County Cork, and then hung over the byres and dwelling houses. Similarly, in the southeast of Ireland, mugwort was gathered on St John's Eve and either kept in the house or thrown on the fire to bring good luck. The smoke was then inhaled as a cure.[2] In Scotland cows were protected from the influence of fairies and witches by having mugwort placed on St John's Eve in their dwellings. It was also made into chaplets which were worn on the heads of both men and beasts to protect them.[3] In Wales it was also the custom to place mugwort and St John's wort over the door on St John's Eve to purify the house from evil spirits.[4] In the Isle of Man mugwort was traditonally worn on 5 July or Tynwald Day, when the annual open air parliamentary assembly on Tynwald Hill was held. The custom of wearing mugwort lapsed, but was revived in 1924 and has continued since.[5] Mugwort was also widely used on May Eve in the Isle of Man to protect people and livestock from harm. It was worn on caps and coats on the day and was pulled around on sleds to expel evil spirits.[6] It was also placed under the tails of animals on May Eve, and used at any time of the year to cure animals thought to be bewitched.

Mugwort was believed to possess various magical powers.[7] It was said to protect the traveller against tiredness, sunstroke, wild animals and evil spirits. The leaves of mugwort were also thought to be magnetic and turn northwards. Medieval English herbals stated that where mugwort was in a house no elves or wicked spirits could dwell there. In England it was also believed that mugwort had the power to turn away the evil eye. Another English belief was that on midsummer eve mugwort secreted a 'coal' beneath its roots, which would protect anyone who dug it up and kept it from lightning, plague and carbuncles.[8] Mugwort was also considered to have great powers to cure female complaints. A Scottish story tells of the funeral of a young woman who had died of consumption. As the procession passed along the firth of Clyde, a mermaid put her head above water and recited the following verse: 'If they wad drink nettles in March,/And eat muggons (mugwort) in May,/Sae mony braw maidens/Wadna gang to the clay.'[9]

LEGENDS AND MYTHOLOGY
The Anglo-Saxons considered mugwort one of the most powerful

herbs against harmful influences, and an eleventh-century herbal credited mugwort with properties: 'Of might against thirty, and against three,/Of might against venom, and the onflying,/Of might against the vile one who fares through the land.'[10] Mugwort was also highly regarded in the Classical world, and the Latin name *Artemisia* derives from the Greek goddess Artemis, the moon-goddess who presided over birth. This is a reference to the use of mugwort for ailments around childbirth.[11] Mugwort was also known in the middle ages as *Cingulum Sancti Johannis* or 'St John's Belt' because it was said to have provided the saint with a belt when he was alone in the desert.[12]

PRACTICAL AND HERBAL USES

Mugwort has been known since ancient times for its ability to restore menstrual flow, ease delivery and cleanse the womb, which earned it its name as the Mother of Herbs.[13] Mugwort is also known for its narcotic qualities, and seems to have been a favourite plant to use as a divinatory throughout Europe since ancient times.[14] It was also used in traditional herbal medicine against palsy, fits, epilepsy and other nervous afflictions. Indeed it was still occasionally used in Ireland as a cure for epilepsy up until recent times.[15] In Ireland mugwort was also often singed and the smoke inhaled by patients as a remedy, and it was used to fumigate the sickroom.[16] Mugwort's aromatic leaves were believed to have the power to repel midges, and the name mugwort is said to mean 'midge plant' in Old English. However, another theory states that 'mug' is a reference to its use in flavouring beer and other drinks before the advent of hops.[17] Mugwort is a member of the daisy family, the *Asteraceae*.

SIMILAR PLANTS

Wormwood – *Mormónta* – *Artemisia absinthium*[18]

ALTERNATIVE NAMES: (E) Southernwood. (I) *Barramótar, Lus an tSeanduine, Subharmant*

Wormwood is famous for its bitter taste, and it is the principal ingredient in the drink absinthe, which is said to taste like pernod, but is notorious for its effects, which include delusions, paralysis and vertigo. In Scotland wormwood was known as *lus an tseanduine* – 'old person's herb' – because its strong smell was used to prevent faintness and weariness, and to keep old people awake in church. In traditional medicine wormwood was used for digestive and stomach complaints, but it has been little used in Irish folk medicine, except in County Mayo for stomach upsets. It has also been used as an insecticide in various parts of the country. Wormwood is a member of the daisy family, the *Asteraceae*.

Yarrow – Athair Thalún

Achillea millefolium

♀ Ruled by the planet Venus in traditional herbal medicine

♎ Associated with the zodiac sign Libra

Yarrow, with its delicate aromatic leaves and flowers, was a favourite plant to use in love charms and for protection against disease and evil influences. It was also valued as a herb for its use in stanching bleeding and for curing a variety of ailments.

SPECIES NAME: As above
ALTERNATIVE NAMES: (E) Angel Flower, Bloodwort, Dog Daisy (Ulster), Herb-of-the-seven-cures, Milfoil, Nosebleed, Old Man's Pepper. (I) *Luibh na nDaitheacha, Lus na Fola, Lus na gCluas*

FOLK BELIEFS AND CUSTOMS
Yarrow was widely used in love divination.[1] In the north of Ireland or Scotland a girl would gather nine sprigs of yarrow after sunset on May Eve, while repeating the following verse:

> Good morrow, good morrow, fair yarrow;
> And thrice good morrow to thee;
> Come tell me before tomorrow
> Who my true love shall be.

The yarrow was then brought home, put into the right-foot stocking and placed under the pillow, whereupon the girl would dream of her future husband that night. However, if she had spoken between pulling the yarrow and going to bed, the charm was broken. In Dublin the belief was that ten sprigs of yarrow must be plucked, and the tenth one thrown over the shoulder. Halloween was also a favourite time for this charm in Ireland, when fortune telling of all kinds was widely carried out. There

were many different versions of the verse, and another popular variation went as follows:

> Good morrow, good morrow, my pretty yarrow!
> I pray before this time tomorrow
> You will tell who my true love shall be.
> The clothes that he wears, and the name that he bears,
> And the day that he'll come to wed me.

In England similar customs prevailed. An ounce of yarrow was sewn in flannel and placed under the pillow before going to bed to ensure the appearance of the future husband or wife in a dream. Sometimes it was believed that the yarrow must be plucked from a young man's grave if the charm was to be effective, while in Cornwall the yarrow must be plucked at the time of the new moon. In Aberdeenshire girls would put a sprig of yarrow at their breasts, so that the first young man that spoke to them would be their true love. Another widespread idea was that if a person's nose was tickled with yarrow and the nose bled it showed that their loved one was true: 'Yarraway, yarroway, bear a white blow / If my love love me, my nose will bleed now.'

In the Scottish highlands yarrow was considered to have powers not only as a love charm, but also to increase beauty. The yarrow was picked with the following verse:

> I will pluck the yarrow,
> That more benign shall be my face,
> That more warm shall be my lips,
> That more chaste shall be my speech,
> Be my speech the beams of the sun,
> Be my lips the sap of the strawberry.

Yarrow was also believed to have powers of protection against evil influences.[3] In Ireland it was believed that yarrow was the first herb that Jesus took into his hand when a child, and so to carry it brought luck and protected against the wiles of enemies. Yarrow could also protect while going on a journey. Before setting out, ten blades of yarrow were plucked, nine were kept and the tenth thrown away. The remaining nine were put in the stocking under the heel of the right foot. If this was done it was believed that the devil would have no power over the traveller. In England, a Cambridgeshire belief was that if yarrow was strewn on the doorstep of the house, no witch would dare to enter. In the Scottish Highlands yarrow was widely used as a charm against the evil eye. In Ireland yarrow was among certain herbs that were boiled and the water given to cows with calf as a preservation against ill-luck and the fairies. In Rath Cairn in County Meath it was believed that going to a fair with some yarrow in your pocket guaranteed that your cow would be sold; while in County Galway it was believed that putting some yarrow into the wool of a sheep would ensure its sale.[4] Yarrow could also retrieve the goodness from the milk if it had been magically stolen, by placing three sprigs of it in a milk churn along with some well water and three sprigs of plantain.[5]

Yarrow was considered an important medicinal herb, and as such it gathered around itself cures that would nowadays be considered more magical than medicinal.[6] For example, it was believed that the fate of a patient with fever could be foretold if a sprig of yarrow was clasped in the right hand while the patient slept. If the yarrow withered overnight it meant that the patient would die. Yarrow was often collected and hung in Irish houses on St John's Eve to ward off illness, and St John's Eve was considered the best time to pick yarrow for medicinal purposes. It was also believed that if yarrow was collected on May Eve it could do great good if the Blessed Trinity was invoked, but if Satan was invoked it had the power to kill. In Ireland yarrow was considered to be one of the seven herbs that nothing natural or unnatural could injure, along with vervain, St John's wort, speedwell, eyebright, mallow and selfheal. It was called the 'herb of seven cures' on account of its many great healing virtues, and was one of the favourite remedies of the fairy doctor against the 'fairy stroke' or evil eye. It was also called 'the father of all herbs' and it was believed that it should only be cut from the ground with a black-handled knife. In Ireland yarrow was also frequently sewn up in clothes to prevent disease.

LEGENDS AND MYTHOLOGY

In Classical legend yarrow was supposed to be the herb used by the Greek hero Achilles to stanch the bleeding wounds of his soldiers, hence the Latin name *Achillea*. Another version has it that the Achilles concerned was a disciple of Chiron, the most learned of the centaurs.[7] The druids were also supposed to use yarrow stalks to forecast the weather.[8]

PRACTICAL AND HERBAL USES

Yarrow has been used to stop bleeding from cuts and wounds since ancient times, and was so valued on the battlefield that it was called by the Romans *Herba militaris*, 'the military herb'.[9] It has continued to be used for this purpose in folk medicine in Britain and Ireland right up to the present day. In Ireland yarrow was used to cure a variety of other ailments.[10] Yarrow has thus been used to stop nose-bleeds, but also to provoke them by putting leaves up the nostrils. The idea behind this was to relieve headaches by lowering the pressure of the blood. In Ireland, yarrow has also been used as a cure for toothache. Drunk as a 'tea', an infusion of yarrow was highly valued as a cure for coughs, colds and fevers, because of its reputation for opening the pores and inducing sweating, and it has also widely been used in Ireland as a remedy for the pains of rheumatism. In Ireland a poultice made of yarrow, fresh grass and a plant called 'finabawn' was mixed with the white of an egg and then put over a whitlow or boil. Yarrow is a member of the daisy family, the *Asteraceae* (or *Compositae*).

SIMILAR PLANTS

Sneezewort – *Lus Corráin – Achillea ptarmica* [11]
ALTERNATIVE NAMES: (E) Bastard Pellitory, White Hellebore, White Weed (Ulster), Wild Fire (Donegal). (I) *Crualus, Roibhe*
Despite its name, no records exist in folk medicine of sneezewort being used to cure colds, although it was used in England as a cure for toothache. Instead, the name apparently derives from the fact that the smell of the flowers was enough to make a person sneeze. An infusion of the flowers and leaves was once a popular drink in the Orkneys, but apparently only for refreshment. Sneezewort is a

member of the daisy family, the *Asteraceae*.

Tansy – *Franclus* – *Tanacetum vulgare* [12]
ALTERNATIVE NAMES: (I) *Annsae, Luibh an Tannsae, Lus na Fraince, Lus na bhFrancach, Tamhsae, Tannsae*

Tansy was traditionally grown around cattle sheds and barns to keep lice and flies away, and the fresh, aromatic leaves were strewn about to deter noxious insects and mice. In traditional medicine tansy was drunk as an infusion to purge the system of intestinal worms, and it was used by women as an aid to conception. In Irish folk medicine it was used in Ulster to restore menstrual flow, and as a cure for indigestion and pains in the joints (by boiling the leaves in salt water and bathing in it). In the Aran Islands the juice of tansy was drunk as a cure for fevers. Tansy was also used to flavour drisheen, the traditional Irish sausage of sheep's blood and milk. Tansy is a member of the daisy family, the *Asteraceae*.

Vervain – Beirbhéine

Verbena officinalis

♀ Ruled by the planet Venus in traditional herbal medicine

Vervain has been considered one of the foremost magical plants in Europe since ancient times, with great powers to protect against harmful influences, and to promote positive ones. It was also used as an effective cure for many illnesses, especially inflammation and fevers, and as an antidote to poisons.

SPECIES NAMES: As above

ALTERNATIVE NAMES: Holy Herb, Juno's Tears, Mercury's Moist Blood

FOLK BELIEFS AND CUSTOMS

Vervain was considered throughout Europe to be a powerful protection against evil and witchcraft.[1] In Ireland in parts of County Kilkenny, the custom on May Eve was to protect the farm from evil influences by walking the boundaries of the farm and sprinkling it with holy well water. A sprig of vervain was carried about on this procedure as an added protection. The cattle were also rounded up and inspected, and if anything suspicious was found on them which could be a bewitched token, like a bramble attached to a cow's tail, it was immediately taken off and burned. A sprig of vervain or rowan was then substituted for it to ward off any intended witchcraft. In Ireland generally, vervain and rowan were considered the best protection for cattle against witchcraft, and they should be tied around the cow's horns or tail. In the Highlands of Scotland it was also believed that vervain was a magical plant that protected against witches. It was taken into their boats by fishermen to bring good luck, and sewn into babies' clothes to protect them against the fairies. In the Isle of Man also, vervain was considered an antidote to evil influences, and people carried pieces of it in their pockets or among their clothes, especially if they were

starting out on a journey or some other enterprise. Medieval Welsh physicians believed that going to battle with vervain about the person would ensure escape from one's enemies. On St John's Eve in Germany there were celebrations and bonfires were lit. People wore chaplets of mugwort and vervain for good luck. As people left the festivities they would take off the chaplet and throw it in the fire saying: 'May all my ill-luck depart and be burnt up with these.' In England garlands of vervain were worn on St John's Eve, and in France vervain was collected before St John's Eve and purified in the smoke of the bonfires on the feast day.

Vervain's magical powers of protection were also believed to be effective for a range of ailments.[2] In Ireland vervain, eyebright and yarrow were favourite remedies of the fairy doctor against the fairy 'stroke' or evil eye. Vervain was one of the seven herbs that nothing natural or supernatural could injure. The others were St John's wort, speedwell, eyebright, mallow, yarrow and self heal. But to be fully effective, they had to be pulled at noon on a bright day near the full moon. However, if they were collected on May Eve and Satan invoked, the same seven herbs could do great harm. In Wales it was believed that hanging vervain about the neck or drinking its juice before going to bed would prevent a person from having nightmares. In England it was believed that people picking it should bless it as a reminder that the plant grew on the hill at Calvary and was used to staunch Christ's blood at the crucifixion. For this reason it was believed to be good at protecting against blasts (facial swellings). In many parts of rural England vervain was also believed to have magical powers as a love philtre.

LEGENDS AND MYTHOLOGY

Vervain was considered by the ancient Gauls to be a powerful magical herb.[3] It was gathered on a moonless night during the dog-days in July and August at the rising of the dog-star Sirius, after an expiatory offering of fruit and honey was made to the earth. An ointment made with vervain was believed to have the power to dispel fevers, prevent diseases, eradicate poisons and to be an antidote against serpents. Vervain was also believed to render the possessor invulnerable from harm. Using a branch of the dried herb to sprinkle about a banqueting hall made the guests more convivial, and it had the power to conciliate enemies. The druids were supposed to have used it in their religious ceremonies, and vows were made and treaties ratified by its means. It was also used by them to cast lots and foretell events. The three herbs held to be most sacred by the druids were water-mint, meadowsweet and vervain. Even today in Wales vervain is called *Llysiau'r Hudol* 'wizard's herb' and *Cas Gangythraul* 'devil's hate'.[4]

In ancient Rome vervain was also considered a powerful herb.[5] It was used to sweep Jupiter's table in the Capitol, and Romans used it to purify their houses and drive away the devil. So much was it used that its Roman name *Verbena* became the word for 'alter-plants' in general. Priests used it for sacrifices and so it was also called by the Romans *herba sacra*. The origin of the name 'vervain' is said by some authors to come from the name *herba veneris*, because it was also believed by the ancients to be an aphrodisiac; but other sources say that the origin is in fact Celtic *ferfaen* from *fer* (to drive away) and *faen* (a stone), from its supposed ability to act against gall stones in the bladder.[6]

Practical and Herbal Uses

There is a sound medicinal basis for some of the healing virtues attributed to vervain, for it contains a substance resembling quinine.[7] In England in particular, vervain applied as a plaster has been valued as a cure for gouty pains, swellings and agues. It has also been widely used in England as a cure for sores.[8] It was believed that vervain worn in a bag around the neck would help a child that was weakly, and that vervain worn as an amulet could cure headaches and tertiary fevers.[9] In Scotland a tea made of vervain was believed to guard against harmful influences.[10] Vervain is not native to Ireland but it has been naturalised in places. Even so it remains scarce here, and the only firm evidence for the use of vervain in Irish folk cures is for allaying fevers in Cavan. However, in Ireland it was also believed that vervain should be worn around the neck as a cure for a scrofula.[11] Gun-flints were boiled with rue and vervain to make them more effective.[12] Vervain is a member of the verbena family, the *Verbenaceae*.

Mallow – Hocas

Malva

♀   Ruled by the planet Venus in traditional herbal medicine.

♉   Associated with the zodiac sign Taurus

*M*allow, with its showy mauve flowers, is a well-known and loved plant of the Irish countryside. It was valued as an important herb since ancient times for its soothing and calming properties, and was used in folk medicine for curing sores, sprains, and inflammations.

SPECIES NAMES:
Common Mallow – *Lus na Meall Muire* – *Malva sylvestris*
ALTERNATIVE NAMES: (E) Horse-button (Donegal), Marsh-Mallow. (I) *Hocas Fiáin, Hocas Mór, Lus na Míol Mór*
Marsh-Mallow – *Leamhach* – *Althaea officinalis*
ALTERNATIVE NAMES: (I) *Leamhan Buí, Leamhnadh, Leann*
Musk Mallow – *Hocas Muscach* – *Malva moschata*
ALTERNATIVE NAMES: (I) *Cál Béatais* (Antrim)
Tree-Mallow – *Hocas Ard* – *Lavatera arborea*

ALTERNATIVE NAMES FOR MALLOW: (E) Hock Leaf. (I) *Milmheacan, Ocas, Ucas*

FOLK BELIEFS AND CUSTOMS
Mallow was seen in Irish folklore as an important herb.[1] Mallow was one of the seven herbs in Irish folklore that nothing natural or supernatural could injure, the others being St John's wort, speed-well, eyebright, vervain, yarrow and self heal. But to be fully effective, they had to be pulled at noon on a bright day near the full moon. However, if the same seven herbs were collected on May Eve and Satan invoked, they could do great harm. A tradition from the middle of County Limerick states that boys would go to the riverbank on May Eve to pick 'marsh-mallows' with which they

struck passers-by. The people being struck did not mind this too
much, as it was supposed to give some form of protection against
illness and fairy influence. The plant concerned was probably the
common mallow, as usually no distinction was made between the
two plants. In England the flowers of mallow were sometimes
used on May Day for strewing before the door and weaving into

garlands.[2] On St John's Eve in Knockaderry, County Limerick, young people would gather the leaf and stem of the *Hocas Fiáin* or mallow, and would go around lightly striking each person they met. The purpose was to protect those who were struck from illness and evil influences during the coming year. Afterwards the stems of the mallow were thrown into the St John's Eve bonfire.[3]

In England the seeds of common mallow were a favourite snack for children. The seeds form a disk of nutlets, which when eaten have a taste similar to peanuts. They were widely known as 'cheeses' or 'bread and cheese'.[4]

PRACTICAL AND HERBAL USES

Mallow was used in Europe as both food and medicine since the earliest times.[5] The young shoots were eaten as a vegetable by the Romans, and the Roman author Pliny recommended mallow sap mixed with water to give protection from aches and pains. In medieval times mallow had a reputation as an anti-aphrodisiac, because its soothing qualities promoted calm and sober conduct. Marsh-mallow (*Althea officinalis*) was once used to make the sweets which still bear its name. The thick, starchy and mucilaginous roots were gathered in England and France and used to make a confectionary paste, which was considered soothing for sore throats, coughs and hoarseness. The modern sweet is simply made of sugar, starch, gelatin, and so on, and does not contain any mallow in it.

The most important use in folk medicine for mallow in both Britain and Ireland was as a soothing poultice for sores, cuts, bruises, ulcers and other skin complaints; and for inflammation of any kind.[6] Usually this involved the leaves or roots (and sometimes the flowers) being pounded and mixed with lard or goose grease to produce an ointment. In Ireland, especially in Leinster, the leaves or roots of mallow were also boiled and the liquid produced was used to bathe sprains. In Counties Derry, Cavan and Waterford, mallow was also used for urinary complaints, while in County Kerry it was used as a tonic to cleanse the system.[7] Mallow gives its name to the mallow family, the *Malvaceae*.

SIMILAR PLANTS

Red Campion – *Coireán Coilleach* – *Silene dioica*[8]
Red campion, with its large red flowers, is a striking sight of the Irish countryside, growing in woodland and near rivers. In Wales it was believed that picking Red Campion would bring snakes into the house, while in the Isle of Man, it was considered unlucky to pick red campion as it was a fairy flower. The Latin name *Silene* derives from the merry, drunken god called Silenus in Greek myth. Red Campion is a member of the pink family, the *Caryophyllaceae*.

Ragged Robin – *Lus Síoda* – *Lychnis flos-cuculi*[9]
Alternative names: (E) Cuckooflower, Male Wild-Williams, Meadow-pink. (I) *Plúr na Cuaiche*
Ragged Robin gets its name from the ragged shape of its bright pink flowers. The Irish name *plúr na cuaiche* or cuckooflower is said to derive from the fact that it flowers when the cuckoo is calling. It was considered unlucky to pick the flowers and bring them indoors. Ragged Robin is a member of the pink family, the *Caryophyllaceae*.

Soapwort – *Garbhán Creagach* – *Saponaria officinalis*[10]
Alternative names: (E) Bruisewort. (I) *Lus an tSiabhainn, Lus Uchta*
Soapwort, with its large pink flowers, is a fairly common sight along streams and hedgerows in Ireland and Britain. Soapwort gets its name from the fact that the leaves will yield a soaplike lather if they are crushed and boiled in water, and it was used for cleaning cloth throughout Europe since ancient times. In Ireland soapwort was used to treat inflammation of the lungs, hence the Irish name *lus uchta*. Soapwort is a member of the pink family, the *Caryophyllaceae*.

Ragwort – Buachalán

Senecio

♀   Ruled by the planet Venus in traditional herbal medicine

*R*agwort, *with its bright yellow, daisy-like flowers and toxic leaves, was regarded as a fairy plant to be treated with caution, and as a noxious weed by farmers. However, it was also valued as a folk cure for several ailments, including jaundice, inflammation, coughs and colds.*

SPECIES NAMES:
Common Ragwort – *Buachalán Buí* – *Senecio jacobaea*
Marsh Ragwort – *Buachalán Corraigh* – *Senecio aquaticus*

ALTERNATIVE NAMES FOR RAGWORT: (E) Balcairean, Bennel, Benweed, Boholawn, Boochelawn (FB), Bulkeshan (Fin), Fairy Horse, James' Weed, James's Wort, Ragged Jack, Ragweed, Seggrum, Staggerwort, Yellow Boy (Donegal). (I) *Balcaiseán, Boglus, Bolcaiseán, Boltán Buí* (Ulster), *Bóthanán, Buabhall(án), Buacalán, Buachaltán, Buafalán, Buafanán, Búclán, Coiseog Bhuí, Deosadán, Fean Talún, Gaosadán, Géasadán, Geosadán, Giúsadán, Lus San Séam*

FOLK BELIEFS AND CUSTOMS
In Ireland it was universally believed that ragwort was used like a horse by the fairies to ride around on.[1] Their favourite time for doing this was on Halloween, and many stories tell of unfortunates abducted and forced to ride around with them all night, only to wake the next morning exhausted, clutching the ragwort in their hands. However, the fairies could also be more generous. A well- known folktale relates how a fairy host takes a man with them on their magical journeys. They give him a special cap and tell him to mount a ragwort as if it were a horse. He finds himself flying with them through the air and landing in a wine cellar in a foreign country. There he drinks his fill, but the next morning he finds himself alone and is then arrested for breaking into the cellar. He is sentenced to

be hanged, but before the rope can be put around his neck he manages to reach into his pocket and put on his fairy cap. He is lifted up into the air and brought back home, to be left standing beside the ragwort at the very spot where he first met the fairies. An old Connaught song describes the fairy ride: 'Is gur shiúil mé na cúig cúigí / Is gan fúm ach buachallán buí' – 'And I travelled through all the provinces, with nothing under me but the ragwort'. A folktale from County Sligo tells of how a man who used ragwort to light his hearth fire was approached on the road one day by two strange men. One of the men said to him: 'We have no horses to ride on and have to go on foot, because you have too much fire.' The man realised that the two men were fairy folk, and that they were referring to the ragwort he was burning. A Sligo saying reflected the caution generally shown in Ireland towards ragwort: 'Don't call it a weed though a weed it may be, 'tis the horse of the fairies, the *boho-laun buidhe*.'

In the Scottish Highlands it was said that the fairies sheltered beside the ragwort on stormy nights, and also rode astride it in their journeys in western Scotland from island to island.[2] In Scotland witches and warlocks were also believed to ride around on ragwort stems as well as the more usual broom.[3] A poem by Robbie Burns describes the devil and his witches and warlocks riding together:[4]

Let warlocks grim, an' wither'd hags,
Tell how wi' you on ragweed nags,
They skim the muirs an' dizzy crags,
Wi' wicked speed.

In Scotland after the Battle of Culloden, the victorious English are said to have named the garden flower 'Sweet William' in honour of their leader, William, Duke of Cumberland. The defeated Scots retaliated by giving the noxious weed ragwort the name 'Stinking Billy'. Alternatively, the Scots maintain that the spread of ragwort throughout Scotland was due to the forage used by the Duke of Cumberland's troops during the Culloden campaign.[5] Ragwort is also the national emblem of the Isle of Man, perhaps because of that island's nickname as *Yn Ellan Shiant* or 'The Fairy Isle'. A more cynical interpretation maintains that it is because there is so much of it in Manx fields.[6]

Ragwort's association with the fairies was believed to give it other magical properties.[7] A Donegal folktale tells of a man with fairy powers who used them to turn a bunch of ragwort into the form of a pig. The man brought the 'pig' to a fair and sold it, but as the unfortunate buyer was driving it home he crossed running water, and the 'pig' instantly turned back into a bunch of ragwort. In Donegal it was said to be bad luck to strike a cow with the flowers of ragwort, because it meant the 'wee folk' would be sure to come and steal the cow's milk. It was commonly believed in Ireland that on Samhain Eve the fairies went about the countryside, and with their breath blasted every growing plant, especially fruits and berries and fairy plants like ragwort and late thistles. In contrast to the usual caution surrounding ragwort, in Meath water was sprinkled on the fire with ragwort to bring good luck. Another common Irish belief was that the favourite place for a leprechaun to mend his shoes was on top of a ragwort on a summer's morning.[8] One folk tale recounts how a man caught a leprechaun and forced him to tell where his crock of gold was hidden. The leprechaun pointed out a particular ragwort growing in a field full of them. The man tied a red garter to the ragwort so that he could locate it again, and rushed home to get a spade. On his return, however, the man was horrified to discover that every single ragwort in the enormous field now also sported a red garter.

Ragwort appears in placenames such as Knocknamoghalaun (*Cnoc na mBuachalán* – hill of the ragwort), County Mayo, and Coolaboghlan (*Cúil an Bhuachaláin* – nook of the ragwort), County Laois.[9]

LEGENDS AND MYTHOLOGY
Ragwort was called the *herba sancti Jacobi*, the herb of Saint James, whose feast day is 25 July when the ragwort is in full bloom. Interestingly, in view of ragwort's role as a 'fairy steed', St James is said to be the patron saint of horses.[10]

PRACTICAL AND HERBAL USES

Ragwort is despised by farmers because its leaves are toxic to livestock. It is considered so dangerous that it is legally classed as a 'noxious weed', and under Irish law landowners must take steps to remove it from their property. Despite this ragwort features in several Irish folk cures.[11] The basal leaves were used in many places as the basis for poultices, and the juice was used for curing cuts, sores and inflammations, including burns, scalds and boils. The flowering head of ragwort could also be put over an ulcer as a cure. Perhaps on account of its yellow flowers, ragwort was also widely considered throughout Ireland as an effective cure for jaundice. Ragwort was also considered good for treating coughs, colds, sore throats, rheumatism and sore joints. In west Cork ragwort was used to make brooms and brushes for sweeping the house.[12] In Scotland and in Ulster ragwort was put in with oats when they were stored to keep mice away.[13] Ragwort is a member of the daisy family, the *Asteraceae*.

SIMILAR PLANTS

Groundsel – *Grúnlas* – *Senecio vulgaris*[14]

ALTERNATIVE NAMES: (I) *Buafanán Ná hEascarann, Crannlus, Gránlus* (Longford), *Gronnlus*

In Scotland old women would make use of groundsel as an amulet against charms to steal the goodness from the milk by putting it in the cream. In Ireland and Britain groundsel was widely used in folk medicine as a poultice to draw matter out of wounds, blisters, boils and so on. The name 'groundsel' has nothing to do with ground, but is the old English for 'pus absorber'. In Ireland groundsel was also used as a hot poultice to ease toothache, and drops of the juice were put in the milk of infants to cure constipation. A traditional belief held that groundsel was also especially good at curing wounds that had been caused by iron. Groundsel was often cut up to use as a food for poultry, and pet birds. Groundsel is a member of the daisy family, the *Asteraceae*.

Goldenrod – *Slat Óir* – *Solidago virgaurea* [15]

Alternative names: (I) *Luibh an Fhall-saora, Luibh an Easa, Luibh Naomh Sheáin*

In traditional medicine an ointment was made out of goldenrod for curing wounds. In Irish folk medicine it was used in County Cavan to cure heart trouble, stomach upsets and kidney problems, and throughout Ulster it was also used as a cure for flatulence. Goldenrod is a member of the daisy family, the *Asteraceae*.

Corn Marigold – *Buíán – Chrysanthemum segetum* [16]

ALTERNATIVE NAMES: (E) Geal-gowan, Geal-seed, Gil-gowan, Marigold-goldins (Ulster), Mogue Tobin (Carlow), Wild Marigold (Ulster), Yellow Oxeye. (I) *Buafanán Buí, Ceannbhán Buí, Íth-bhláth, Íth-órga, Liathán*

Corn marigold used to be a common feature of croplands, but better farming methods have made it scarce now in the wild. Indeed, it first appears to have spread thoughout Europe from western Asia along with the introduction of agriculture. The County Carlow name 'Mogue Tobin' refers to a farmer who was said to have been driven out of his farm when it was unable to grow anything else. In England corn marigold was used in garlands at midsummer and hung up in houses. Corn Marigold is a member of the daisy family, the *Asteraceae*.

Heather – Fraoch

Calluna/Erica

♑ Associated with the zodiac sign Capricorn

*H*eather, with its strong purple flowers and tough, springy branches, is a symbol of fierceness, resilience, and independence. It was highly prized, especially in Ireland and Scotland, for its many uses which included providing material for brooms, bedding, fuel, fodder for livestock and even beer.

SPECIES NAMES:
Heather – *Fraoch Mór – Calluna vulgaris*
ALTERNATIVE NAMES: (E) Scotch Heather, Ling. (I) *Fraoch na Lochlannach*
Bell Heather – *Fraoch Cloigíneach – Erica cinerea*
ALTERNATIVE NAMES: (I) *Fraoch Coitianta, Fraoch Corcra, Fraoch Dearg, Fraoch Fireann*
Cross-leaved Heath – *Fraoch Naoscaí – Erica tetralix*
ALTERNATIVE NAMES: (I) *Fraoch ar Inse*
Irish Heath – *Fraoch Camógach – Erica erigena*
ALTERNATIVE NAMES: (E) Mediterranean Heather
St Dabeoc's Heath – *Fraoch na hAon Choise – Daboecia cantabrica*

ALTERNATIVE NAMES FOR HEATHER: (E) Heath (I) *Asair, Fraochlach* (Donegal)

FOLK BELIEFS AND CUSTOMS
Given its mountainous habitat, it is no surprise that heather is associated in folklore with poor land.[1] A saying from the north of England has it that: 'Where there's bracken there's gold, where there's gorse there's silver, where there's heather there's poverty.' A similar saying from County Kerry states: *An t-ór fe'n aiteann, an t-airgead fe'n luachair agus an gorta fe'n bhfraoch* – Gold under furze, silver under rushes and famine under heather. A similar saying, also

from Kerry, states: *mac rí an t-aiteann, mac bodaigh an fraoch* – Furze is the son of a king, heather the son of a lout.' How heather first became linked to mountains is related in a well-known folktale.[2] It states that at the time of creation no plant was willing to cover the bare mountain tops. The heather, which was a shy plant with no flowers, felt sorry for the mountains and so covered them with its modest green. As a reward for this unselfish act, God then granted the heather its thousands of little flowers, so that it could cover the mountains every autumn in a mantle of royal purple.

A well-known inhabitant of heather moorland is the red grouse, and the bird's mournful cries are explained in various stories.[3] In Scotland it is said that the grouse lives off the tops of the heather, and despite the acres of the plant all around it, it lives in perpetual fear of famine, crying and bemoaning its lot. A similar version of the story from Tyrone has the grouse crying out:

A Mhairéad! A Mhairéad! A Mhairéad,
Tá an fraoch ag dul go hAlbain,
Tá an fraoch ag dul go hAlbain.
Caomhain é, caomhain é, caomhain é,
Bain sop, bain sop, bain sop!

Margaret! Margaret! Margaret!
The heather's going to Scotland,
The heather's going to Scotland,
Save it, save it, save it,
Pluck a wisp, a wisp, a wisp!

A Munster saying quotes the grouse as an example of unnecessary frugality: *Spáráil na circe fraoigh ar an bhfraoch is an saol go léir ag ithe* – As sparing as the grouse with the heather while the whole world eats.' In Munster it is also said that the grouse's endless complaining is because of the decision of a powerful local chief, Ó Caoimh Dhúth' Alla, who alloted his lands between the different birds of the air. The grouse was displaced from the fertile woods to the bare heathery hilltops, and ever after cries out the following: *Ó Caoimh, Ó Caoimh, Ó Caoimh cómhachtach / Thug a'choill, thug a choill, thug a' choill dóibhsean / agus an sliabh domhsa!* – 'O'Keeffe, O'Keeffe, O'Keeffe, so strong / You gave the wood, the wood, the wood to them / and the mountain to me!'

Notwithstanding its link with poor soil, a common folk belief in

Britain and Ireland is that it is lucky to wear heather or to bring it into the house, and that to find it will bring happiness.[4] In Scotland people put a sprig of heather under their beds for luck. White heather in particular is considered very lucky, and in Scotland most bridal bouquets have a sprig of it. A bunch of white heather was also a symbol of friendship or love when given as a present. In Britain, many people return from moorland districts with a sprig of the lucky white heather in their buttonhole or tied to the front of their cars. One reason white heather is said to be lucky is that it is the only variety which is free of the bloodstains of the Picts who were so brutally slain on Scotland's heaths.[5] However, another Scottish belief (although rare) is that white heather is actually unlucky, because a sprig of it was given to Bonnie Prince Charlie when he landed in August 1745.[6]

The Gaelic word for heather – *fraoch*, also means wrath, fury and anger in both Scotland and Ireland.[7] A Scots Gaelic phrase for a hero of the fiercest wrath is *laoch bu gharg fraoch*. The war cry of the McDonalds was simply *Fraoch!*, and heather was the badge of Conn of the Hundred Fights. In light of this it is not surprising that heather was a favourite plant to use as a clan badge.[8] Heather is the badge of the MacDonald, MacDonell and Macalister clans, while bell heather is the badge of the Macdougall clan. The Macphersons have white heather as their clan badge, and the Menzies (not surprisingly) have Menzies heather as theirs. However, despite this, heather's association with bloodshed led to the belief that heather would never grow over the graves of the clans. Heather was also often carved into handles for the ceremonial Scottish dirk.[9]

In Ireland heather featured in some 'Garland Sunday' customs.[10] Garland Sunday was generally the last Sunday in July, when people gathered on hill tops all over Ireland to celebrate the first fruits of the harvest with food and drink and the lighting of bonfires. In County Leitrim heather flowers were picked on the hilltop during the festivities, tied into bunches and carried home, where they were strewn at the doors of the outhouses to bring good luck. In County Mayo, sprigs of heather were picked at the start of the celebrations, worn throughout them, and then discarded before descending the hillside.

Heather was also said to be a favourite plant of the fairies.[11] In Scotland the fairies were said to prize the tops of heather as food, while in Wales the fairies were said to play on the heather tops. In Brittany heather is the emblem of St Anne, who was especially revered by the Bretons (St Anne is the mother of the Virgin Mary).[12]

LEGENDS AND MYTHOLOGY

One of the best-known Irish stories concerns the legend of the Danish heather beer.[13] According to the legend, after the battle of Clontarf there were only two Vikings left in Ireland – an old man and his son. They were therefore the only two people in Ireland who knew the secret method which the Vikings had of making beer from wild heather. Under the threat of torture, the old man agreed to tell the secret. However, he asked that his son be put to death first, so that he would not have the shame of letting his son see him submit. The son was then put to death, but instead of divulging the secret, the old man demanded to be killed himself as he would never tell. The Irish had no option but to oblige, and the old man was killed, taking the secret of the heather beer with him.

A hero called Fraoch mac Idath (Heather son of Cherry) features in the eighth-century Irish legend 'The Cattle Raid of Fraoch'.[14] Fraoch was the handsomest warrior in Ireland and Scotland, and so great was his beauty that Fionnabhair, the daughter of Queen Maedhbh and King Ailill of Connaught, fell in love with him. Fraoch went to Ailill seeking Fionnabhair's hand in marriage, but Ailill demanded all of Fraoch's wealth as a bridal price. Fraoch refused this price as too high, and Ailill, fearing that he would take away Fionnabhair without permission, planned treachery against him. He asked Fraoch to bring him rowan berries from a rowan tree that grew on the far side of a river, knowing that a monster dwelt in the river at that spot. As Fraoch swam across he was attacked in the middle of the river by the monster, and cried out for his sword. Fionnabhair dived into the river with the sword, and Fraoch was able to slay the monster. When he came ashore, his mother and a group of otherworld women took him to an otherworld dwelling where he was healed of his wounds. Fraoch then returned to the royal court of Connaught and succeeded in winning

Ailill's consent to have Fionnabhair's hand in marriage.

Heather's many practical uses also feature in some Irish legends.[15] In 'The Pursuit of Diarmaid and Gráinne', at one point Diarmaid made a bed out of heather for himself and Gráinne down by the sea. This was to fool Fionn, who had the magical ability to see the couple in visions. When Fionn saw them lying on heather, he was convinced that they were hiding in the mountains, and so searched for them there in vain. Heather also features in the eighth-century poem about the hermit Marbán. In the poem Marbán describes his simple hut in the woods, stating that its two doorposts are made of heather. This may not be as strange as it sounds, as heather was traditionally used in wattle and daub construction, and for thatching.[16]

Heather's many uses were sufficient to earn it a place in the Old Irish Brehon Laws on trees and shrubs as one of the 'bushes of the wood'.[17] This meant that the unlawful clearing of a whole field of heather was subject to a fine of one *dairt* (or year-old heifer) under the laws. The Irish for bilberry (*fraochán*) is very similar to heather (*fraoch*), so it is probable that bilberry was included in the laws along with heather. Heather was also linked by some medieval scholars with the ancient Irish Ogham alphabet.[18] Each letter of the alphabet was named after a different native tree or shrub, and the letters *Onn* or O and *Úr* or U were said by some authorities to be named after heather.

PRACTICAL AND HERBAL USES

Notwithstanding its association with poverty, heather in Ireland was seen as adding to the value of land in certain circumstances. A Civil Survey of 1654 classified land with both furze and heath on it as being part profitable, as opposed to being worthless wasteland.[19] In both Ireland and Scotland heather had a myriad of uses.[20] Heather was used to make brooms, beds were made with its springy branches, and it served as fuel for the hearth. The blossoms of heather were used to make a yellow dye for yarn, and it was used to tan leather. Heather also provided good fodder for livestock. In addition, Scottish highlanders used heather to make a kind of ale from its tender tops. Heather ale was once one of the staple drinks of the Highlands, and was traditionally drunk from cattle horns. It may have been first brewed by the Picts as long as 4,000 years ago. In Scotland honey made from heather was also especially prized, and beekeepers would move hives from place to place on the mountains to get the best flavour. Heather was used to cure a variety of ailments, usually by making a tea from the young tops or flowers. In Ireland, heather was used in County Clare against a weak heart, in County Wicklow it was used to cure coughs, while in County Tipperary it was considered a cure for asthma.[21] Heather gives its name to the heath family, the *Ericaceae*.

SIMILAR PLANTS
Bog-Rosemary – *Lus na Móinte* – *Andromeda polifolia*
ALTERNATIVE NAMES: (E) Marsh Andromeda. (I) *Fraoch Corraigh*
With its pretty pink, bell-shaped flowers, bog-rosemary looks like a heather, though in fact it is as closely related to bilberry and cranberry as it is to heather. The Latin name *Andromeda* refers to a beautiful maiden in Greek myth who became the wife of Perseus (son of Zeus), after Perseus saved her from being sacrificed to a sea monster. Bog-rosemary is a member of the heath family, the *Ericaceae*.

Bilberry – Fraochán

Vaccinium Myrtillus

♃ Ruled by the planet Jupiter in traditional herbal medicine

*Bilberry, with its dark, juicy and edible berries, is a symbol of the good-
ness of the first fruits of the harvest, and the period of pleasure and
relaxation before the hard work of the harvest begins in earnest. Bilberries,
or fraughans, have been valued in Ireland as a tasty and nutritious food
source since the earliest times.*

SPECIES NAME: As above

ALTERNATIVE NAMES: (E) Blackwhorts, Blaeberry, Blueberry,
Coraseena (Donegal), Dogberries, Fraughan, Fraun (Ulster), Fruogs,
Heatherberries, Hurs, Hurts, Mossberry (Donegal), Mulberries,
Whorts, Whortleberry. (I) *Breileog, Broileog, Dearc Fraoigh, Lusra na
bhFraochán, Mónadán, Mónann, Mónarán*

FOLK BELIEFS AND CUSTOMS

In folklore bilberry, whortleberry or fraughan, is associated above
all else with the Celtic festival of Lúnasa. Although in modern times
the names and dates of the celebration of Lúnasa vary from place to
place, they can all be shown to have their origins in the festival once
held on 1 August. In recent times the festival was generally held on
the last Sunday in July, or the first Sunday in August, and had a
wide variety of names such as Fraughan Sunday, Garland Sunday,
Hill Sunday and Domhnach Chrom Dubh. Máire Mac Neill in her
groundbreaking work *The Festival of Lunasa*, outlined the traditions
surrounding the festival from all over Ireland, which generally
involved people gathering on hilltops to celebrate the first fruits of
the harvest with food and drink, sports and games, and the lighting
of bonfires. Bilberries played a prominent role in this, and indeed
very often the picking and eating of bilberries on the hilltop was the
ostensible reason for the merry making. It was often believed that if
there was a good crop of bilberries it meant there would be a good

harvest, but if the crop was poor then the harvest would be also. In some places a special basket called the 'fruog basket' was made out of rushes in preparation for picking the fruit.[1]

Courtship between young people naturally played a part in the festivities, and in Donegal bilberries had a role to play. The boys made bracelets of bilberries for the girls with short threads brought for the purpose, and competed to make the prettiest girls wear them. However, the bracelets were only worn during the festivities and the custom was to take them off and leave them on the hilltop before going home.[2] At Knockfeerina in County Limerick the young people laid bilberries and flowers on a small cairn called the 'strickeen', which was reputed to cover the entrance to the underground palace of Donn Fírinne, the chief of the fairies in the locality.[3] The Lúnasa bonfire was then lit nearby as the evening festivites began. Lúnasa customs were not just confined to Ireland.[4] In the Isle of Man bilberries were also gathered on the first Sunday in August in a similar way; and in Cornwall the August festival of Morvah also involved the picking of bilberries and the courtship of the young.

In most places a lot of the bilberries that were gathered were brought home to be eaten afterwards.[5] The berries were often made into 'fraughan cakes', and in County Kilkenny the cakes were specially eaten by young girls at a bonfire dance. In County Mayo a girl was chosen to make the bilberry pies, which were given the nonsense names *Pócaí Hócaí* or *Rólaí Bólaí*. In Counties Down and Monaghan, the berries were brought home to be made into preserves, while in County Longford they were made into a 'wine' with sugar. This drink was considered a great treat for young lovers and to drink it was to hasten the wedding day. In many parts of Munster and south Leinster the 'fraughans' were taken home and eaten as an 'after course' or dessert, mashed with fresh cream and sugar. Another reason for taking some bilberries home was to give them to those who could not attend because of old age or illness.[6] In Donegal and Armagh the bilberries were taken home for this purpose after being strung onto long stalks of grass. In County Armagh it was considered good luck to bring the berries home as it ensured a good crop for the coming season. On the other hand, it was very bad luck if someone fell and destroyed their berries on the way home.

A widespread tradition stated that bilberries should not be picked after 1 August, and that very bad luck would befall anyone who ate them after that date.[7] It was believed that after that date they had the curse of Crom Dubh on them, and the devil's spit – a kind of spume or mould – was to be seen on them. According to folklore, Crom Dubh was a pagan nobleman who opposed St Patrick in an encounter at Lúnasa, and naturally came off the worst. Originally, however, Crom Dubh was an image of the devil, and the name means 'the dark stooping one'. In Laois and Offaly it was believed that bilberries should not be eaten after Garland Sunday because the fairies spat on the fruits on that night. More generally it was believed that bilberries simply lost their flavour after Garland Sunday. It is interesting to note how these traditions echo the widespread similar beliefs surrounding the eating of blackberries after Halloween.

In Scotland bilberry, or blaeberry as it is more commonly known there, is the badge of many Highland clans.[8] Among the clans concerned are the Buchanans, the Dundas', the Maclaines and the Scotts. Bilberry is also the badge of the Comyn clan. According to legend there is a spot at the end of Loch Pityoulish in Rothiemurchus where nothing will grow but blaeberry, because a contingent of Comyns were slain by the Shaws and buried in the hollow there. In the Scottish Highlands too, at the harvest feast of St Michael (29 September), a cake called the Struan Michael was traditionally baked, which included in it cranberries, bilberries, blackberries, carroway seeds and wild honey.[9]

Bilberry appears frequently in Irish placenames. Examples include Froghanstown (*Baile Fraochán*), County Westmeath; Freehans (*Na Fraocháin* – the bilberries), County Waterford; and Gortnavreaghaun (*Gort na bhFraocháin* – field of the bilberries), County Clare.[10]

LEGENDS AND MYTHOLOGY

Bilberry features in the eighth-century poem about the hermit Marbán.[11] In the poem Marbán describes his simple life in the woods, and mentions bilberries as one of the wild fruits he depended on for survival. The Old Irish text the 'Book of Rights' states that bilberries from a place called Brigh Leithe were given as a ritual gift to the king of Tara at Lúnasa.[12]

The Irish for bilberry (*fraochán*) is very similar to heather (*fraoch*), so it is probable that bilberry was included along with heather as one of the 'bushes of the wood' in the Old Irish Brehon Laws on trees and shrubs.[13] This meant that the unlawful clearing of a whole field of bilberry or heather was subject to a fine of one *dairt* (or year-old heifer) under the laws. In confirmation of this, an Old Irish legal text defined bilberries as a sweet (*cumra*) fruit, along with cultivated apples and plums, blackberries, hazelnuts and strawberries.[14] Other fruits like wild apple, sloe and haws were defined as rough (*fíadain*).

PRACTICAL AND HERBAL USES

Bilberry, or fraughan as it is more commonly known in Ireland, has been valued as a food source in Ireland and Britain from ancient times right up to the present day.[15] The berries have a sweetish flavour with a tart aftertaste and have traditionally been relished. Their consumption was by no means confined to rural areas. The Irish naturalist Threkeld, writing in 1726 noted that: 'The poor women gather them in autumn and cry them about the streets of Dublin by the name of fraughan'. In Exmoor in England, and in the Galtee Mountains in Ireland, bilberries were still picked up until recent times to be commercially sold. In Ireland the fruit was usually picked for jams and dyes, and the branches were used as brooms, and for spraying potatoes. In Scotland too, the berries of bilberry were used by Highlanders for making into tarts and jellies, often mixed with whiskey to give an added relish. In both Ireland and Scotland bilberries were also picked for their medicinal qualities.[16] In Ireland bilberry was used as a diuretic to deal with kidney troubles in Counties Wicklow and Kilkenny, and against gravel stones elsewhere. It was also used against jaundice in County Cavan, asthma in County Carlow, and as an antidote to pain in County Wexford. In Scotland 'blaeberry tea' was also used for urinary complaints, and in the Western Isles as a treatment for diarrhoea. In the Hebrides the leaves were dried and used as a substitute for tea. Bilberry is a member of the heath family, the *Ericaceae*.

SIMILAR PLANTS

Cranberry – *Mónóg* – *Vaccinium oxycoccos*[17]

ALTERNATIVE NAMES: (E) Bogberry, Kraanberry (FB), Moorberry,

Mossberry, Red Whorts. (I) *Blainsneog, Crúibín* (Aran Is), *Maonóg, Móineog, Mónadán, Mónann, Mónarán, Muineog, Múnóg, Plainseog* (Donegal, Mayo)

Cranberry features several times in early Irish legends. For example, in the eighth-century poem about the hermit Marbán, cranberry is mentioned as one of the wild fruits he depends on for survival. Similarly, in the legend *Suibhne Geilt* or 'Mad Sweeney', Sweeney is a king who has been driven mad by a curse and taken to living in the wilds. He lives off the various wild plants and herbs for survival, and particularly relishes the cranberries he finds. At one point he says: *Sásaidh saicchimsi, suairc an monarán,* 'a meal I seek, pleasant the bogberry', and later on he declares: *Mian luim ná monainn co mbloidh, at millsi na maothnatoin,* 'I love the precious bogberries, they are sweeter than any'. Despite this, cranberry does not seem to have been eaten in Ireland as much as bilberry. In Scotland the berries were frequently eaten, but the fruit is very acid and was believed to occasionally cause headaches and giddiness. In Scotland cranberry is the badge of the MacFarlane and Davidson clans. Cranberry is a member of the heath family, the *Ericaceae*.

Cowberry – *Bódhearc* – *Vaccinium vitis-idaea*[18]
ALTERNATIVE NAMES: (E) Keady-atchin (Donegal), Moonog
The berries of cowberry are very sharp in taste, but nevertheless are edible and were sometimes used in Britain to make an excellent jelly. Cowberry is a member of the heath family, the *Ericaceae*.

Bearberry – *Lus na Stalóg* – *Arctostaphylos uva-ursi*[19]
ALTERNATIVE NAMES: (E) Bear Whortleberry, Blanchnog (Donegal), Burren Myrtle, Moanagus (Donegal). (I) *Lusra na Geire Boirnighe, Stalóg*
Since the eighteenth century the leaves of bearberry have been used in official medicine for troubles of the bladder. In Scotland bearberry is the badge of the Mackintosh clan. Bearberry is a member of the heath family, the *Ericaceae*.

Crowberry – *Lus na Feannóige* – *Empetrum nigrum*[20]
ALTERNATIVE NAMES: (E) Blackberried Heath, Crakeberry, Corisraan

(Donegal) Deer's Grass (Donegal), Monnocs-heather (Ulster), Moonogs (Ulster), She-heather (Donegal). (I) *Fraoch na bhFraochóg, Fraochóg, Lus na Fionnóige*

The berries of crowberry were sometimes eaten in the Scottish Highlands, but were not considered very desirable. However, if they were boiled in allum-water, the berries yielded a black dye suitable for yarn. Crowberry gives its name to the crowberry family, the *Empetraceae*.

Dog-Rose – Feirdhris

Rosa Canina

♃   Ruled by the planet Jupiter in traditional herbal medicine

♐   Associated with the zodiac sign Sagittarius

The dog-rose, with its pretty pale pink or white flowers, is a well-loved sight in Irish hedgerows in summer; and its close relation, the cultivated or garden rose, is an ancient symbol of love and beauty. The bright red rosehips of dog-rose were considered a useful source of food in Ireland in earlier times, and have now regained recognition as a important source of vitamin C.

Species name: As above
Alternative names: (E) Briar, Buck-brier, Bucky (Ulster, US), Dog-brier, Hip-tree. (I) *Cocán* (rosebud), *Coindris, Conrós, Earradhreas, Eirrdhris, Fáirdhris, Fírdhris, Foirdhris, Oirdhris, Sceach Mhadra*

Alternative names for rosehips: (E) Buckie-berries (Ulster), Buckie-lice, Itchy-backs (Cork), Itchy-berries (US), Itchypoo (Ulster, US), Jacky Dorys (Cork), Johnny Magorys, Lucky-briar Berry, Puckies, Skeeory. (I) *Caor Madra, Caor Sceiche, Mogóir, Muc-chaor, Mucóid, Mucóir, Mucos, Mugóir, Sceach-chaor, Sceach Muc, Sceachóid, Sceachóir, Sceamhachóir (Madra), Sceicheoid, Sceochóir*

Folk Beliefs and Customs
The rose appears in many Irish folk songs as a symbol of love and beauty. In a famous ballad Ireland herself is praised as the lovely *Róisín Dubh* or 'dark Rosaleen' (little rose), and is told not to sigh or weep, as help from the Pope and Spanish wine will gladden her heart. The ballad reflects the sixteenth-century hope that perhaps the Spanish and their armada would free Ireland's Catholics from English rule. In a well-known love song from the nineteenth century called 'The Flower of Sweet Strabane' the songwriter describes

his love's beauty in a way typical of these songs: 'Her cheeks they are a rosy red, her hair golden brown/And o'er her lily white shoulders it carelessly falls down/She's one of the loveliest creatures of the whole creation planned/And my heart is captivated by the flower of sweet Strabane'. Of course, it would be impossible not to mention one of the most famous Irish ballads here, 'The Rose of Tralee'. This became so popular that it has inspired the town of Tralee in County Kerry to host annually its own beauty contest. It is the cultivated or garden rose that is usually referred to in these songs rather than any of the native wild roses, which have unfortunately tended to be overshadowed.

The red rose has been the national emblem of England since the reign of Henry VII (1485-1509), when it became a symbol of the British monarchy and so England herself.[1] Henry VII was the first Tudor monarch, and the red rose was originally a Tudor emblem. Nowadays the red rose is occasionally worn on St George's Day (23 April), the national day of England. This can lead to confusion, however, because the red rose is also the symbol of socialism and the British Labour Party. In England various superstitions surround the garden rose.[2] For example, it was believed that if someone was holding a rose and the petals fell, leaving only the stem, it was an omen that that person was going to die shortly. Garden roses were also used in love divination. It was believed that if a girl picked a rose without speaking on midsummer eve, carried it home and carefully wrapped it in white paper, and did not open it until Christmas Day, it would be as fresh as the day she picked it. If she then wore the rose going out, the man who came and took it from her would be her future husband. In Cheshire and Lancashire dog-rose is considered unlucky, and any plan formed while sitting near one is sure never to work. In Scotland the red rose is the badge of the Erskine Clan, while the four-petalled rose is the badge of the Matheson clan.[3]

Wild rosehips were considered a useful source of food in ancient Ireland, but they have not usually been used in recent times by anyone but children. Throughout Britain and Ireland, school children have traditionally enjoyed tormenting their fellows by playing a game or prank with the seeds of rosehips. The hairy seeds were put down the the neck of the unwitting victim between the skin and clothes, which would cause the most unbearable itching. The only cure for this was a change of clothes! In Cork rosehips got the name 'itchy-backs' on acount of this game, while Ulster names include 'itchy-berries' and 'itchypoos'.[4] A common name for rosehips in both Irish and Scots Gaelic is *muc-chaor* or 'pig-berry', and this is apparently because the bristly seeds resemble a pig's hairs.[5] Another common local name for rosehip in Ireland is 'Johnny Magory' (probably from Irish *mugóir*) which led to a favourite chant of children: 'I'll tell you a story about Johnny Magory'.[6] 'Buckie' or 'Puckie' are both local names in Ulster for rosehips, and in Ulster Scots something useless was traditionally descibed as: 'Naw worth a buckie.'[7] Rosehips were also used by schoolboys as 'bullets' to be fired out of their 'guns' or peashooters made from the stems of hogweed.[8] In Britain the hips and young shoots of dog-roses were sometimes eaten by children. The skins especially were prized for being soft and very sweet.[9]

There are two explanations given for the name 'dog-rose'.[10] The first is that the name derives from the ancient tradition put forward by the Roman naturalist Pliny that the root of a wild rose could cure the bite of a mad dog. The second is that the name was originally 'dag-rose' ('dag' being a dagger) because of the sharpness of its thorns. The name then became changed to 'dog' by people who did not understand its significance.

LEGENDS AND MYTHOLOGY
Roses appear sometimes in Celtic myth as a symbol of beauty, but usually it appears to be the cultivated rose that is meant.[11] For example, in one tale the Fianna are greeted by Niamh of the Golden Head, daughter of the king of Tír na n-Óg (the Land of Youth). She is described as having golden hair and 'cheeks redder that the rose, and her skin whiter than the swan upon the wave'. In the legend of Tristan and Isolt, the doomed lovers are buried together after their deaths in the same grave. A rose grows up over Isolt and a vine over Tristan, and the two plants grow together so that they cannot be parted. Cultivated roses have been known in Europe since ancient times, so it seems that they became symbols of love and beauty a long time ago. Dog-rose does appear in one Irish folktale, however. The folktale describes how three hags enchant the Fianna by each winding a magic coil of yarn around a stick of dog-rose. Each warrior is put into a trance the moment he sets eyes on the yarn.[12]

The cultivated rose probably originated in Persia in ancient times, and roses were well known to the Greeks and Romans.[13] Rose petals were strewn at Roman feasts and celebrations, and at Roman weddings both bride and groom were crowned with roses. Rosettes and roses were also carved on Greek and Roman tombstones as a symbol of spring and rebirth beyond the grave, and there is evidence that roses held a similar symbolism to the ancient Celts.[14] For example, rosettes appear on Celtic tombstones in Alsace, and a sculpture in Gloucester shows rosettes alongside ravens, a recognised symbol of death. Rosettes also appear with Celtic goddesses, probably as an image of beauty. Depictions of the Celtic horse-goddess Epona sometimes show her with rosettes, and Classical writers state that devotees to her cult often offered roses to her. Rosettes also appear on clay figurines of the Celtic 'Venus' figure. The resemblance between rosettes and the sun also led to them appearing as a solar symbol. For example, at Tresques in southern Gaul, a dedication to the Celtic Jupiter bears a sun wheel symbol and a rosette.

Dog-rose may have been considered sufficiently useful to earn a place in the Old Irish Brehon Laws on trees and shrubs as one of the 'bushes of the wood', probably on account of its rosehips.[15] The unlawful clearing of a whole field of one of the 'bushes of the wood' was subject to a fine of one *dairt* (or year-old heifer) under the laws. However, there is some doubt over the place of dog-rose as the plant referred to in the laws is *spín*, which is generally translated as gooseberry. Nevertheless, there is evidence that wild rosehips were eaten in ancient Ireland. An Old Irish legal text defined rosehips as a rough (*fíadain*) fruit, along with wild apple, sloe, acorn, haws, and rowanberries.[16] Other fruits like cultivated apples and plums, blackberries, and strawberries were defined as sweet (*cumra*). An excavation of an eleventh-century site at Winetavern Street in Dublin found the seeds of rowan, blackberries, wild apples, sloes, haws and rosehips. The rose was also linked by some medieval scholars with the ancient Irish Ogham alphabet.[17] Each letter of the alphabet was named after a different native tree or shrub, and the letter *Ruis* or *R* was said by some authorities to be named after the rose.

PRACTICAL AND HERBAL USES
In modern times wild rosehips are recognised as an important source of vitamin C. During the Second World War in the northeast of England, rosehips were gathered on a commercial basis for the manufacture of rosehip syrup. Rosehip syrup is still manufactured in Britain, but nowadays the rosehips are imported from Chile.[18]

The link with vitamin C was not a traditional part of country folk-lore, but in Ireland wild rosehips were nevertheless sometimes used for making jam.[19] In Ireland dog-rose does not seem to have had any herbal uses, but as it was traditionally lumped in with bramble under the common name of 'brier', it is possible that some of the herbal remedies for that plant in fact involve dog-rose. In England the gall of wild rose was said to cure whooping cough or toothache, while in Wales it was said that if the gall was put under the pillow, it would guarantee a good night's sleep to someone suffering from insomnia.[20] In Ireland the wood of dog-rose was traditionally used to make 'clams' for use in the castration of animals.[21] Dog-rose is a member of the rose family, the *Rosaceae*.

SIMILAR PLANTS

Sweet-Briar – *Dris Chumhra* – *Rosa rubiginosa*[22]

ALTERNATIVE NAMES: (E) Eglantine, Rose-of-Jerusalem (I) *Rós na Banríona Muire, Sceach Chumhra*

Sweet-briar is noted for its sweet scent, and its praises were sung in many older English poems under the name 'eglantine'. It was also traditionally believed to be the 'rose-of-Jerusalem' that provided Christ with His crown of thorns. Sweet-briar was taken as a decoction in County Longford for curing jaundice. Sweet-briar is a member of the rose family, the *Rosaceae*.

Burnet Rose – *Briúlán* - *Rosa pimpinellifolia*[23]

ALTERNATIVE NAMES: (E) Scotch Rose. (I) *Stancán*

Burnet rose gets it name from having small divided leaves like salad burnet. The rosehips are also purple-black instead of the red of dog-rose. Burnet Rose is a member of the rose family, the *Rosaceae*.

Field Rose – *Rós Léana* – *Rosa arvensis*[24]

Field rose is a common sight in Irish hedgerows and can be distinguished from dog-rose by its trailing habit and white, almost scentless flowers. Field Rose is a member of the rose family, the *Rosaceae*.

Bramble – Dris

Rubus Fruticosus

♀ Ruled by the planet Venus in traditional herbal medicine

♈ Associated with the zodiac sign Aries

*The bramble or blackberry, with its dark, juicy berries, has been consid-
ered a valuable food source since the earliest times. Despite the nui-
sance of its whip-like thorny branches, it has also been valued for its other
uses, which include providing dyes and for wickerwork, and curing ailments such as diarrhoea and skin complaints.*

SPECIES NAME: As above
Alternative names: (E) Blackberry, Brammle (Ulster), Briar, Brier,
Brimel(es) (FB). (I) *Dreas, Drisleog, Fan-go-Fóill* (?), *Pras, Preas, Sceach
Talún, Sméardhris*

ALTERNATIVE NAMES FOR BLACKBERRIES (*Sméara Dubha* in Irish): (E)
Blackas (Cork), Scaldberries. (I) *Sméar Ciaráin*

FOLK BELIEFS AND CUSTOMS
A universal belief throughout Ireland was that blackberries should
not be eaten after the feast of Samhain or Halloween (31 October).[1]
The practical reason behind this belief is the fact that the berries
begin to rot around this time and so become unwholesome to eat.
However, in popular lore the usual reason given for the prohibition
was that at Halloween a fairy called the *púca* or pooka spat on the
berries and made them inedible. In other places it was believed that
the pooka urinated on the fruits instead. Alternatively it was often
said to be the devil that did the damage. Sometimes the belief in
Ireland was that Michaelmas (29 September) was the correct date,
and that the pooka rode around the country defiling the berries on
that night. It was also said that the reason they should not be eaten
was that the devil put his foot on the blackberries at Michaelmas, or
cast his club over them.[2] In England similar ideas were held usually
also about eating blackberries after Michaelmas.[3] For example, in

Devonshire it was considered taboo to eat blackberries after the last day of September because after that date 'the devil enters into them'. Another English belief was that the devil fell into a blackberry thicket, and so left his curse on the thorns which injured him. In Scotland it was said that the devil covers the blackberries with his cloak and renders them unwholesome in late autumn.[4] In Brittany the reason for the prohibition was said to be *à cause des fées* – 'because of the fairies'.[5]

In Ireland blackberries were universally eaten, and several Irish phrases reflect this. In Irish the best part of any collection is called *an sméar mullaigh* or 'the topmost blackberry', while something very common is described as *chomh fairsing le sméara* – 'as widespread as blackberries'.[6] Blackberries are not always appreciated, however, as another phrase describes useless things as *ní fiú sméar san fhomhair é* – 'it's not worth an autumn blackberry', though perhaps this refers to later blackberries when they have become overripe. Despite the prohibitions on eating blackberries after the festival, in Ireland the festivities of Halloween often included foods such as apple cake, nuts and blackberry pie.[7] In the Scottish Highlands too, blackberries were used at the harvest feast of St Michael (29 September), when a cake called the Struan Michael was traditionally baked, which included in it blackberries, bilberries, cranberries, carroway seeds and wild honey. It was baked on a fire of oak, rowan, bramble and other woods considered blessed.[8] Despite this custom, it was commonly believed in the Scottish Highlands that each blackberry contained a poisonous worm.[9] In north Wales too, blackberries were often considered poisonous.[10] In England, however, not only were blackberries eaten, but the young stalks of bramble were also relished by children. When peeled they were considered to be sweet and juicy. The young shoots were also traditionally eaten in England as a cure for fastening loose teeth.[11]

An arch of bramble or briar which had rooted at both ends (sometimes called a 'double-headed' bramble) was commonly considered in folklore to have special powers.[12] A widespread belief in Ireland was that those who wished to invoke evil spirits could do so by crawling through such a briar arch on Halloween night while making their unholy request. It was also believed that the devil would grant special powers, such as great musical ability or luck at cards, to the person who invoked his name while carrying this out – but at the high price of giving up one's soul! In England it was believed that a double-headed bramble could be used to cure various ailments. For example, a child with whooping cough could be cured by passing it under the bramble arch three times before breakfast for nine days in succession. Alternatively it must be done at sunrise while facing the rising sun. Another version states that the child must be passed seven times through the arch, while saying: 'In bramble, out cough, here I leave the whooping cough.' In Somerset hernia could be cured by passing the patient under the bramble arch, while in Dorset boils could be cured by doing the same thing three mornings in a row. In Wales children with rickets were made to crawl or creep under blackberry bushes three times a week.

Bramble was generally considered to have special powers, both good and bad.[13] In Ireland it was believed that one farmer could wish bad luck on another by standing under a wild briar and invoking the devil's aid. In many parts of Ireland a bramble found attached to a cow's tail on May Eve was considered suspicious, as it might be a bewitched token put there to steal the goodness from the animal. In England it was widely believed that the period when blackberries were ripe was inauspicious. Animals, especially cats, that were born at this time were likely to be sickly and troublesome, while many people were more prone to depresssion. Bramble could also have powers for good, however. In Scotland it was believed that a sprig placed under a milk pail prevented the goodness from being stolen. In the Scottish Highlands also a wreath made of either woodbine or bramble, ivy and rowan was placed over the lintels of the cow-house and under the milk vessels to protect both cows and milk from witchcraft, the evil eye, and murrain. In the Scottish Highlands also on the eve of the feast of St Brigid, an image of the saint called the *dealbh Bride* was made out of straw and decorated in her honour. A small white rod called *slachtan Bride* or Bride's Wand was placed beside the image. The wand was generally made of birch, broom, bramble, white willow or some other wood considered to be sacred. In England in ancient times blackberries were supposed to provide protection against all 'evil runes' if gathered at the right time of the moon.

Various other superstitions have also attached themselves to bramble.[14] In Cornwall it was believed that blackberry stains would never disappear while the fruit was in season, and that hair was prone to fall out during the blackberry season! It was also believed in Cornwall that a good blackberry season meant a good herring season. In some parts of England bramble was planted on graves to cover more unsightly weeds and to deter grazing sheep. Local folklore maintained, however, that it was done also to keep the dead in and the devil out. A Cornish cure for scalds and burns involved gathering nine bramble leaves and putting them in a vessel of clear spring water. Each leaf was then passed over the affected area while saying three times: 'Three came from the east, one with fire and two with frost, out with the fire and in with the frost, in the name of the Father, Son and Holy Ghost.' A widespread belief maintained that Christ used a bramble switch on his donkey on the way into Jerusalem, and that he also used it to drive the moneylenders out of the temple.[15] In Ireland the flower of the blackberry was a symbol of beauty to the Gaelic poets, and a well-known love ballad has the name *Bláth na Sméar*, or 'Flower of the Blackberry'.[16]

LEGENDS AND MYTHOLOGY

Bramble and blackberries are mentioned frequently in Irish legends.[17] In the legend *Suibhne Geilt* or 'Mad Sweeney', Sweeney is a king who has been driven mad by a curse and taken to living in the wilds. In a well-known poem he describes the trees and plants around him, and usually praises their beauty. However, what he has to say about the thorny briar shows that he is not so fond of it:

> O briar, little arched one,
> thou grantest no fair terms,
> thou ceasest not to tear me,
> till thou hast thy fill of blood.

Bramble's thorns also feature in a tale called 'The Death of King Fergus', when at one point in the story Iubhdan, the king of the leprechauns, recites a poem about the properties of various woods: 'Bending wood the vicious briar, burn it sharp and fresh, cuts and flays the foot, keeps everyone enmeshed.' The thorns of briar prove useful, however, in a tale from the Lays of Fionn which relates how the Mainí, the seven sons of Queen Meadhbh, hold a hostile force at bay by erecting a fence of briars and blackthorns until help arrives. Blackberry, meanwhile, features in an amusing incident in the legend of 'The Cattle Raid of Cooley' or the *Táin*. The legend tells how the youthful hero Cúchulainn fooled his opponents by smearing blackberry juice over his lower jaw and chin to make it look like he had a beard. He did this because no warrior would fight him if they knew he was too young to have a beard of his own. In the 'Lives of the Saints' a story about the life of St Senan tells of how his mother started eating blackberries at a well. At this the unborn saint speaks to her from the womb with the rebuke: 'Stay from that O mother, for that is refection before the proper hour.'

Bramble was sufficiently useful to earn a place in the Old Irish Brehon Laws on trees and shrubs as one of the 'bushes of the wood', probably on account of its blackberries.[18] This meant that the unlawful clearing of a whole field of bramble was subject to a fine of one *dairt* (or year-old heifer) under the laws. In confirmation of this, an Old Irish legal text defined blackberries as a sweet (*cumra*) fruit, along with cultivated apples and plums, bilberries, hazelnuts and strawberries.[19] Other fruits like wild apple, sloe and haws were defined as rough (*fíadain*). In Dublin, an excavation of an eleventh-century site at Winetavern Street found the seeds of blackberries, rowan, wild apples, sloes, haws and rosehips.[20] Blackberries are also mentioned as food in several legends.[21] In an eighth-century Irish poem the hermit Marbán speaks of his simple life in the woods, and describes the 'manes of bramble with good blackberries' that help to sustain him. A story called 'Cael and Credhe' about the Fianna, the warriors of ancient Ireland, describes how they feasted on 'beautiful blackberries, haws of the hawthorn, nuts of the hazels of Cenntire, and tender twigs of the bramble bush'. Elsewhere an early Irish poem describes how blackberries formed a fragrant crop for the women of the Fianna.

PRACTICAL AND HERBAL USES

Blackberries have been eaten as food since the earliest times, either eaten directly or made into jams and tarts.[22] Blackberry seeds have been found in the stomach of a Neolithic man dug up at Walton-on-the-naze in Essex. In Ireland blackberries were traditionally eaten mashed up with oatmeal in a kind of porridge, but in later times they were mainly used for making jams. Bramble has also been put to other uses.[23] In the Scottish Highlands and Ireland the roots of bramble have been used to make an orange (with other plants) or dark green dye for the treatment of wool. In Ireland the root of bramble has also been used as the core for hurling balls and for pipes, while the long shoots have been used for wickerwork and for securing thatching. Bramble also had some medicinal uses.[24] In traditional medicine blackberry jelly was used to cure dropsy and blackberry cordial was considered to have great restorative powers. In Ireland the leaves of bramble were used to cure diarrhoea in people and cattle, and for a variety of ailments in different parts of the country, such as cuts in Counties Offaly and Louth, swellings in County Wicklow and sore feet in County Leitrim. In Britain bramble has also been widely used as a cure for diarrhoea, but in addition it has been used for coughs and colds. In the southwest of England bramble was used for a variety of skin complaints, like burns and scalds, shingles, boils and spots. In Scotland too, the leaves were placed on burns and scalds. Bramble is a member of the rose family, the *Rosaceae*.

SIMILAR PLANTS

Stone Bramble – *Sú na mBan Mín* – *Rubus saxatilis*[25]
ALTERNATIVE NAMES: (E) Dwarf Mountain Bramble, Lady's Berry, Raspis. (I) *Crúibíní Sionnaigh*
In Scotland the red-berried stone bramble is the plant badge of the McNab clan. Stone Bramble is a member of the rose family, the *Rosaceae*.

Dewberry – *Eithreog* – *Rubus caesius*[26]
ALTERNATIVE NAMES: (I) *Gormdhearc*
Dewberry can be distinguished from blackberry by the large size of the grains, and the waxy bloom which covers them. The taste of the berries is said to be insipid. Dewberry is a member of the rose family, the *Rosaceae*.

Cloudberry – *Eithreog Shléibhe* – *Rubus chamaemorus*[27]
ALTERNATIVE NAMES: (I) *Lus na nEithreog*
Cloudberry actually gets its name from Old English *clud* meaning a hill. In the Scottish Highlands the orange-berried cloudberry was gathered to eat and considered a 'most grateful fruit'. Cloudberry is a member of the rose family, the *Rosaceae*.

Raspberry – *Sú Craobh* – *Rubus idaeus*[28]
Wild raspberry appears as a valued food in several early Irish legends and poems. In the legend *Suibhne Geilt* or 'Mad Sweeney', Sweeney is a king who has been driven mad by a curse and taken to living in the wilds. He lives off the various wild plants and herbs for

survival, and raspberry is one of the foods mentioned. At one point he says: *Subha craobh, is fiach féile* – 'raspberries, they are the due of generosity'. An old Irish poem in praise of a glen called Gleann Ghualainn mentions raspberries as one of the fruits that grew there at the time of the Fianna, the legendary warriors of Ireland. In British folk medicine a tea made from the leaves of raspberry was drunk to alleviate labour pains. Raspberry is a member of the rose family, the *Rosaceae*.

Bracken – Raithneach Mhór

Pteridium aquilinum

☿   Ruled by the planet Mercury in traditional herbal medicine

♊   Associated with the zodiac sign Gemini

Bracken, and ferns in general, were seen as strange and magical plants because they bear neither flowers nor fruit; and produce mysterious, almost invisible seeds (technically spores). Bracken was also valued for providing fertile ash after burning, and bedding in the autumn, when the dry fronds turn many shades of red and brown on our hillsides.

SPECIES NAME: As above
ALTERNATIVE NAMES: (E) Brake Fern, Female Fern, Fern-of-God, Mary's Fern. (I) *Raithín, Raithneach Mhuire* (Cork).

Alternative names for Fern: (E) Fearn (FB), Galapa (TC) Grinlesk Muni (TC), Vearne (FB)

FOLK BELIEFS AND CUSTOMS
A widespread belief in Britain and Ireland was that fern seed gathered on St John's Eve would make the bearer invisible.[1] The reasoning behind this was that because fern seed itself is practically invisible, it could bestow the same property on those who carried it. In Ireland Samhain Eve or Halloween was also a good time to collect the seed. The seed had to be carefully collected on white paper at midnight, and the paper then folded up and carried in the pocket. The carrier could then enter homes and buildings and plunder money and treasures without being discovered. But there was a difficulty in collecting the seed, because all the powers of evil and darkness would do their best to frighten off the collector. Although they could not touch him, unearthly yells, screams, whirlwinds and fiendish apparitions were employed to make the person lose their nerve. Indeed stories relate how those who successfully collected the seed often lost their wits in the process. In Ireland it was also believed that carrying fern seed about would bring good luck at

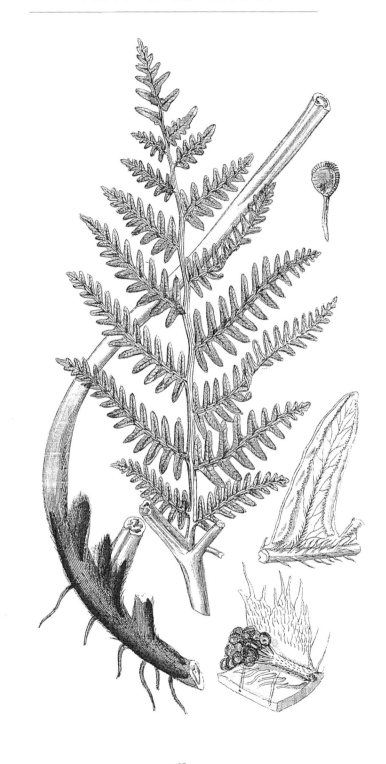

cards to the person who carried it.[2] Many similar customs were found throughout Europe, where the tiny round golden seeds of fern linked it in folklore to gold and treasure.[3] In Bohemia it was believed that on St John's Day fern seed bloomed like gold, and that whoever collected it and ascended a mountain holding it in their hand on Midummer Eve would discover a vein of gold. In Brittany treasure seekers would gather fern seed on Midsummer Eve, and keep it until the following Palm Sunday. If they then strewed it on the ground at a likely spot the seed would reveal where the treasure was hidden. In Switzerland it was believed that if a person waited by a fern on St John's night the devil would appear and present them with treasure.

A common superstition holds that holy initials can be seen on a stem of bracken when it is cut, though the details vary in different places.[4] In Ireland people believed that the letters GOD could be seen on the stem of cut bracken, and in Scotland it was the letters JC for Jesus Christ that appeared. Similarly, in England, a stem of bracken was often used as a charm against witches because the markings at its foot were said to spell out the Greek letters CHI, which is the beginning of Christ's name in Greek. One story explains that bracken would not adore the Creator and so was deprived of the flowers it once had. However, it repented and was forgiven, and so God's monogram can be seen forever afterwards in its stem as a token of this forgiveness. In England ferns are associated with thunder and lightning, and they were hung about the house to prevent storms. However, if they were burnt it was believed that they would bring on rain. As late as 1636, during a visit of Charles I to Staffordshire, it was commanded that no ferns should be burnt in the county to ensure fine weather during the king's stay.[5] Fern or bracken is noted for its ability to spread, and thus in Ireland it became a byword for prolificity.[6] An old saying describing something abundant was *comh rathmhar leis an raithnigh* – 'as prolific as the fern'. Similarly, a saying from the north of England has it that: 'where there's bracken there's gold, where there's gorse there's silver, where there's heather there's poverty.'

Bracken was widely valued in folklore for its benevolent powers.[7] In Ireland bracken is called Mary's Fern because it was believed that St Joseph used it as bedding for the Virgin Mary and the Christ child. As such it was blessed and nothing that slept on it would ever catch a cold. In Wales wagoners would put a bunch of fern over the horses' ears, or on their collar, to 'keep the devil away' and to baffle witches. In the south of Scotland fern was believed to be among those plants avoided by witches. Bracken or fern was also used in love charms.[8] In the Scottish Highlands nine stems of fern that had been cut with an axe were among the ingredients used in a love charm; and the root of bracken was also considered a valuable ingredient in love philtres. An old Gaelic song goes: 'Twas not the maiden's matchless beauty / That drew my heart nigh / Not the fern-root potion / But the glance of her eye.' In England an old belief was that if a woman put a leaf of bracken she had gathered on St John's Eve in a man's left shoe, she would make him love her. In Cornwall it was believed that if a person went to the first fern that appeared in the spring and bit it down to the ground, they would suffer no toothache for the following year.[9]

However, fern also had the reputation of being a fairy plant, so it was not always regarded benignly.[10] In Ireland it was believed that a fairy changeling who had been successfully banished into a river or lake would turn into a clump of fern or yellow iris. In parts of Britain it was believed that for a traveller to tread on a fern would cause him to become confused and lose his way. In Staffordshire ferns were known as 'Devil's Brushes', and it was considered bad luck to gather them for fuel or to touch them. In the Scottish Highlands fern is the plant badge of the Chisholm clan and bracken the plant badge of the Robertson clan.[11]

LEGENDS AND MYTHOLOGY

The use of fern for making fires appears several times in Irish myth.[12] One legend tells of how Nechtan, the king of Munster, successfully deceived Bres, the king of Ireland, who had levied a tax on the milk of every hornless dun cow in Ireland. Nechtan avoided paying the tax by singeing all the cows of Ireland over a fire of fern, and then smearing them with the ashes of flax seed to make them look dark brown instead of dun. A story from the Life of St Patrick tells of how he was given a site for a church on the west side of the river Bann at 'the place where the children are burning the fern'. The site was called Cúl Raithin (Coleraine) from then onwards. Bracken's use as a bedding also appears in Irish myth.[13] In the Irish legend *Suibhne Geilt* or Mad Sweeney, Sweeney is a king who has been driven mad by a curse and taken to living in the wilds. In a well-known poem he describes the trees and plants around him, and praises their beauty. However, he considers that the bracken provides him with little welcome:

O tall, russet fern,
Thy mantle has been made red,
There is no bed for an outlaw,
In the branches of thy crests.

Fern also appears in Irish myth as a fairy or magical plant.[14] In the tale 'The Cattle Raid of Cooley' the warrior Nera enters a fairy mound at Samhain (or Halloween). It is summer in fairyland, so he returns from the mound carrying flowers of summer with him as proof of his stay. The flowers he brings are golden fern, wild garlic, and primrose. In a tale called 'The Death of Muirchertach', the king of the same name falls under the spell of a fairy woman. She shows her powers by turning the waters of the Boyne into wine, and making enchanted pigs out of ferns. She also conjures up an illusion of two armies fighting one another with stones, ferns and sods, and Muirchertach exhausts himself battling against these shadows. Other enchantments then follow which ultimately lead to the king's death.

Bracken's many uses were sufficient to earn it a place in the Old Irish Brehon Laws on trees and shrubs as one of the 'bushes of the wood'.[15] This meant that the unlawful clearing of a whole field of bracken was subject to a fine of one *dairt* (or year-old heifer) under the laws. Excavations have found that bracken was used as bedding for both people and animals in Viking Dublin. Bracken or fern was also linked by some medieval scholars with the ancient Irish Ogham alphabet.[16] Each letter of the alphabet was named after a different native tree or shrub, and the letter *Gétal* (which had a sound like *Gw*) was said by some authorities to be named after bracken.

Fern may also have been used to brew ale in ancient Ireland.[17] In the *Lebor Gabála*, or 'Book of Invasions of Ireland', the first brewer in Ireland was named as Malaliach and he was said to be the first person in Ireland to make *lind ratha* or 'fern ale'. The Old Irish word for bog-myrtle (*rait*) is very close to that for fern (*raith*), so it is possible that bog-myrtle is in fact the proper translation. The evidence is ambiguous, however, because although there is no record of either ferns or bog-myrtle being used to make ale in Ireland, both plants have been used for that purpose elsewhere. In Norway the fronds of both male fern and bracken were used to make beer, while the branches of bog-myrtle were used to flavour beer in France, Wales and England (especially Yorkshire).

PRACTICAL AND HERBAL USES

Bracken had a variety of traditional uses.[18] It was widely used for animal bedding in Ireland, and was also used for making beds and thatching cottages in the Scottish Highlands. In Ireland bracken was burnt at St John's Eve, and the potash-rich ash collected and used for bleaching linen, or spread on the soil as a fertiliser. The ash from fern was also often mixed with lard to make soap. The selling of fern led to the first example of the secret speech of the Irish Travellers, called Travellers' Cant or Shelta being recorded by scholars.[19] In 1877 the linguist and scholar C.G. Leland met a traveller at Aberystwyth in Wales. When Leland asked him what he did for a living the man replied 'shelkin' gallopas'. When Leland asked him what language he was speaking the man replied that it was Travellers' Cant for 'selling ferns', and he then went on to provide Leland with the first recorded vocabulary of the speech. In traditional herbal medicine a decoction of the root of bracken mixed with honey was recommended as a vermicide for those troubled with worms.[20] However, bracken was not usually used in folk medicine as it is in fact poisonous to humans and animals, often containing cyanide.[21] Bracken is a member of the family *Hypolepidaceae*, of the order Pteridophytes, which includes ferns, horse tails and club mosses.

SIMILAR PLANTS

Royal Fern – *Raithneach Ríúil* – *Osmunda regalis*[22]

ALTERNATIVE NAMES: (E) Bog Onion, Water Fern. (I) *Bior-raithneach, Gall-Raithneach* (Clare Is), *Oinniún Múin, Raithneach an Rí, Raithneach Capaill, Raithneach Gallda* (Clare Is), *Raithneach Uisce, Rí-raithneach.*

Royal fern gets its Latin name from a story telling how a boatman called Osmund hid his family safely from marauding Vikings on an island covered with the fern. In County Galway royal fern or 'bog onion' was believed to flower at night in June but the flowers were said to disappear mysteriously before daybreak, leaving only the seeds behind. In Ireland and Britain, the rhizomes of royal fern were used in folk medicine as a cure for sprains, dislocations and bruises by boiling them in water and bathing the effected part with the resulting liquid. In Ireland royal fern has also been used as a cure for rickets, rheumatism and sciatica. Royal fern is a member of the family *Osmundaceae*.

Maidenhair Fern – *Dúchosach* – *Adiantum capillus-veneris*[23]
ALTERNATIVE NAMES: (E) Black Footed Fern. (I) *Ceannbhán Dubh Chosach, Cos-dhubh, Failteann Fionn, Tae Scailpreach* (Aran Is)
The dried fronds of maidenhair fern have traditionally been used in the Aran Islands to make a tea. Curiously, it was believed that anyone who collected the fern for use should ask for payment from the recipient, as not to do so would risk death! Maidenhair fern is a member of the family *Adiantaceae*.

Maidenhair Spleenwort – *Lus na Seilge* – *Asplenium trichomanes*[24]
ALTERNATIVE NAMES: (E) White Maidenhair. (I) *Lus an Chorráin*
In Ireland maidenhair spleenwort was used to cure coughs in County Derry, and was boiled with honeysuckle and oatmeal to make a decoction for curing dysentry in County Cavan. Maidenhair spleenwort is a member of the family *Aspleniaceae*.

Wall-rue – *Luibh na Seacht nGábh* – *Asplenium ruta-muraria*[25]
ALTERNATIVE NAMES: (E) Herb-of-the-seven-gifts, Tentwort. (I) *Ráib Chloiche*
In Ireland wall-rue was believed to cure seven different ailments in County Tipperary, hence the name 'herb-of-the-seven-gifts' or *luibh na seacht ngábh*. It was also boiled in milk and taken to treat epilepsy in County Cavan. The name 'tentwort' refers to its use in traditional medicine to cure 'taint' or rickets. Wall-rue is a member of the *Aspleniaceae* family.

Hart's Tongue Fern – *Creamh na Muice Fia* – *Phyllitis scolopendrium* [26]
ALTERNATIVE NAMES: (E) Cow's-tongue. (I) *Craobh Muice Fia, Teanga Fia*
In Irish folk medicine the fronds of hart's tongue fern were traditionally boiled and made into an ointment to cure burns and scalds. It was also used in County Donegal to soothe insect stings, in County Wexford for dog bites, and in County Meath to cure warts. Hart's tongue fern is a member of the *Aspleniaceae* family.

Moonwort – *Lus na Míosa* – *Botrychium lunaria* [27]
ALTERNATIVE NAMES: (I) *Dealtlus, Éasclus, Luanlus*
Moonwort was believed by the ancients to be a plant of magical power if gathered by moonlight, and it was traditionally used by

witches and wizards in their incantations. It was believed to have the power to open locks and unshoe horses who tread upon it. According to one Irish story a man from Clonmel, County Tipperary, was able to open the the locks in Clonmel jail and escape using moonwort. Moonwort is a member of the *Ophioglossaceae* family.

Polypody – *Scim Chaol – Polypodium vulgare*[28]
ALTERNATIVE NAMES: (E) Oak-fern, Polypody-of-the-oak, Wall-fern. (I) *Scamh, Sceamh, Scim Darach, Scim na Crainn, Scim na gCloch*.
Polypody was used in Irish folk medicine to cure burns and scalds in Counties Cavan and Leitrim, and as a mild laxative in County Donegal. Although they are the same species, the ordinary fern which grew on walls was supposed to be much less potent than the 'polypody-of-the-oak' which grew on mature oak trees. In County Galway it was believed to make an excellent tonic, but it had to be pulled at the full moon and the roots left buried in porridge for the night, before it would work. Polypody is a member of the *Polypodiaceae* family.

Ivy – Eidhneán

Hedera Helix

♄   Ruled by the planet Saturn in traditional herbal medicine

♑   Associated with the zodiac sign Capricorn

Ivy, with its dark, evergreen leaves, is a symbol of enduring fertility and life, especially at Christmas when it is traditionally used for decoration. Its clinging nature has made it a symbol of fidelity and loyalty since ancient times, and its binding properties made it a symbol of restraint. Ivy has been used for a variety of folk cures in Ireland, including for corns, skin complaints, and coughs and colds.

SPECIES NAME: As above

ALTERNATIVE NAMES: (I) *Aighneán, Eibheann, Eidheann, Feidhneán, Iashlat*

FOLK BELIEFS AND CUSTOMS

In Ireland and Britain ivy was a traditional decoration at Christmas time, when long fronds of ivy were used as garlands to decorate the house, especially around the windows and the walls.[1] Sometimes in Ireland the berries of the ivy were whitened with starch to give an added festive air, and loose leaves of ivy, holly, bay and laurel were strung on twine, or sewn onto pieces of linen to form patterns and seasonal motifs. A widespread belief was that it was unlucky to have ivy in the house at any other time than Christmas. In Ireland the widespread custom of 'hunting the wren' involved groups of mummers or 'wren boys' going from door to door on St Stephen's Day (26 December) singing songs in exchange for money, food or drink. Originally this involved the cruel custom of catching and killing a real wren, which was then carried around, attached to a holly bush, or when that was not available, a bush of ivy.[2] Thankfully, in later times the use of a real wren was generally dispensed with. One story to explain the custom states that St Stephen was hiding from soldiers in an ivy-covered tree. As the soldiers passed by, a wren rustled the ivy and so attracted the soldiers'

attention. The wren was said to be cursed thereafter on account of this. Ivy was also linked to All Saints' and All Souls' Day after Halloween, as a widespread custom among Catholics was to visit the graves of departed relatives on those days and place wreaths of ivy on them.[3]

Ivy was used in love divination in many parts of Britain and Ireland, usually at Halloween.[4] An Irish rhyme provides a method of divination involving nine ivy leaves:

Nine ivy leaves I place under my head
To dream of the living and not of the dead,
To dream of the man I am going to wed,
And to see him tonight at the foot of my bed.

In Wales ivy was also used for love divination at Halloween. A pointed ivy leaf representing the man and a round ivy leaf representing the woman were put together into the fire. If they jumped towards each other as they burned, it meant marriage. If they jumped away, it meant hatred. A rhyme from the south of Scotland outlines another divination procedure:

Ivy, ivy I love you
In my bosom I put you,
The first young man who speaks to me
My future husband he shall be.

Love divination was not only carried out by women. In England it was believed that a man could see his future love if he collected ten leaves of ivy at Halloween, threw one away, and slept with the other nine under his pillow. Alternatively in Ireland the divination could be carried out on New Year's Eve, when holly or ivy leaves were put under the pillow and the following charm said: 'Oh ivy green and holly red,/Tell me, tell me whom I shall wed.' Ivy was also used for death divination at Halloween.[5] In Ireland this involved nominating an unblemished ivy leaf for each member of the family, and each person putting their leaf in a glass or cup of water to stand overnight. In the morning if the leaf was still spotless the person who set it in the water was sure of life for the next year. However, if the leaf had become stained or spotted, the person it represented would surely die in the next twelve months. An English variation of this had the leaves standing in the water for twelve days from New Year's Day. If there were any spots on the leaf on the twelfth night it meant sickness for the coming year.

Ivy was generally believed to have powers of protection in folklore.[6] In Scotland a piece of ivy was nailed over the byre door to prevent witches putting a spell on the cattle, and to protect them from diseases. In the Scottish Highlands ivy was plucked with a charm to increase milk: 'I will pluck the tree-entwining ivy/As Mary plucked with her one hand.' Ivy, woodbine and rowan were also woven into a wreath and placed over the lintel to protect the cow house and under the milk vessels to protect the milk. In the south of Scotland ivy was generally believed to be avoided by witches. A widespread belief in Britain and Ireland was that ivy growing on a house would protect against witchcraft and general misfortune; and in Wales in particular it was believed that financial loss was expected for the inhabitants if ivy should wither on a house wall. On the other hand, exactly the opposite was also often believed, with ivy growing on the wall of the house thought to bring bad luck or sickness.[7] In Somerset it was said to be bad luck to ever pick an ivy leaf off a church, as this would bring sickness. In County Wicklow it was said that ivy growing on a house would drain the energy from the inhabitants. In Ireland too, ivy was a symbol of those who were devout but hard hearted: *Béal eidhinn, croí cuilinn* – 'ivy mouth, holly heart' went an old saying.[8]

Over the centuries, various customs and superstitions have attached themselves to ivy.[9] Ivy had associations in Classical legend with the Roman god Bacchus, the god of wine, and so traditionally throughout Europe an ivy sprig was often hung outside a vintner's or innkeeper's premises. In Irish folk tradition it was said that the elder tree once refused to shelter Christ while the ivy did, so the elder is the last tree to come into leaf while the ivy is evergreen. In England it was believed that cups or bowls made of ivy wood would protect against cramp and whooping cough. In Ireland it was believed that cattle could be cured of sore eyes by hanging an ivy leaf over the fireplace. As the ivy shrivelled up, so the sore eyes would get better. Ivy taken from a hawthorn bush was also believed to be a good cure for eye ailments. In Ireland ivy leaves were also traditionally made into a musical instrument by children (though exactly how isn't clear). In Scotland ivy is the plant badge of the Gordon clan.[10]

LEGENDS AND MYTHOLOGY

Being an evergreen, ivy makes a good shelter against cold and wind, and this features in several Irish legends.[11] According to the 'Lays of Fionn' the young Fionn MacCumhaill was nursed in hiding by his foster mother Bodhmann in the hollow of a tall, ivy-clad tree. He was given the nickname 'the lad of the hollow' on account of this. In the legend *Suibhne Geilt* or 'Mad Sweeney', Sweeney is a king who has been driven mad by a curse and taken to living in the wilds. He frequently describes the trees and plants around him, usually praising their beauty, and naturally ivy is not excluded from this: 'O ivy, little ivy / Thou art familiar in the dusky wood.' At one point Sweeney even asserts that his food includes ivy berries. In particular, however, Sweeney values ivy for the shelter it provides. He speaks of living 'alone in the top of the ivy' and later declares the following verse:

A proud ivy bush
Which grows through a twisted tree –
If I were right at its summit,
I would fear to come out

Ivy features in a famous Welsh version of the Celtic legend 'How Trystan Won Esyllt'.[12] In the story Isolt has left her husband March and eloped with her lover Tristan. March goes to King Arthur to complain about this insult to his honour, but the lovers steadfastly refuse to be parted. Eventually Arthur resolves the difficulty by ruling that Isolt should be with one of the rivals while the leaves are on the trees, and with the other while the trees are bare, and that March as her lawful husband should have first choice. March chooses the time when the trees are bare, because the nights would be longest at that time. When Isolt hears this she triumphantly declares 'Blessed be the judgement and he who gave it', and sings the following verse:

There are three trees that are good,
holly and ivy and yew;
they put forth leaves while they last,
And Tristan shall have me as long as he lives.

And so March lost Isolt to Tristan for good.

Ivy's use as winter fodder was sufficient to earn it a place in some versions of the Old Irish Brehon Laws on trees and shrubs as one of the 'bushes of the wood'.[13] This meant that the unlawful clearing of a whole stand of ivy was subject to a fine of one *dairt* (or year-old heifer) under the laws. Ivy was also linked by some medieval scholars with the ancient Irish Ogham alphabet.[14] Each letter of the alphabet was named after a different native tree or shrub, and the letters *Gort* or *G* and *Ór* or *Ó* were said by some medieval authorities to be named after ivy.

Ivy was an important plant in Classical legend as it was dedicated to Bacchus, the Roman god of wine.[15] Devotees of Bacchus wore a wreath of ivy, because it was believed that binding the brow with ivy prevented intoxication. Ivy was also sacred to Dionysus, the Greek equivalent of Bacchus, and his followers carried fir branches spirally wreathed in ivy in his honour at their autumn revels. Ivy was a symbol of fidelity in ancient Greece and Rome, and Greek priests presented a wreath of ivy to newly-wed couples. In ancient Egypt too, ivy was a sacred plant.[16] It was dedicated to the god Osiris and called his plant because it was evergreen , and was also linked to the god Attis, whose eunuch priests were tattooed with a pattern of ivy leaves.

PRACTICAL AND HERBAL USES

An ability to smother grape-vines convinced early herbalists that the berries of ivy could overcome the effects of alcohol. As a result of this, goblets made of ivy wood were believed to neutralise the effects of bad or poisoned wine.[17] In folk medicine in both Britain and Ireland the main use for ivy has been in the treatment of corns.[18] Usually this involved soaking the leaves in vinegar and then binding them on as a poultice. In Ireland tying ivy around a corn was also said to be a good method of curing it. Ivy was also used in Ireland for treating a wide variety of other ailments.[19] Burns and scalds were treated with an ointment made from the boiled leaves and fat, while ivy was also widely used to staunch bleeding and reduce inflammation. Ivy berries were eaten in County Offaly and other midland counties as a cure for aches and pains; and ivy was generally valued as a cure for coughs, colds and bronchitis. In Ireland and parts of the Scottish Highlands, a cap made from ivy leaves was often placed on the head of a child suffering from eczema. In County Monaghan a heated ivy leaf was used as a cure for boils and abcesses. One side of the leaf was applied to draw out the pus, while the other side was then applied to promote healing. In Britain and Ireland the juice of ivy leaves was also brushed into fabrics like serge to restore its appearance by removing the shine.[20] Ivy gives its name to the ivy family, the *Araliaceae*.

SIMILAR PLANTS

Ground-ivy – *Athair Lusa* – *Glechoma hederacea*[21]
ALTERNATIVE NAMES: (E) Alehoof, Gill-go-by-ground, Robin-run-in-the-hedge, Wandering Jew. (I) *Eidhneán Talún*
Despite its name, ground-ivy does not bear much resemblance to real ivy, and the name seems to derive from its ability to act as ground cover. The name 'alehoof' derives from the fact that its bitter taste made it an alternative to hops in flavouring ale. Ground-ivy was used in folk medicine in Britain and Ireland to clear the head of 'stuffiness' and mucus, as an inhalant for coughs and colds, and as a general tonic for cleansing the system. It was also used in Ireland to clean up skin complaints, sores and blisters. In Scotland ground-ivy was supposed to be effective in healing the bites of serpents. Ground-ivy is a member of the dead-nettle family, the *Lamiaceae*.

Large Bindweed – *Ialus Mór* – *Calystegia silvatica*
ALTERNATIVE NAMES: (E) Devil's Garters, Great Bindweed, Robin-run-the-hedge, (I) *Corrán Casta*, *Feidhneán Talún* (Cork)

Hedge Bindweed – *Ialus Fáil* – *Calystegia sepium*
ALTERNATIVE NAMES: Campanelle, Great Withywind, Hedge Bell, Hedge Lily, Old Man's Nightcap, Scammony The Tormentor (Fermanagh).

Field Bindweed – *Ainleog* – *Convolvulus arvensis*
ALTERNATIVE NAMES: (E) Cornbind, Jack-run-the-country, Ropewind, Small Bindweed. (I) *Duillmheal*, *Feidhneán Talún* (Cork), *Lusán Siúltach*
Bindweeds are hated by farmers and gardeners on account of their invasive habits and ability to regenerate from even the tiniest piece of root left in the soil – hence names like 'Devil's garters'. It is possible, however, to appreciate the beauty of their white or pink trumpet-shaped flowers when they are growing in the wild, and not choking cultivated plants by climbing up their stems and completely covering them. Hedge bindweed was used as a remedy for kidney trouble in County Fermanagh, where it was known as 'the tormentor' on account of its habit of gripping other plants and choking them.[22] Bindweeds give their name to the bindweed family, the *Convolvulaceae*.

Minor Plants in Folklore

Houseleek – Lus an Tóiteáin

Sempervivum Tectorum

♃   Ruled by the planet Jupiter in traditional herbal medicine

♓   Associated with the zodiac sign Pisces

SPECIES NAME: As above
ALTERNATIVE NAMES: (E) Roofleek (Cork), Sengreen, Waxplant (Offaly, Westmeath). (I) *Buachaill Tí* (Galway), *Glan-eagla, Luibh an Tóiteáin, Norp, Orp, Plúirín Sliogán* (?), *Sincín, Teineagal, Tincín, Tin-eaglach*

FOLK BELIEFS AND CUSTOMS
In Ireland and throughout Europe houseleek was believed to pro-tect against fire and lightning.[1] In Ireland affixing houseleek to the roof preserved the house from fire and protected the inhabitants from burns and scalds. Indeed, houseleek was often deliberately encouraged to grow on the roof of thatched houses for this purpose. If the roof was made of some other material, special niches or nooks were made in or about the roof or porch of the house. In England it was also believed that houseleek growing on the roof protected the house from fire and thunder, and that to cut it down would be invit-ing trouble. In Wales it was thought that having houseleek growing on the roof would bring luck to the house. In Europe, houseleek's protective powers were so strongly believed in, that the emperor Charlemagne was said to have ordered that it be planted on the roof of every house in his realm.

LEGENDS AND MYTHOLOGY
The protective attributes of houseleek have ancient origins.[2] The Romans called houseleek *Iovis caulis* – 'Jupiter's Plant' and believed that it had fallen down from Zeus or Jupiter to protect the house from the lightning he wielded. For that reason it was often grown in sand on the roof tiles of Roman houses.

PRACTICAL AND HERBAL USES
In traditional herbal medicine houseleek or 'sengreen' was used to soothe ulcers, burns, scalds and inflammations.[3] In Ireland

houseleek was widely used as a treatment for lumps and swellings, including corns, warts and chilblains.[4] Generally the leaves were used as a poultice, or the juice mixed with cream or fat to make an ointment. In Ireland it was also widely believed that bathing the eyes in the juice of houseleek was good for relieving soreness.[5] Houseleek has also been used to cure headaches in County

Roscommon, kidney trouble in County Cavan and as an abortifacient in County Mayo.[6] Houseleek is a member of the stonecrop family, the *Crassulaceae*.

Similar Plants

Navelwort – *Cornán Caisil* – *Umbilicus rupestris*[7]
Alternative names: (E) Kidneyweed, Kidneywort, Pennygrass, Pennyleaf, Pennyleaves, Wall Pennywort. (I) *Coinneal Mhuire, Cornán Leacáin, Lamhainn-cat-leacain, Lann Cleite* (Donegal), *Leacán, Luan Chait* (Ulster)
The Romans called navelwort 'Venus' navel', and used it in spells to procure love. In traditional medicine navelwort was valued as a cure for kidney complaints, particularly to aid the passing of kidney stones, hence its names 'kidneyweed' and 'kidneywort'. Navelwort was also used like houseleek, to cure skin complaints. In Ireland navelwort was used to cure corns and chilblains in Counties Wicklow, Wexford and Carlow, and sore eyes in Counties Wicklow and Leitrim. Like houseleek, the leaves were applied as a poultice, or mixed with cream or fat to make an ointment. Navelwort was also used to cure jaundice in County Waterford and tuberculosis in County Wicklow. Navelwort is a member of the stonecrop family, the *Crassulaceae*.

Orpine – *Tóirpín* – *Sedum telephium*[8]
Alternative names: (E) Heal-all (Ulster), Livelong, Lusonalee (Fin), Red Orpiment. (I) *Sanarc, Tirpín, Toirpín*
Orpine was used for love divination throughout Europe on St John's Eve or midsummer. The plants were placed in pairs in pots, and if they grew towards each other it meant love, if they grew apart it meant aversion. In England, orpine was used as a remedy against fever, sterility in women, and too-profuse menstruation. Orpine is a member of the stonecrop family, the *Crassulaceae*.

Biting Stonecrop – *Grafán na gCloch* – *Sedum acre*[9]
Alternative names: (E) Wall-pepper. (I) *Lusra an tSionnaigh, Lus(ra) na Seangán*

Reflexed Stonecrop – *Grafán Crom* – *Sedum reflexum*
Alternative names: (E) Indian Fog, Indian Moss (Donegal), Yellow Stonecrop

In Britain the leaves of reflexed stonecrop were eaten as a green salad. In Ireland stonecrops have been used in Counties Cavan, Leitrim, and Wexford as a way of ridding the system of worms. They were also used in County Westmeath for kidney problems. Stonecrops give their name to the stonecrop family, the *Crassulaceae*.

Meadowsweet – Airgead Luachra
Filipendula ulmaria

Scarlet Pimpernel – Falcaire Fiáin
Anagallis arvensis

Foxglove – Lus Mór
Digitalis Purpurea

Honeysuckle – Féithleann
Lonicera periclymenum

St John's Wort – Beathnua

Hypericum perforatum

Mugwort – Mongach Meisce
Artemisia vulgaris

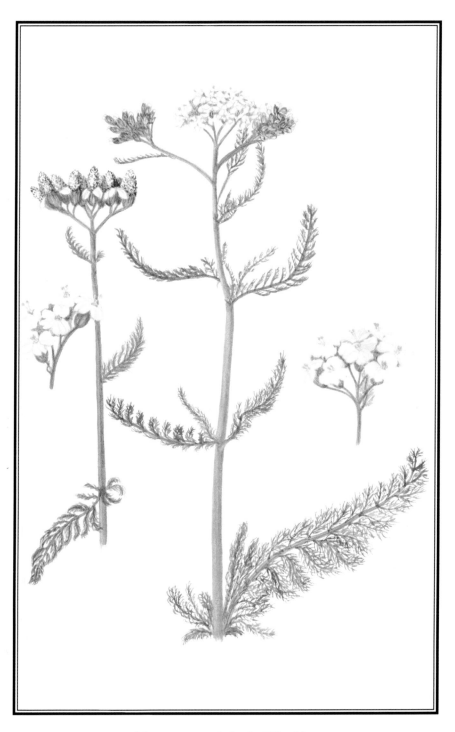

Yarrow – Athair Thalún
Achillea millefolium

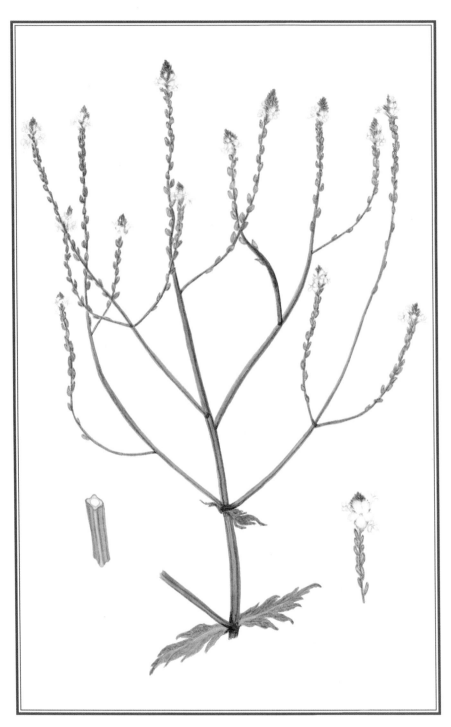

Vervain – Beirbhéine
Verbena officinalis

Sea Wrack – Feamainn

Fucus

Not ruled by any planet in traditional herbal medicine

SPECIES NAMES:
Bladder Wrack – *Feamainn Bhoilgíneach* – *Fucus vesiculosis*
ALTERNATIVE NAMES: (E) Blistered Seaweed. (I) *Barrchonlach, Builgeog, Feamainn, Faimleach* (Sligo), *Turscar Dubh na gClog*

Channel Wrack – *Caisíneach* – *Pelvetia canaliculata*
ALTERNATIVE NAMES: (I) *Dualamán, Dúlamán, Dúlamán Fada, Dúlamán Gaelach, Dúlamán na Beanna Buí, Feamainn Cháilíneach, Muiríneach na Muc*

Strap Wrack – *Coirleach* – *Laminaria digitata*
ALTERNATIVE NAMES: (E) Oarweed, Tangle. (I) *Corrlach, Feamainn Dhearg, Langach* (*Lobhair*), *Leathach, Liach* (Clare Is), *Liadh, Liagh, Múrach, Ribín, Scoth Buí, Scraith Buí*

Serrated Wrack – *Míoránach* – *Fucus serratus*
ALTERNATIVE NAMES: (E) Black Wrack, Toothed Wrack. (I) *Turscar Ladharach*

Knotted Wrack – *Feamainn Bhuí* – *Ascophyllum nodosum*
ALTERNATIVE NAMES: (E) Egg Wrack, Knobbed Wrack. (I) *Turscar na Ruadhóg*

ALTERNATIVE NAMES FOR WRACK: (E) Kelp, Wore (Fin). (I) *Ceilp, Stiallach* (Connaught), *Trioscar, Troscar, Truscar, Turscar, Tuscar*

FOLK BELIEFS AND CUSTOMS
Seaweed was considered a valuable source of fertiliser and food for coastal communities in both Ireland and Britain.[1] In Ireland the spring tide nearest St Brigid's Day (1 February) was believed to be the greatest tide of the year; and coastal dwellers were quick to take the opportunity of cutting and gathering the seaweed and of collecting shellfish and other shore produce at this time. In many

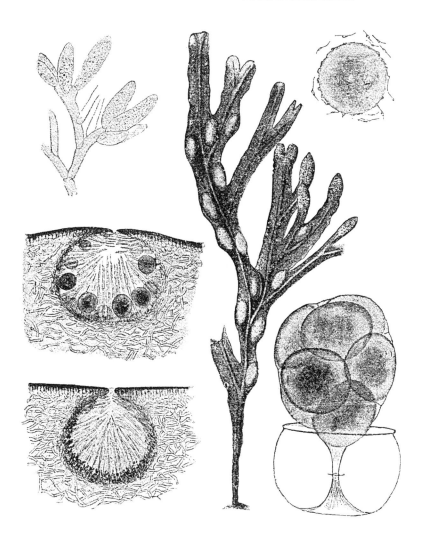

coastal areas of Ireland shellfish and edible seaweed appeared along-side the potatoes instead of meat during the fasting season of Lent; and many coastal communities had only shellfish and edible seaweed as their main meal on the fast day of Good Friday before Easter.

Many superstitions surrounded the gathering of seaweed in Ireland.[2] A particularly strong belief was that seaweed should not be gathered on a Sunday or other Holy Days, and various stories illustrate this point. One tells of a group of men gathering seaweed who work through the night into early Sunday morning. They are accompanied in their work by a strange man who works further down the beach. When they have collected a large amount of sea-weed and are about to leave, the strange man suddenly disappears, and a huge wave sweeps in and carries away all the seaweed they have collected, leaving them with nothing for their labours. Other stories tell of how nothing but weeds would grow on land that had been spread with seaweed gathered on a Sunday. On the other hand, various stories tell of how people who observed the prohibi-tion were rewarded. One story tells of a man who refused to collect a large amount of seaweed that had washed up on the beach because it was the start of the Christmas season. When the twelve days of Christmas were over, the man returned to the spot where the seaweed lay. Instead of the seaweed being dried out and rotten as it should be, it was as fresh as the day he first saw it.

Gathering seaweed was also particularly important in the Scottish Highlands.[3] Every year the inhabitants of the Isle of Lewis carried out a custom at Halloween which involved a sacrifice to a sea being called 'Shony'. They would gather at the local church at night time before the festivities began, and then one person would wade out into the sea crying out: 'Shony, I give you this cup of ale, hoping you will be so kind as to send us plenty of seaweed for enriching our ground the following year'. The person would then throw the cup into the sea, and the festivities would begin. The name Shony is believed to derive from Sjoni, the norse god of the sea, and reflects the Norse influence on the western isles of Scotland. Seaweed was also gathered in the Scottish Highlands with the following traditional prayer:

> Come and come is seaweed,
> Come and come is red sea-ware,
> Come is yellow weed, come is tangle,
> Come is food which the sea entraps.

Seaweed was also linked to the fairies.[4] In Scotland the fairy being called the water-horse or kelpie was said to look like a horse except it was covered in seaweed. If it took human form it could be identified by the strands of seaweed still in its hair. In Brittany the fairy beings or hairy imps called the Korrigans were said to ride across the sea on boats of seaweed doing mischief to fishermen.

A widespread belief, particularly in England, is that seaweed is a great indicator of weather if kept in the porch of a house. It is believed to dry up and shrivel if the weather is to be fine, and swell up and feel damp to the touch if wet weather is on the way.[5] In Cornwall and Devon, seaweed was dried and placed on the mantlepiece to protect the house from fire.[6] In Wiltshire it was believed that you would never be without a friend as long as you had seaweed about the house.[7]

LEGENDS AND MYTHOLOGY

Seaweed's use as food appears in some Irish legends.[8] In the legend *Suibhne Geilt* or 'Mad Sweeney', Sweeney is a king who has been driven mad by a curse and taken to living in the wilds. He lives off the wild nuts and berries around him, but at one point he also mentions seaweed (*femar*) as one of the foods which provide his sustenance. In the legend 'The Cattle Raid of Cooley'or *Táin Bó Cúailnge*, the warrior Cuchulainn welcomes his rival Fergus as a guest at one point and offers him a handful of watercress, seaweed (*femmaig*) and brooklime to eat. As we have seen, seaweed was considered sufficiently valuable as a food and fertiliser in ancient Ireland to attract laws protecting it from unlawful collection.

Seaweed appears as a magical plant in Welsh myth.[9] In the Welsh tale 'Math son of Mathonwy' the magician Gwydon conjured up an enchanted ship made from red seaweed and kelp in order to sail unopposed into the harbour of the fortress of his enemy, Queen Aranrhod.

PRACTICAL AND HERBAL USES

In western coastal areas of Ireland sea wrack was traditionally gathered to fertilise the land, specially for growing crops like potatoes.[10] The seaweed would be cut by hand and then loaded onto a horse and cart for transporting to the field. Sometimes the work was carried out from a boat with a scythe specially made for cutting underwater, or the gatherers would wade out in the sea up to their shoulders to haul up the seaweed in nets. In places the seaweed was even 'cultivated' by placing large stones along a beach to encourage the growth of the seaweed. Seaweed could also be burnt and the ashes, known as 'kelp' were then spread as the fertiliser.[11] In Ireland an industry traditionally existed in the export of kelp as fertiliser to England. In more recent times in Ireland the seaweed industry exists to provide algal products which have a wide variety of uses, from stabilising ice cream, paper making and pharmaceuticals, to preserving a good 'head' on a pint![12] In traditional medicine the jelly-like mucilage in the swollen vesicles of bladder wrack was considered an effective cure for rheumatism, bruised limbs and sprains.[13] Generally the seaweed was boiled into an oily lotion, or placed hot against the skin, or put into a bath of hot water. Seaweed baths were traditionally very popular in Ireland to relieve aches and pains, and many people took them every week on fair day. Baths were situated around the coast in places like Westport, Ballybunion and Dún Laoghaire.[14] Despite their plant-like appearance seaweeds are a kind of algae, and as such are classified separately from true plants in a 'kingdom' called the Protista, along with organisms such as amoebas and slime-moulds. Wracks are members of the Brown Algae, of the division *Chromophycota*.

SIMILAR PLANTS

Carrigeen – *Carraigín* – *Chondrus*[15]
ALTERNATIVE NAMES: (E) Irish Moss. (I) *Cosáinín* (*Chondrus crispus*), *Ceann Donn*, *Clúimhín Cait*.
Carrigeen or Irish moss has traditionally been gathered in Ireland, both to eat and for use in folk medicine as a cure for coughs, colds, sore throats and chest ailments. The plants were boiled in milk or water, and the decoction strained and drunk hot. It was also the basis of a teetotal drink called 'sobriety'. In Ireland it was said that carrigeen was one of the three plants that kept some people from starving during the famine, the others being charlock and nettle. Carrigeen is a member of the Red Algae, of the division *Rhodophycota*.

Dulse – *Duileasc* – *Rhodymenia palmata*[16]
ALTERNATIVE NAMES: (E) Dillisk, Dullice (Ulster). (I) *Creathneach*, *Rapán* (Donegal)

Pepper Dulse – *Míobhán* – *Laurencia pinnatifida*
ALTERNATIVE NAMES: (I) *Miabhán*, *Milseán Mara*, *Milseán Trá*, *Mímheán*, *Míobán*.
Dulse or dillisk has been eaten in Ireland since ancient times. An eighth-century Irish law text mentions dulse as making up part of the commoners' diet. Later, the Dublin botanist Caleb Threkeld

wrote in 1727 that 'in Dublin men chew it like tobacco when dry – it destroys worms, and gives a relish to beer and it is recommended against women's longings'. Dulse was (and is) eaten raw, fresh or dried, or cooked like spinach, and was valued as a protection against ill health in general. In the west of Ireland dulse was also given to pigs to eat, while pepper dulse was considered by some to be the best kind of dulse to eat, and was also sold as food. Dulse is a member of the Red Algae family, of the division *Rhodophycota*.

RED LAVER – *Sleabhac Dearg – Porphyra laciniata* [17]
ALTERNATIVE NAMES: (E) Purple Laver, Slake, Sloak (US), Sloke, Sloucan. (I) *Slabhac* (Donegal), *Slabhcán, Sleabhac, Sleabhcán, Slodhac, Sludhac.*
In Ireland purple laver was eaten as a vegetable, being stewed for hours until tender and then dressed with butter, vinegar and pepper. In the Aran Islands purple laver was used as a cure for indigestion. Red laver appears in the placename Coomatloukane (*Com an tSleabhcán* – hollow of the laver), County Kerry. Red laver is a member of the Red Algae family, of the division *Rhodophycota*.

Green Laver – *Glasán – Ulva lactuca*
ALTERNATIVE NAMES: (E) Sea-lettuce. (I) *Bó-shleaidige, Sleaidí*
Despite its alternative name of 'sea lettuce' green laver does not seem to ever have been eaten. The name instead refers to the thin green fronds which are said to resemble lettuce. Green laver is a member of the Green Algae family, of the division *Chlorophycota*.

Grasses – Féara

Gramineae

☿ Couch Grass ruled by the planet Mercury in traditional herbal medicine

♄ Darnel Grass ruled by the planet Saturn in traditional herbal medicine

SPECIES NAMES:
Quaking Grass – *Féar Gortach – Briza media*
ALTERNATIVE NAMES: Cowquakes

Common Couch – *Broimfhéar – Elymus repens*
ALTERNATIVE NAMES: (E) Brome Grass, Dog's-grass, Quitch Grass, Scutch Grass, Switch Grass, Swutch Grass (US). (I) *Cruithneacht Bhruimsean, Féar Gaoil*

Creeping Bent – *Feorainn – Agrostis stolonifera*
ALTERNATIVE NAMES: (E) Fiorin (Kerry). (I) *Faorthann* (Mayo), *Feoirthín, Fiorthann, Fiothrán*

Timothy – *Tiomóid – Phleum pratense*
ALTERNATIVE NAMES: (I) *Féar Capaill*

Darnel – *Roille – Lolium temulentum*
ALTERNATIVE NAMES: (E) Bearded Darnel, Raygrass. (I) *Breallán, Raidhle, Raighle, Raoile, Ríle, Roilléire, Ruíllé*

Marram – *Muiríneach – Ammophila arenaria*
ALTERNATIVE NAMES: (E) Bennet, Bent, Helm, Matweed. (I) *Biríneach, Muirín, Muraineach, Tráithnín*

ALTERNATIVE NAMES FOR GRASS: Glask (TC), Shirk (TC)

FOLK BELIEFS AND CUSTOMS
A widespread belief unique to Ireland was the existance of *Féar Gorta* or Hungry Grass.[1] It was said to be a patch of grass which caused great faintness and hunger to come upon the person who

stepped on it. According to custom, the only way to counteract it was to carry a handful of oaten meal, which should be eaten immediately the weakness was felt. Usually hungry grass was found high up in the mountains in remote areas, and anyone found dead in the mountains from exhaustion or exposure was said to be a victim of it. Famous locations in Ireland where hungry grass grew include Mount Brandon, and between two cairns in the mountains near Omeath. Hungry grass could also occasionally be found growing near holy wells. Various theories existed to explain the phenomemon. Hungry grass was said to grow where a dead body had touched the ground, or where a meal had been eaten and no crumbs left behind for the fairies. Alternatively it was said to be where a famine victim had been buried.

It seems, however, that there is some medical basis for the phenomemon of hungry grass. It is believed to be a condition of faintness or exhaustion likely to occur after a long day working in the mountains. The sufferer feels weak and may even lose consciousness, but it passes if the sufferer sits and rests. As custom relates, the attack may be prevented or cut short by bringing a cake of oaten bread and eating it when the attack begins. Hungry grass has been identified by some with the species quaking grass, but it appears more likely that no one species of grass is especially linked to it. A variation on the *Féar Gorta* was the *Fóidín Mearaí* or 'sod of confusion'. It was said to be a particular piece of ground or turf that if a traveller trod on it while out walking, he or she would be led astray.[2]

Grass features in some children's games.[3] One favourite is blowing on a blade of grass held taut between the fingers to produce a piercing sound. In England children also played a divination game to see whom they would marry. Each seed of a certain kind of grass was touched in turn moving up the stalk, while saying 'tinker, tailor, soldier, sailor, rich man, poor man, beggarman, thief'. The person they named when they reached the last seed would be the person they would marry. Children were also fond of chewing the soft and juicy ends of grasses to quench their thirst, particularly the species called bent grass.

A widespread belief was that an abundance of grass at Christmastime foretold a large number of deaths in the following year.[4] A County Kerry saying put it like this: 'A green Christmas, a fat churchyard.' The idea behind this was that hard, frosty weather was better for killing off germs.

LEGENDS AND MYTHOLOGY

Ireland's reputation for being a green country goes back a long way.[5] The Norman cleric Gerald of Wales, writing in the twelfth century in his well known 'History and Topography of Ireland', has this to say: 'The island is … richer in pastures than in crops, and in grass than in grain … The plains are well clothed with grass, and the haggards are bursting with straw.'

Later he says: 'This is the most temperate of countries … The grass is green in the fields in winter, just the same as in summer.' Finally, among the wonders of Ireland, he recounts the miraculous qualities of some plains called 'Brigid's pastures'. The pastures possess the marvellous property that 'even though all the animals of the whole province have eaten the grass down to the ground, nevertheless when morning comes they have just as much grass as ever'. It seems it has never taken much in Ireland to make the grass grow!

Grass features in the lore surrounding the legendary cow called the *Glas Ghaibhleann*.[6] The *Glas Ghaibhleann* was a cow that belonged to the Irish smith god Goibhniú, and was said to be able to provide an inexhaustible supply of the best quality milk. According to folklore, in any field it slept in, the cow passed on some of its fertile qualities to the grass. An old saying therefore, about any rich pasture is that *Chodail an Ghlas Gaibhneach ann* – 'the *Glas Gaibhneach* (or *Gaibhleann*) slept there'. In a similar vein, Irish folklore about the reign of the just king Cathal Crobh-dhearg states that 'the grass was so abundant that it reached above the horns of the cattle when they lay down in the field'. The belief that the reign of a good king brought abundance and good growth has its origins in the pagan belief of the fertile 'marriage' of the rightful king to the land.

PRACTICAL AND HERBAL USES

The main use for grass has always, of course, been as food for livestock. Nowadays cultivated grass species are grown in pastureland, rather than any wild varieties; and green grass in the form of silage is used rather than dried grass or hay as winter fodder. Couch grass was also used in Ireland by poor people as fodder for the donkeys in winter.[7] Grass did have other uses, however.[8] For example, grass was traditionally used for rope-making and thatching in Ireland. Marram grass, with its tough, wiry fibres, was particularly favoured for this, and it was plaited into strips to make mats, baskets and even stools. Darnel grass was said to produce drunkenness and it was sometimes used to adulterate malt and other liquors. Grass generally did not have many medical uses.[9] In Ireland a poultice of fresh grass, yarrow and a plant called 'finabawn' was mixed with the white of an egg, and then put over a whitlow or boil to cure it. In Ireland and in parts of Britain, an infusion made from the bruised rhizomes of couch grass was used to cure kidney and genito-urinary infections. It was also believed that if a dog ate something poisonous it would cure itself by eating some couch grass, which would then cause it to vomit up the poison. Grasses give their name to the grass family, the *Gramineae* or *Poaceae*.

SIMILAR PLANTS

Common Cotton-Grass – *Ceannbhán* – *Eriophorum angustifolium*[10]
ALTERNATIVE NAMES: (E) Bog-cotton, Bog-down, Bog-silk, Cotton-sedge, Crushy-bracken (US), Flowans (US), Hare's-tail. (I) *Buinneán Bán, Canach Móna, Flocas* (Cork), *Scathóg Fiáin, Scathóg Fionnaidh, Síoda Móna, Scothóg Fiáin, Scothóg Fionnaidh, Tóin Fhionn*
Cotton-grass or bog-cotton, with its pure white downy tufts, is a well-loved and even iconic feature of Irish boglands. In Gaelic Scotland it was a symbol of purity and beauty, and the complexion of maidens was often said to be 'as white as the cotton grass' in Scots Gaelic poetry. In Ireland 'bog-cotton' as it is usually known, was said to be cursed by St Patrick, but it was nevertheless used for filling mattresses and pillows. Common cotton-grass is a member of the sedge family, the *Cyperaceae*.

Knotgrass – *Glúineach Bheag* – *Polygonum aviculare*[11]
Alternative names: (E) Little Bird's Tongue, Sparrow's Tongue. (I) *Féar Altach, Féar Craobhach, Teanga Éanáin, Teanga Gealbhain*
The alternative names for knotgrass, 'sparrow's tongue' and 'little bird's tongue', are said to derive from the fact the little pointed leaves resemble the tongues of birds. Knotgrass was used in traditional medicine to cure ulcers and sores, and was also given to pigs to eat when they were sick and off other foods. Knotgrass is a member of the dock family, the *Polygonaceae*.

Cleavers – *Garbhlus* – *Galium aparine*[12]
ALTERNATIVE NAMES: (E) Catchweed, Claiver (US), Devil's Garters (Ulster), Goosegrass, Jack-at-the-hedge, Roabin-rin-the-hedge (US), Robin-run-the-hedge, Sticky Backs, Sticky Billy (Ulster), Sticky

Willies, Willy-run-the-hedge. (I) *Airmeirg, Airnéisí, Brioslán, Caol-fhail, Garbhach, Lus Garbh, Sop an tSéaláin* (Galway), *Sop Séaláin* (Meath), *Uirlis Chríonna* (Kerry)

Cleavers, goosegrass, or robin-run-the-hedge is a well-known and often disliked weed, on account of the many tiny hooks on its leaves and seeds, which catch in clothing and animals' fur. In England, cleavers was given to goslings to eat, hence the name 'goosegrass'. In Ireland, eating the leaves of cleavers was said to make fat people thin. However, cleavers was not seen as very palatable. In Munster it was said of a greedy person that: *d'iosfaidh se an gharbhach* – 'he would even eat cleavers'. Nevertheless, in the eighteenth century the seeds of cleavers were roasted to make coffee, which is not as strange as it sounds, since cleavers is in fact a distant relative of coffee. In ancient Greece shepherds were supposed to have used the stalks of cleavers to sieve animal hairs out of milk, and it may have a similar use in Ireland as the name *sop an tséaláin* means 'wispy strainer'. In Irish folk medicine cleavers was used to cure burns in Counties Westmeath and Wicklow, swellings in County Wicklow, inflammation of the bowels in children in County Donegal, and stomach ache in County Limerick. Cleavers is a member of the bedstraw family, the *Rubiaceae*.

Dandelion – Caisearbhán

Taraxacum Officinale

♃ Ruled by the planet Jupiter in traditional herbal medicine

♐ Associated with the zodiac sign Sagittarius

SPECIES NAME: As above

ALTERNATIVE NAMES: (E) Clock, Heart-fever Grass (Ulster), Monk's Head, Pee-the-bed (Antrim), Pishamoolag (Donegal), Pish-the-bed (Ulster, US), Piss-a-bed, Piss-in-the-beds (Offaly), Pisterbed (Longford), Priest's Crown, Wet-the-bed. (I) *Bearnán Beárnach, Bearnán Bríde, Bláth Buí, Caisreabhrán, Gais-shearbhán, Gathánn Gabhainn* (head), *Lus Bhríde, Searbhán (Muc)*.

THE SEEDS OF DANDELION ARE ALSO KNOWN AS: (E) Jimmyjoes (Dublin), Jinnyjoes (Dublin)

FOLK BELIEFS AND CUSTOMS

Dandelion is known in both Irish and Scots Gaelic as *Bearnán Bríde* – 'the indented one of Brigid' on account of the serrated edge of its leaves or petals.[1] In Ireland the link with Brigid was believed to be due to the fact that it is almost the first wild flower to come into bloom following her festival. In Scotland the link was explained by saying that its milky sap nourished the early lamb, just as Brigid protected the young livestock. In the Scottish Highlands a hoop made of milkwort, butterwort, dandelion and marigold was bound with a triple cord of lint and placed under the milk vessels to prevent witches spiriting away the substance of the milk.

The fluffy seedheads of dandelions or 'clocks' were used in a number of children's games in both Britain and Ireland.[2] The games usually involved seeing how many puffs it took to blow away all the seeds. The most popular game involved telling the time with the seeds, each puff signifying an hour of the clock – three puffs meant it was three o'clock and so on – hence the name 'clock' for the dandelion. Alternatively, the number of puffs could signify the number of years until the person would get married. Another game involved saying 'love me', 'love me not', with each puff in turn,

until the last one decided the result.

Dandelion is well known for its diuretic properties, and this has led to the universal notion among children that picking the flowers will lead to bed wetting.[3] This explains the many names found in Britain and Ireland like piss-the-bed, wet-the-bed, etc. The same idea also exists in mainland Europe, as such names as French *pis-senlit* and Dutch *pisse-bed* confirm. Some other dandelion folk cures also developed a more magical aspect. One cure for warts decreed that the juice of the dandelion had to be applied nine mornings in a row, and that prayers had to be said while applying the juice. The dandelions also had to be gathered before dawn. It was also believed that chickenpox could be cured with a medicine containing dandelion, but only if a man gave the medicine to a woman sufferer and vice versa.

The name dandelion comes from the Latin *dens leonis,* 'lion's tooth' (or *dent de lion* in French), but it is not clear if this refers to the jagged leaves, the tap root or the parts of the flower.[4] In Ireland dandelion appears in the placenames Moneysharvan (*Muine Searbhán –* thicket of the dandelion), County Derry and Toberataravan (*Tobar an tSearbháin –* well of the dandelion), County Roscommon.[5]

PRACTICAL AND HERBAL USES

Dandelion has been used in a wide variety of traditional herbal cures, but it was particularly well known throughout Europe for its diuretic properties in promoting the flow of urine and thus assisting kidney and associated troubles.[6] The next most widespread cure was applying the milky sap to warts in order to remove them.[7] Dandelion was also widely used to cure coughs and colds, and as a tonic to 'cleanse the blood'.[8] In Ireland dandelion was used for liver trouble, jaundice, stomach upsets, rheumatism and even 'consumption', as tuberculosis was known. Indeed, a Dublin cure for tuberculosis involved eating a sandwich of bread and butter and fresh dandelion leaves.[9] Dandelion was also used in various parts of Ireland for a range of different cures.[10] Among other things, it was used for cuts in Counties Cavan, Wicklow, Limerick and Kerry; for sprains and swellings in Counties Kildare and Limerick; and for diabetes in County Kilkenny. In Ireland a stye could also be cured by bathing the eye in the milky sap of the dandelion. The regard for dandelion in Ireland goes back a long way. In ancient Ireland a cure called 'Diancecht's Porridge' was prescribed for fourteen different disorders of the stomach, as well as for colds, sore throats and worms, amongst other disorders. It was a brew made from a mixture of dandelions, hazel buds, chickweed, wood sorrel and oatmeal. Dandelion flowers were also widely used in Britain and Ireland to make a very potent but most palatable wine.[11] The young leaves of dandelion can be eaten as a salad, while the roots can be dried and roasted to make 'coffee'.[12] Dandelion is a member of the daisy family, the *Asteraceae*.

SIMILAR PLANTS

Mouse-Ear Hawkweed – *Searbh na Muc* – *Hieracium pilosella*[13]
ALTERNATIVE NAMES: (E) Creeping Mouse-ear, Great Hawkweed, He-dandelion (US). (I) *Caisearbhán na Muc, Cluas Luch, Cluas Liath, Srubhán, Sruth na Muc.*
Mouse-ear hawkweed is one of the commonest members of the hawkweeds, the large number of plants that look like dandelions, but in fact aren't. In Irish folk medicine mouse-ear hawkweed was used in Counties Meath and Limerick to cure whooping cough, in Counties Roscommon, Westmeath, and Wicklow for urinary troubles, and in County Cavan to cure sores. Mouse-ear Hawkweed is a member of the daisy family, the *Asteraceae*.

Goat's-beard – *Finidí na Muc* – *Tragopogon pratensis*[14]
ALTERNATIVE NAMES: (E) Go-to-bed-at-noon. (I) *Féasóg Gabhair, Gabhar-ulcha*
Goat's-beard is one of the many plants that to the untrained eye resemble dandelion, but are nevertheless clearly different. The name 'goat's-beard' derives from the seedhead, while the name 'Go-to-bed-at-noon' comes from the fact that the flower closes up after midday. Goat's-beard is a member of the daisy family, the *Asteraceae*.

Common Cudweed – *Cáithluibh* – *Filago vulgaris*[15]
ALTERNATIVE NAMES: (E) Chaffweed, Cotton-down, Herb Impious. (I) *Cadhluibh, Canach Bán, Canach Móna, Canach Sléibhe, Cáthluibh Gnabhlus, Gnamhlus*
Cudweed gets its name from the fact that it was put into the mouths of cattle that had lost their cud. It also had the name 'herb impious' because the later flowers spring up higher than the earlier ones and crowd them out, 'as many wicked children do unto their parents'.

In traditional medicine cudweed was used to heal chafing of skin, hence the name 'chaffweed'. Common Cudweed is a member of the daisy family, the *Asteraceae*.

Nipplewort – *Duilleog Bhríde* – *Lapsana communis*[16]
ALTERNATIVE NAMES: (E) Dock-cress, Tetterwort. (I) *Duilleog Mhaith, Duilleog Mhín*
Nipplewort gets its name from the fact that Prussian herbalists used it to heal the ulcers on the nipples of women's breasts. This may be an example of sympathetic magic, as the buds of nipplewort in fact resemble nipples. Similarly, in the Scottish Highlands nipplewort was used to ease the soreness of the nipples of nursing mothers, and in the Isle of Man nursing women used it to increase the flow of milk. Nipplewort is a member of the daisy family, the *Asteraceae*.

Colt's-Foot – *Sponc* – *Tussilago farfara*[17]
ALTERNATIVE NAMES: (E) Coughwort, Fohanan (Donegal), Pish-the-bed (US), Spunk (Dublin). (I) *Adhann, Cluas Liath, Comann, Copóg Shleamhain* (Ulster), *Fáthlán, Gallán Greannchair, Luibh-in-aghaidh-casachtaigh, Sponclus*
Colt's-foot was traditionally used as a tinder on account of the downy undersurface of its leaves – hence the name 'spunk' (or spark). The leaves were traditionally coated in salt-petre (gunpowder) and then dried out before use. In addition, the leaves of colt's-foot were often dried and used as a substitute for tobacco, or mixed in with tobacco. The smoke from colt's-foot tobacco was held to be very good against a dry cough, and the leaves were used as a soothing ingredient in throat lozenges until recently. In Irish folk medicine the leaves were soaked in water or boiled in milk, and the resulting liquid drunk as a cure for asthma. The name 'colt's-foot' refers to the shape of the leaves. Colt's-foot is a member of the daisy family, the *Asteraceae*.

Buttercup – Fearbán

Ranunculus

♂ Ruled by the planet Mars in traditional herbal medicine

♈ Associated with the zodiac sign Aries

SPECIES NAMES:
Creeping Buttercup – *Fearbán Reatha* – *Ranunculus repens*
ALTERNATIVE NAMES: (E) Crowtoe (Donegal), Sitfast

Meadow Buttercup – *Fearbán Féir* – *Ranunculus acris*

Bulbous Buttercup – *Tuile Thalún* – *Ranunculus bulbosis*

Goldilocks Buttercup – *Gruaig Mhuire* – *Ranunculus auricomus*
ALTERNATIVE NAMES: (I) *Garbhlus na Móna*

Lesser Spearwort– *Glasair Léana Bheag* – *Ranunculus flammula*
ALTERNATIVE NAMES: (E) Cowgrass (Ulster), Meadow Crowfoot. (I) *Lasair Léana*

Common Water Crowfoot – *Néal Uisce Coiteann* – *Ranunculus aquatilis*
ALTERNATIVE NAMES: (E) Eelweed (Donegal), Water-lily (Donegal). (I) *Fliodh Uisce, Líon na nAbhann, Niúl Uisce*

ALTERNATIVE NAMES FOR BUTTERCUP: (E) Butterflower, Crowfoot, Goldcup, King's Knobs. (I) *Cam an Ime, Cearbán, Cos Cromáin, Cos Préacháin, Crobh Préacháin, Fearbóg, Gairgín*

FOLK BELIEFS AND CUSTOMS
In Ireland buttercups, like primrose and marsh marigold, were sometimes picked on May Eve and brought home to decorate the house and farm buildings.[1] The flowers were made into bouquets and put on windowsills or doorsteps to provide protection against the fairies and other evil influences. In Ireland buttercup was also sometimes rubbed on cows' udders on May day to protect them.[2] In

addition, during the May Day festivities girls decked themselves with wreaths of daisies, marsh marigolds and buttercups.[3]

Traditionally, the scent of the flowers of meadow buttercup were thought to cause madness, probably on account of the acrid nature of its sap, which is a trait shared by all the buttercup family.[4] On account of this a common name for them in England was 'crazies', and it was widely believed to be bad luck to pick the flowers. Paradoxically it was also believed in ancient times that buttercups could cure lunacy when worn in a bag around the neck.[5] More benignly, another common belief was that a pasture full of buttercups eaten by cattle would give a golden colour to the milk and butter produced by their milk, but there is no basis for this as buttercups are generally avoided by livestock.[6]

A favourite children's game was to use the flowers of buttercup to see 'who likes butter'.[7] A flower was held by one child under the chin of another to see if a yellow glow was visible. If a glow appeared on the chin – which it usually did when the sun was shining – then it was taken as proof that the child did indeed like butter. The name buttercup needs no explanation, but up until recent times 'crowfoot' was in fact the more widely used name for the various species of *Ranunculus*. The name derives from the shape of the leaves which were said to resemble a crow's foot. The Irish name *fearbán* comes from *fearb*, meaning a weal or welt, on account of the acrid nature of the plants' sap.[8] The lesser spearwort features in an Irish proverb to descibe anything bright and shiny: *mar ghlasair léana i bpoll portaigh* – 'like a lesser spearwort in a bog'.[9]

LEGENDS AND MYTHOLOGY

Buttercup appears in some Irish legends.[10] In one legend the goddess of the land, after her symbolic wedding to an Irish king, changes from an ugly hag into a beautiful, young maiden with buttercup yellow hair, wearing a mantle of matchless green. More prosaically, in the legend 'The Cattle Raid of Cooley' or *Táin Bó Cúalnge*, the warrior Cuchulainn is described as scattering his enemies like 'buttercups in a meadow'. In Classical mythology buttercup was dedicated to Hymen, the god of marriage and attendant of Venus.[11]

PRACTICAL AND HERBAL USES

All the species of buttercup are known for the biting and acrid qualities of their sap, which can produce blistering. For this reason they were valued in folk medicine (especially lesser spearwort) for their ability to raise blisters and act as a counter irritant for all rheumatic afflictions.[12] The counter irritant qualities of buttercups were also put to use in Ireland to relieve headaches. The leaves were rubbed on the temples and forehead, even at the price of blistering the skin. The blistering powers of lesser spearwort were also put to other uses quite opposed to healing. A favourite trick of beggers and tramps was to beat their hands with lesser spearwort to produce swellings, in order to invoke greater pity in those they begged from.[13] Buttercups were also put to a variety of other herbal uses in different parts of Ireland, like curing warts in County Louth, heartburn in Counties Clare and Limerick, and kidney trouble in County Meath.[14] In Ireland buttercup was also widely used to cure jaundice, probably on account of its yellow flowers.[15] Buttercups give their name to the buttercup family, the *Ranunculaceae*.

SIMILAR PLANTS

Wood Anemone – *Lus na Gaoithe* – *Anemone nemorosa*[16]

ALTERNATIVE NAMES: (E) Nedcullion (Antrim, Donegal), Star-of-Bethlehem, Windflower. (I) *Nead Cailleach, Nead Coille*

The name 'anemone' comes from the Greek word for the god of the wind (hence the other common name 'windflower'), and in Greek legend he sent his namesakes on the earliest spring days as a token of his coming. In Counties Clare and Galway the leaves of wood anemone were laid on the head to alleviate a headache. Wood anemone is a member of the buttercup family, the *Ranunculaceae*.

Dock – Copóg

Rumex

♃   Ruled by the planet Jupiter in traditional herbal medicine

SPECIES NAMES:
Broad-leaved Dock – *Copóg Shráide* – *Rumex obtusifolius*
ALTERNATIVE NAMES: (E) Butter Dock (Dublin), Common Dock, Sharp-pointed Dock. (I) *Bileog Sráide, Copóg Coiteann, Copóg Rua*

Water Dock – *Copóg Uisce* – *Rumex hydrolapathum*
ALTERNATIVE NAMES: (I) *Bior-chopóg*

Curled Dock – *Copóg Chatach* – *Rumex crispus*
ALTERNATIVE NAMES: (E) Yellow Dock

Clustered Dock – *Copóg Thriopallach* – *Rumex conglomeratus*
ALTERNATIVE NAMES: (I) *Copóg Géar*

ALTERNATIVE NAMES FOR DOCK: (E) Docken, Dockroot, Dogroot, Phorams, Sour Dock (Donegal), Sturdy (US). (I) *Eireaball Madra Rua, Pór* (the seed) (Meath), *Puinneog*

FOLK BELIEFS AND CUSTOMS
Perhaps the most widely-known folk cure of all in these islands is the belief that rubbing dock leaves on a nettle sting can cure them.[1] Very often a rhyme had to be said while rubbing the leaf, and there were many different variations. For example, in Ireland a common rhyme was: 'Docken, docken in and out/Take the sting of the nettle out.' Two examples in Irish were: *Neantóg a dhóig mé agus copóg a leighis mé* – 'nettle burnt me and dock healed me'; *Te, te neantog, fuar, fuar copóg* – 'hot, hot nettle, cold, cold dock.' In England a common rhyme was: 'Nettle in, dock; Dock in; Nettle out; Dock rub nettle out'. This led to the phrase 'In dock, out nettle' to suggest inconstancy. A Cornish rhyme goes: 'Dock leaf, dock leaf, you go in; sting nettle, sting nettle, you come out.'

Despite its status as an unwanted weed, dock is associated with good soil.[2] A folktale tells of a blind man thinking of giving his daughter's hand in marriage. He is taken to the farm of the young man seeking to marry his daughter, and begins to walk the land with his helper and a few others. The people with the blind man are puzzled because he would stop every few paces, kneel down and search about him. They ask him what he is looking for, and he replies 'I'm looking for docks or thistles – any land that doesn't have them is not worth farming'. The young man's family then hurriedly bring him back inside before the match is refused! The dock also features in a stock phrase in Irish folktales to denote a moonlit night and its lengthening shadows: *An gearrán bán ag dul ar scáth na copóige agus an chopóg ag dul uaidh* – 'the white gelding (i.e., the moon) seeking the shade of the dock, and the dock receding from it'.[3] In Scotland dock was credited with great powers to break the fairy spell over a child.[4]

PRACTICAL AND HERBAL USES

Apart from curing nettle stings, dock has also been used for a variety of other folk cures.[5] It was used to staunch bleeding in parts of Britain and Ireland, and in Ireland drinking a decoction of the seeds was also believed to cure bronchitis, coughs and colds of all kinds. A decoction of the roots of dock was used to cure liver troubles in Counties Cavan and Meath, and jaundice in Counties Monaghan and Limerick. In County Wicklow dock root was also used to cure boils, skin complaints, liver complaints, rheumatism and diarrhoea. In County Wexford the juice of curled dock was squeezed out of the leaves and out on to a cloth which was then tied around a stone bruise. The powdered root of water dock was used by the Romans as a remedy for loose teeth, and an ancient belief held that a sachet of dock seed tied to the left arm of a woman would prevent her from being barren.[6] Dock leaves were also widely used to wrap up butter after it came from the churn; and the broad-leaved dock is still called 'butter dock' in Dublin on account of this.[7] Docks give their name to the dock family, the *Polygonaceae*.

SIMILAR PLANTS

Common Sorrel – *Samhadh Bó* – *Rumex acetosa*[8]

ALTERNATIVE NAMES: (E) Cow Sorrel, Cuckoo Sorrel, Meadow Sorrel, Poor Man's Herb, Red Sourleek, Soorag (US), Soorlick (Ulster), Sour Bellies (Dublin), Sour Sallys (Dublin), Sourleeks (Antrim), Sourlick (Ulster), Sourock, Sturdy (US), Sweetie Souries (Kerry). (I) *Puinneog, Ribleachán* (?), *Sabhadh, Sail na gCuach, Samhóg, Sealbhóg, Sealgán*

Sorrel has been an important food in Ireland since the earliest times. In early Ireland sorrel was regularly collected from the wild and eaten raw, or cooked in a soup or broth. In the legend of *Suibhne Geilt* or 'Mad Sweeney', the eponymous Sweeney was a County Antrim king who lost his wits and fled from society to live in the wilderness. Sorrel is mentioned as one of the wild plants he ate to survive. According to legend, St Kevin lived for seven years on nothing but nettles and sorrel. Sorrel appears in a few placenames like Carrowtavy (*Ceathrú an tSamhaidh* – quarter of the sorrel), County Sligo, and Lissatava (*Lios an tSamhaidh* – fort of the sorrel), County Mayo. Sorrel was used in Irish folk medicine for a variety of purposes. It was used to cleanse the system in Counties Wicklow and Cavan, and to heal sores and bruises in Counties Limerick and Sligo. It was also used in the southeast of the country in a poultice for boils, septic sores, and chickenpox. Common sorrel is a member of the dock family, the *Polygonaceae*.

Common Bistort – *Stóinse* – *Polygonum bistorta*[9]

ALTERNATIVE NAMES: (E) Snakeroot, Snakeweed. (I) *Copóg Nimhe, Luibh an Nathar Nimhe, Lus na hImirche*

In Ireland bistort or 'snakeweed' was plucked when going on a journey, while saying a charm that described it as: *an chéad luibh a ghlac Mhuire 'na láimh* – 'the first herb the Virgin Mary took into her hand'. Bistort was used in the Scottish Highlands as a cure for urinary complaints. Common bistort is a member of the dock family, the *Polygonaceae*.

Water-pepper – *Biorphiobar* – *Polygonum hydropiper*[10]

ALTERNATIVE NAMES: (E) Lakeweed, Redshank (Ulster), Spotted

Arsesmart, Smartweed. (I) *Glúineach Mór, Glúineach The.*
The pungent, acrid leaves of water-pepper were used to repel fleas, and so were often put into clothing and linen. This gave rise to its other name of 'arsesmart' as the green leaves are irritating when touched against bare skin! It was also believed that if water-pepper was put under a horse's saddle the horse would cope longer with hunger or thirst. In traditional medicine it was used as a cure for sores, ulcers, swellings and toothaches. Water-pepper is a member of the dock family, the *Polygonaceae.*

Redshank – *Glúineach Dhearg* – *Polygonum persicaria*[11]
ALTERNATIVE NAMES: (E) Bloodweed (Donegal). (I) *Loirgneach Dhearg*
According to legend redshank received the spots on its leaves because it grew at the foot of the cross, and drops of Christ's blood fell upon them. Redshank was used in County Limerick to stop bleeding, and was probably used for the same purpose in County Donegal, as the local name there 'bloodweed' would indicate. Redshank is a member of the dock family, the *Polygonaceae.*

Fat Hen – *Blonagán Bán* – *Chenopodium album*[12]
ALTERNATIVE NAMES: (E) Lamb's Quarter, Milds (Ulster), Miles (Ulster), White Goosefoot. (I) *Cál Slapach, Ceathramha Caorach, Cos Ghé, Lus Coise Gé Bán, Praiseach Fiáin, Praiseach Mín.*
Fat hen, with its broad leaves and spikes of green flowers, resembles dock but is unrelated. Fat hen has been used as a green food in Europe since ancient times, and traces of it have been found at Bronze Age sites in Britain. In Ireland fat hen was used as a food since before the Normans, as Pre-Norman sites often contain traces of it. A decoction of its stems was drunk in County Dublin as a cure for rheumatism. Fat hen is a member of the goosefoot family, the *Chenopodiaceae.*

Good King Henry – *Praiseach Bhráthar* – *Chenopodium bonus-henricus*[13]
ALTERNATIVE NAMES: (E) All-good, English Mercury, Wild Spinach
Good King Henry, with its broad leaves and spikes of green flowers, resembles dock but is unrelated. Good King Henry was traditionally eaten as a pot herb thoughout Europe. Its Irish name *praiseach bhráthar* or 'monk's spinach', indicates it was brought to Ireland to be used as a food in monasteries. Good King Henry is a member of the goosefoot family, the *Chenopodiaceae.*

Charlock – Praiseach Bhuí

Sinapis Arvensis

☾ Ruled by the moon in traditional herbal medicine

SPECIES NAME: As above
ALTERNATIVE NAMES: (E) Corn Kale (Dublin, Limerick), Field Mustard, Gill (US), Prassha Bwee, Preshagh (Fin), Prushia, Skillocks (Donegal), Skillogs (Donegal), Sprashach (US), Wild Kale, Wild Mustard, Yella-weed (US). (I) *Braiste, Corrán Buí, Garbhán Bodaigh, Garbhóg, Lus na Súl mBuí, Nóinín Buí, Praiseach Gharbh, Súil Buí*

FOLK BELIEFS AND CUSTOMS

Charlock, or *prassha bwee,* as it is still more widely known in Ireland, was generally considered a useless plant and a serious pest to the farmer, and it was a source of shame to have it growing on one's land.[1] One of the points held against it was the difficulty in eradicating it from land because of the great tenacity of its seeds. An Irish children's rhyme about charlock reflects this common view of it as a rough weed: 'Spell *prassha bwee* : P-h-am, p-h-a-m, r-o-u-g-h-am, w double-e wee – *prassha bwee*!

However, charlock was not always held in such low esteem. The Irish herbalist K'eogh, writing in the seventeenth century, stated that it was 'boiled and eaten by the common people in spring'; while another Irish herbalist, Caleb Threkeld, writing in 1727, recorded that 'it is called about the streets of Dublin before the flowers blow, by the name corn-cail, and used for boiled sallet (salad)'.[2] More usually though, charlock was only eaten when other foods were scarce, particularly in times of famine.[3] In County Galway, for example, a mixture of charlock, nettles and a few grains of yellow meal were eaten by people when times were hard. In addition, one of the disadvantages of charlock was that eating too much of it gave a person a yellowish complexion. However, for all charlock's status as a famine food, many people in Ireland had reason to be greatful for it. A widely-held view was that three plants above all kept many people alive during the Great Famine when no other food was available. The plants were charlock, nettle and the seaweed, carrigeen. In Scotland, in the Orkney Islands, during the three months of the year

when grain supplies had run out, bread called 'reuthie' bread was made from the seed of charlock – 'reuth' being a local name for the seeds.

The Irish name *praiseach* comes from the Latin *brassica* or cabbage, and charlock was so widely used that the name came to mean any kind of vegetable pottage.[4] From this it developed the secondary meaning of a mess or shambles, and to this day to make a mess of something in Irish is to make a *praiseach* of it! Charlock appears in the placenames Cloonprask (*Cluain Praisce* – meadow of the charlock), County Galway and Trafrask (*Trá Phraisce* – Strand of the charlock), County Cork.[5]

PRACTICAL AND HERBAL USES

In Ireland charlock was used to cure jaundice, probably on account of its yellow flowers. The flowers were boiled and strained and the resulting water drunk.[6] In County Limerick, its juice was drunk as a spring tonic to keep the system free of diseases for the rest of the year.[7] Charlock is a member of the cabbage family, the *Brassicaceae*.

SIMILAR PLANTS

Woad – *Glaisín- Isatis tinctoria*[8]
ALTERNATIVE NAMES: (I) *Glaisean*

Woad now appears to be extinct in Ireland, but it was once an important plant to the Irish on account of the bright blue dye that it yields. References to woad occur several times in early Irish texts. For example, an eighth-century text mentions that the queen of Tara had her own woad garden. Another example occurs in a story about the famous Irish king Cormac Mac Art, which relates the first wise judgement he gave. The case involved the compensation that was due to a queen because a sheep had eaten up her woad garden. Cormac ruled that, instead of the sheep being given up as forfeit for the lost woad, the more just compensation was that the shearing of the sheep should be given. This was because, like the wool, the lost woad would grow back. Woad also appears in the life of St Kieran. In the story, Ciarán's mother is making dye from woad and asks him to leave the house, as it is considered unlucky to have men in the same house as cloth being dyed. Ciarán does so, but as he is leaving he turns the dye dark grey. At his mother's protests he again changes the colour of the dye, this time to a white 'whiter than bone'. The third time he relents and turns the woad dye into the 'best blue colour ever seen'. Woad was not only used to dye clothes in ancient times. In a famous reference, Caesar in his *De Bello Gallico* reported that British warriors painted themselves with woad, and the Roman naturalist Pliny stated that the wives and daughters-in-law of Britons stained their bodies blue with woad. Similarly, an eighth-century poem about the Irish poet Ameirgin mentions his blue-tattoed shank. The use of woad as a dye in Europe was only superceded in recent centuries by the advent of the indigo plant. Woad is a member of the cabbage family, the *Brassicaceae*.

Shepherd's Purse – *Lus an Spáráin* – *Capsella bursa-pastoris*[9]
ALTERNATIVE NAMES: (E) Caseweed, Clappedepouch, Lady's-purse, Pick-purse. (I) *Luibh na nAosán, Lus Coiscthe na Fola, Lus na Fola, Sráidín*
Shepherd's purse gets its name from the resemblance of the seed cases to a purse, pouch or bag. As it is a common weed of little value the pouch was held to belong to a poor person – like a shepherd. The name 'clappedepouch' is of Irish origin, and refers to the begging of lepers, who stood at crossroads with a bell or clappers looking for alms, which they received in a cup attached to the end of a pole. The seed cases are also heart-shaped, and a common children's game throughout Europe was for one child to make another pick a seed case, and when it broke open, to tell him 'now you have broken your mother's heart'. In herbal medicine shepherd's purse was valued for stopping bleeding and excessive menstrual discharge – hence the Irish names *lus coiscthe na fola* and *lus na fola*. In Irish folk medicine shepherd's purse was drunk as a tea in County Limerick, or chewed for kidney troubles. Shepherd's purse is a member of the cabbage family, the *Brassicaceae*.

Violet – Sailchuach

Viola

♀ Violet ruled by the planet Venus in traditional herbal medicine

♎ Violet associated with the zodiac sign Libra

♄ Pansy ruled by the planet Saturn in traditional herbal medicine

♒ Pansy associated with the zodiac sign Aquarius

SPECIES NAMES:
Common Dog-Violet – *Fanaigse* – *Viola riviniana*
ALTERNATIVE NAMES: (E) Purple Violet. (I) *Bíodh-a-leithéid, Cogal Gorm, Plúirín, Sailchuach Chon*

Wild Pansy – *Goirmín Searraigh* – *Viola tricolor*

Field Pansy – *Lus Croí* – *Viola arvensis*
ALTERNATIVE NAMES FOR V. ARVENSIS AND TRICOLOR: (E) Heart's-ease, Herb Constancy, Herb Trinity, Love-in-idleness, Shasaigh-na-criodh (Donegal), Three-faces-under-a-hood

Sweet Violet – *Sailchuach Chumhra* – *Viola odorata*

ALTERNATIVE NAMES FOR VIOLET: (I) *Salchuach, Sálchuach*

FOLK BELIEFS AND CUSTOMS
The dark purple colour of violets linked them to sadness and death in popular belief.[1] It was believed in England that violets flowering in the autumn were an omen of death for the people on whose land they are growing. It was also thought to be bad luck to see a dog-violet flower in the autumn as it was an indication of plague or sickness, and to bring a single dog-violet into the house would bring bad luck to the family. In England it was also thought to be bad luck to bring anything less than a full handful of flowers indoors, as bringing only one or two would cause any young chicks or ducks to

die. This idea may be similar in origin to the idea held about primrose that the number of flowers brought into a house was an omen of how many eggs would hatch. On the other hand it was believed that to give violets showed goodwill on the part of the giver; while to dream of violets meant riches would soon come your way.[2]

Despite their dark colour, the beautiful scent of sweet violets meant they could not be seen in a wholly negative light, and indeed they have been associated with love since ancient times. Violets

were also a symbol of modesty, both on account of their sombre
colour and their drooping flower heads – hence the expression, a
'shrinking violet'. One explanation for this characteristic is that violets hung their heads shyly when the baby Jesus passed them, and
have done so ever since.[3] The Irish name for violet *sailchuach* is
believed to derive from the resemblance of the spur on the flower to
an old Irish drinking horn.[4] Alternatively it may mean 'cuckoo's
heel' instead because of a supposed resemblance, and several
British names like 'cuckoo's shoe' and 'cuckoo's stocking' reflect
this. The name 'dog-violet' is believed to have arisen because this
species of violet has no scent, so it was given the disparaging name
to distinguish it from its more favoured cousin.[5]

The wild pansy was a symbol of remembrance in European folklore, and the English name 'pansy' comes from the French *pensée* or
'thought'.[6] It symbolised faithfulness, and its corolla (the whorl of
leaves forming the inner envelope of the flowers) was a symbol of
the Holy Trinity.[7] It was also dedicated to the Holy Trinity because
of its three colours – purple, yellow and white. This symbolism
explains the name 'herb Trinity', and pansy was also called 'herb
constancy' because it symbolised fidelity. It was also a symbol of
love, hence its alternative name of 'heart's-ease', and it was dedicated to St Valentine.[8] In fact, the wild pansy was valued in ancient
times for its potency in love charms.[9] In Shakespeare's *A Midsummer
Night's Dream*, Oberon squeezes the juice of pansy or 'love-in-idleness' into Titania's eye so that she would fall in love with the ass-
headed Bottom when she awoke. In England it was believed that
pansies should not be picked when the weather is good, as it would
cause rain before long.[10]

LEGENDS AND MYTHOLOGY

Violet appears as a symbol of beauty in the Irish legend 'The
Wasting Sickness of Cúchulainn', when the warrior Labraid is
described as having a cheek 'like the beautiful colour of violet'.[11] To
the ancient Greeks and Gauls violets were the symbol of virginity,
and the flowers were used to embellish the nuptial bed.[12] Violets
were said to have sprung from tears shed by Adam after his ban-
ishment from the Garden of Eden. Alternatively they were said to
have sprung from the blood of the Egyptian god Attis. However, in
Greek myth sweet violets were a symbol of Aphrodite, the goddess
of love, and of the city of Athens.[13] The name 'violet' comes from

the Latin *Viola*, which is a Latin form of the Greek *Ione*. According to legend, Jupiter turned his beloved maiden Io into a heifer for fear of Juno's jealousy, and caused these flowers to spring up from the earth to be food for her, and to bear her name.[14]

PRACTICAL AND HERBAL USES

In traditional medicine since ancient times the strongly-scented sweet violet was made into 'violet balls' and used to revive those who had fainted, despite the fact that the same scent is known to induce faintness or giddiness in some people.[15] Naturally, sweet violet has also been used as an ingredient in perfumes for many centuries.[16] The ancient Britons used violets as a cosmetic, and they were steeped in goat's milk to increase female beauty.[17] In more recent times, in British folk medicine violets were widely used to cure cancerous tumours, both externally in a poultice and internally by drinking an infusion.[18] In Ireland violets were used for this purpose only in Counties Westmeath and Tipperary. Elsewhere, in Ireland, violets were used as a poultice to cure boils in County Westmeath and as a decoction to cure a 'pain in the head' in County Limerick. Perhaps on account of their sombre colour, people would traditionally wear violets around their necks to avoid drunkenness.[19] In Ireland the name 'heart's-ease' generally applied to self-heal (*Prunella vulgaris*), instead of pansies, which does not seem to have featured in Irish folk medicine. Violets give their name to the violet family, the *Violaceae*.

SIMILAR PLANTS

Butterwort – *Bodán Meascáin* – *Pinguicula vulgaris* [20]
Large-Flowered Butterwort – *Leith Uisce* – *Pinguicula grandiflora*
ALTERNATIVE NAMES: *Liath Uisce* (Clare Is)

ALTERNATIVE NAMES FOR BUTTERWORT: (E) Bog Violet, Mountain Sanicle, St Patrick's Spit (Ulster), St Patrick's Staff (Ulster), Steepgrass (Ulster), Steepweed (Ulster), Steepwort (Ulster). (I) *Im-go-huileanna, Meascán, Sadhbhóg Sléibhe, Uachtar-go-tóin, Úthacha* (Kerry)

In Ireland butterwort or bog violet is known in Ulster as 'St Patrick's Staff' from the resemblance of the shape of the flower to a staff, and it was said that one of the flowers sprang up wherever St Patrick's own staff touched the ground on his travels over the bogs. In the Scottish Highlands butterwort or *mothan* was considered a powerful herb. It had the power to ward off evil, particularly witches or fairies who might steal the good from the milk of the dairy. So effective was it that the milk of a cow who had earlier eaten butterwort was even thought to be protected against fairy spells. Indeed, if a person ate the cheese from such a cow, they too would be secure from any fairy agency. Butterwort was also a powerful love charm in Scotland. A woman wanting to win a man would pluck it and weave it into a *cuach* or hoop. She would then put the hoop into her mouth, and if she could get the man to kiss her, he would be hers forever. On the other hand, butterwort was traditionally disliked by sheep farmers as it was supposed (wrongly) to give them the liver disease sheep-rot if they ate it. Butterworts are members of the bladderwort family, the *Lentibulariaceae*.

Water-Lily – Bacán

Nymphaeaceae

☽   Ruled by the Moon in traditional herbal medicine

♋   Associated with the zodiac sign Cancer

SPECIES NAME:
White Water-Lily – *Bacán Bán* – *Nymphaea alba*
ALTERNATIVE NAMES: (E) Lough Lily (Donegal). (I) *Buail Bán, Buail-lile, Duilleog Bháite, Bobailín* (the bud), *Bun-ribe* (the root)

Yellow Water-Lily – *Cabhán Abhann* – *Nuphar lutea*
ALTERNATIVE NAMES: (I) *Liach Lobhar, Liach Loghar*

FOLK BELIEFS AND CUSTOMS
To European poets the white water-lily was a symbol of purity of heart.[1] In Scotland it was thought that water-lily could facilitate the fairy spell and cause a child to become 'fairy-struck' or *buailte*.[2] The yellow water-lily was said to destroy or remove the sexual drive if taken.[3] It seems for this reason to have been adopted as a symbol of celibacy as it appears in carvings on the roof bosses of Bristol Cathedral and Westminster Abbey, and in the Angel Choir at Lincoln. Another name for yellow water-lily in England is 'brandy bottle' because the flowers are said to smell of the stale dregs of brandy.[4]

LEGENDS AND MYTHOLOGY
A surviving carving dedicated to the British Celtic water goddess Coventina depicts her as holding a water-lily in one hand with a pitcher of water beside her. Coventina was worshipped throughout Britain, Gaul and parts of Spain.[5]

PRACTICAL AND HERBAL USES
In traditional medicine the root of yellow water-lily was used to calm fits or feelings of lust and passion.[6] In Ireland the roots of water-lily were used in County Cavan to staunch bleeding and to

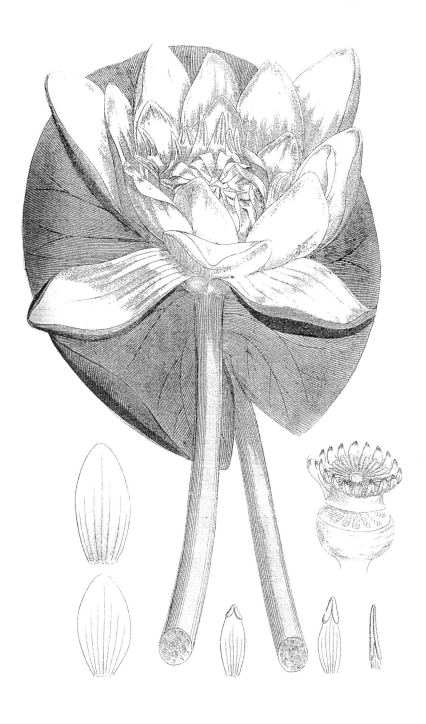

draw out a boil.[7] In Scotland the roots of white water-lily were boiled to produce a black dye for dyeing wool and yarn.[8] In England the roots of yellow water-lily were rubbed with milk to produce an effective deterrent to cockroaches and crickets.[9] Water-lilies give their name to the water-lily family, the *Nymphaeaceae*.

SIMILAR PLANTS

Bogbean – *Báchrán* – *Menyanthes trifoliata*[10]
ALTERNATIVE NAMES: (E) Boagbean (US), Bognut, Buckbean, Marsh Trefoil. (I) *Bearnán Lachán, Pónaire Chapaill, Pónaire Chorraigh, Pónra, Pór an Chapaill, Práta Portaigh*
Bogbean resembles a water-lily with its large, but delicate white blossoms tinged with pink, but it is in fact unrelated. In Welsh myth, the beautiful maiden Olwen was said to have palms and fingers 'whiter than shoots of marsh trefoil against the sand of a welling spring'. Its intense bitterness has led to it being used as a substitute for hops in brewing beer, and bogbean may have been used for that purpose in ancient Ireland. In Ireland and Britain the roots of bogbean were collected and boiled for a tonic to cleanse the system, assist digestion and cure boils and other skin troubles. In Ireland bogbean has also been used as a remedy for rheumatism, heavy coughs and colds. Bogbean gives its name to the bogbean family, the *Menyanthaceae*.

Bog Pondweed – *Liach Mhóna* – *Potamogeton polygonifolius*[11]
ALTERNATIVE NAMES: (E) Blackweed (Donegal), Dulaman (Donegal), Liagh-roda (Donegal), Slanlis, Lady Wrack (Donegal). (I) *Duilleog Féithe*
In British folk medicine the leaves of bog pondweed were boiled in cream to make an ointment for healing burns and scalds. Bog pondweed is a member of the pondweed family, the *Potamogetonaceae*.

Canadian Waterweed – *Tím Uisce* – *Elodea canadensis*[12]
ALTERNATIVE NAMES: (E) American Weed (Donegal), Cat's-tails, Glorus (Donegal), Raave, Swanweed (Donegal), Water Thyme.
As its name suggests, Canadian waterweed is an invader from the New World, being first recorded in Ireland in 1836. For a while it was invading waterways throughout Britain and Ireland, but it later diminished in growth as it found its niche. Canadian waterweed is

a member of the frogbit family, the *Hydrocharitaceae*.

Common Duckweed – *Ros Lachan* – *Lemna minor*[13]
ALTERNATIVE NAMES: (E) Duck's Meat. (I) *Grán Lachan, Grán Tonnóige, Lus-gan-athair-gan-mháthair, Mac-gan-athair-gan-mháthair, Ros Uisce*
The eighth century Irish text 'Cormac's Glossary' give the origin of the Irish name for duckweed *ros* as *ro-fhos* or 'great rest', as it is always on top of stagnant water. In Ireland duckweed was used in County Leitrim to cure swelling, and in County Cavan as a tonic to cleanse the system. Common duckweed gives its name to the duck-weed family, the *Lemnaceae*.

Mint – Mismín

Mentha

♀   Ruled by the planet Venus in traditional herbal medicine

♎   Associated with the zodiac sign Libra

SPECIES NAME: As above
Water Mint – *Mismín Mionsach* – *Mentha aquatica*
ALTERNATIVE NAMES: (E) Bog Mint, Water-ebony. (I) *Cartláid, Mismín Dearg, Samhadh Feárna*

Corn Mint – *Mismín Arbhair* – *Mentha arvensis*
ALTERNATIVE NAMES: (E) Apple Mint, Smearmint, Spearmint

ALTERNATIVE NAMES FOR MINT: (I) *Cartlainn, Cobhlán, Meantas, Miontas* (*Fiáin*)

FOLK BELIEFS AND CUSTOMS
An Irish love charm involved a man holding a sprig of mint in his hand until it grew warm and moist. The man then took hold of the hand of the woman he loved, making sure that their two hands were closed over the herb. Silence then had to be maintained for ten minutes between the two parties to give the charm time to work. Once this was done she would be sure to follow him for ever.[1] In Ireland mint was supposed to protect against the 'evil eye' and a sprig of mint tied around the waist was supposed to keep away diseases of the stomach.[2] It was also believed in Ireland that a sprig of mint tied around the wrist kept away infection and disease.

LEGENDS AND MYTHOLOGY
In Greek mythology, Menthe, or mint, was a pretty nymph who was turned into a humble creeping plant by Persephone when she noticed Pluto's interest in her. Pluto consoled the nymph by ensuring that she would give out a delicious smell however hard she was trodden down.[3] The Greeks and Roman also liked to crown themselves with peppermint at their feasts.[4] Water mint, meadowsweet and vervain were said to be the three herbs held most sacred by the druids.[5]

PRACTICAL AND HERBAL USES

In medieval England mint was traditionally strewn in bed chambers for its refreshing fragrance, and in 'places of recreation, pleasure and repose, and where feasts and banquets are made'.[6] In Ireland mint was used to banish fleas and keep moths out of clothing, while in England it was frequently placed in rooms to keep away flies.[7] In Ireland sprigs of corn mint were also placed in corn stacks to keep away mice.[8] In Britain and Ireland water mint has mainly been used in folk medicine to counter coughs and colds, and as a cure for indigestion and stomach ache.[9] Usually this took the form of drinking the juice or making a tea from the dried leaves. The juice from nine sprigs of mint strained through a cloth was used in Ireland to cure deafness. A thimbleful of the juice was put into each ear.[10] Mint has also been used in Ireland to cure jaundice in County Limerick, measles in County Cavan, and nettle stings in County Dublin.[11] Mints are members of the dead-nettle family, the *Lamiaceae* (or *Labiatae*).

SIMILAR PLANTS
Wild Thyme – *Tím Chreige* – *Thymus praecox*[12]
ALTERNATIVE NAMES: (E) Mother-of -thyme

Basil Thyme – *Lus Mhic Rí* – *Acinos arvensis*
ALTERNATIVE NAMES: (I) *Lus Mhic Rí Breatain, Lus Mhic Rí na mBrat.*
The pleasant scent of thyme has made it a symbol of love in folklore. In England girls would wear thyme, mint and lavender to attract suitors. In Scotland, the scent of thyme had the reputation of giving strength and courage, and Scottish Highlanders drank an infusion of it to prevent disagreeable dreams. Similarly, in ancient Rome, soldiers would bathe in thyme-scented water to increase their valour. The scent of thyme was also traditionally believed to enliven the spirits, and the Romans gave it to people who suffered from melancholy. For all its positive associations, thyme was held to be very unlucky by gypsies in Britain, and was never brought by them into their waggons or tents. Despite its later link to love in folklore, thyme was associated with sacrifice in ancient Greece and was planted by them on graves, and this custom was also carried on in Wales. In British and Irish folk medicine an infusion of thyme was drunk, both as a sedative and for coughs and respiratory ailments. Thymes are members of the dead-nettle family, the *Lamiaceae.*

Marjoram – *Máirtín Fiáin* – *Origanum vulgare* [13]
In traditional herbal medicine marjoram was highly valued for making a tea that was drunk to counter indigestion, ear ache, coughs, dropsy and bladder problems. In Irish folk medicine marjoram tea was drunk in Ulster as a remedy for indigestion and acidity. Marjoram is a member of the dead-nettle family, the *Lamiaceae*.

Selfheal – *Duán Ceannchosach* – *Prunella vulgaris*[14]
ALTERNATIVE NAMES: (E) All-heal, Blue-curls, Cailleach's Tea, Heart's-ease, Keanadha-hassog (Donegal), Minerac (Offaly), Minyayruck (Offaly, Kildare), Touch-and-heal (Ulster), Wood Sage (Ulster). (I) *Ceannbhán Beag, Duáinín an tSeanchais, Duán Donn, Lus Croí, Sásadh-na-croí* (Donegal), *Tae an Chnoic, Tae Maide, Tae na gCailleach* (Mayo), *Tae na nGarraithe, Tae na nGarrantaí* (Mayo)
In traditional medicine selfheal was regarded as one of the best plants to heal wounds and was therefore called 'selfheal', as it was a means whereby a person could safely treat themselves. It was also used for heart complaints, and selfheal was widely known in Ireland as 'heart's ease' for this reason. In County Mayo a tea was traditionally made of selfheal, which was held to be good for a weak heart or heart palpitations. In Ireland selfheal was also considered a good cure against any sudden blow or 'stroke' that might befall a person, and for children that were sickly or wasting away, perhaps as a result of being 'fairy struck'. In addition, to cure fevers in children, the leaves were rubbed against the palms and soles three times, and a distillation of selfheal was given to children to rid them of worms. Selfheal was also widely supposed to cure fevers and tuberculosis in adults in Ireland. Selfheal is a member of the dead-nettle family, the *Lamiaceae*.

Wood Sage – *Iúr Sléibhe* – *Teucrium scorodonia*[15]
ALTERNATIVE NAMES: (E) Mountain Sage, Wild Sage. (I) *Ceannbhán Cinn Coille, Sáiste Chnoic, Sáiste Coille, Sáiste Fiáin, Sáiste Muice*
In traditional medicine wood sage was used as a remedy for wounds, broken veins, ulcers and scurvy. It was also used in brewing ales and beers before the use of hops became widespread. In Irish folk medicine wood sage was widely used for coughs, colds, indigestion and palpitations. It was also used in County Cork for rheumatism. Wood sage is a member of the dead-nettle family, the *Lamiaceae*.

Umbellifers – Umbalaigh

Umbelliferae

♄   Hemlock ruled by the planet Saturn in traditional herbal medicine

♑   Hemlock associated with the zodiac sign Capricorn

☿   Wild Carrot ruled by the planet Mercury in traditional herbal medicine

SPECIES NAMES:
Hemlock – *Moing Mhear* – *Conium maculatum*
ALTERNATIVE NAMES: (E) Conine, Dho (Fermanagh). (I) *Áthabha, Binn Mhear, Cornán Fáil, Forán* (Connaught), *Mil Bhear, Mil Mhear, Min Mhear, Moing Bhearra, Mongach Mhéar, Muin Mhear*

Wild Carrot – *Mealbhacán* – *Daucus carota*
ALTERNATIVE NAMES: (E) Bird's-nest. (I) *Bleamhacán, Bliúcán, Crallacóg, Cuirdín Fiáin, Milbheacán, Miodhlucán, Muadhonn, Mugomán*

Hogweed – *Feabhrán* – *Heracleum sphondylium*
ALTERNATIVE NAMES: (E) Cow Parsnip, Dryland Scout (Ulster), Odhran (Ulster), The Singer (Kerry). (I) *Faidhf na Madaí, Fiúran* (Dublin), *Fleabhrán, Fuarán, Gleorán, Odhrán, Pleascán*

Pignut – *Cúlarán* – *Conopodium majus*
ALTERNATIVE NAMES: (E) Arnut, Cuckoo Potato (Donegal), Earth Chestnut, Earthnut, Fairy Potatoes, Harenut, Harnothe (FB), Kippernut, St Anthony's Nut. (I) *Clórán, Cnó Arcáin, Cnó Milis, Cnó Talún, Cútharlán, Práta Cluracáin, Práta Clutharacháin, Práta Lurcáin, Práta Lutharacháin.*

Cow Parsley – *Peirsil Bhó* – *Anthriscus sylvestris*
ALTERNATIVE NAMES: (E) Da-ho (Ulster), Girns (US), Ha-ho, Hi-how, Keeshion (Ulster), Lady's-lace, Maggie-da-ho (US), Queen Anne's Lace. (I) *Pearsáil, Cos Uisce*

Hemlock Water-Dropwort – *Dathabha Bán* – *Oenanthe crocata*

ALTERNATIVE NAMES: (E) Water Hemlock, Wild Rue (Donegal). (I) *Áthabha Bán, Feallabhog, Táthabha Bán, Tréanlus*

Shepherd's Needle – *Gob an Ghoirt* – *Scandix pecten-veneris*
ALTERNATIVE NAMES: (E) Adam's-needle (Tipperary), Lady's-comb (Donegal), Venus Comb.

Ground Elder – *Lus an Easpaig* – *Aegopodium podograria*
ALTERNATIVE NAMES: (E) Ashweed, Bishop's Weed, Farmer's Plague
(Ulster), Garden Plague (Ulster), Goutweed, Herb-gerard. (I) *Gúta*,
Lus an Ghúta

Rock Samphire – *Craobhraic* – *Crithmum maritimum*
ALTERNATIVE NAMES: (E) Creevereegh (Donegal), Semper (Donegal). (I)
Cabáiste Faille, Cnámhlus, Craoracán, Geirgín na Trá, Griolóigín, Lus na gCnámh

FOLK BELIEFS AND CUSTOMS

Umbellifers are a well-known sight in our hedgerows in early summer, with their white caps of lacy flowers. For many people, however, some effort is needed to learn to recognise the different
species, as they can be hard to tell apart. In folklore by far the most
important umbellifer is hemlock (*Conium maculatum*), on account of
its strongly poisonous nature.[1] Hemlock can be identified from
other umbellifers by its smooth, purple blotched stems. In Ireland,
so feared was hemlock that it was believed to be dangerous to
show it to anyone or it might do them harm. Indeed so great was
the danger from it thought to be that if a plant was desired, a cord
was tied around it and attached to a dog. The dog was then set running in order to pull up the plant, so that any harm that came from
the act would fall only on the dog. However, in Ireland it was also
believed that hemlock could be used as a cure for evil, but only in
conjunction with other herbs. Despite its poisonous nature, hemlock was used in Ireland in a rather perilous love charm. Ten leaves
of hemlock, dried and powdered and mixed with their food or
drink would make the person you desired love you in return. In
England hemlock was associated with witchcraft and devil wor-
ship, and it was said that to take a mouthful of it would make a
man Satan's servant for life. According to an old English legend the
purple spots of hemlock represent the brand put on Cain's brow
after he committed murder. In the south of Scotland, hemlock was
said to be favoured by witches, while it was also believed that
Scottish fairies used to dip the heads of their arrows in the dew that
lay on the hemlock.

Also important in folklore is wild carrot (*Daucus carota*).[2] In Ireland the root of wild carrot was traditionally eaten and savoured for its sweet taste. In the Scottish Highlands wild carrot was relished as well, and the Sunday before the feast of St Michael (29 September) was called 'Carrot Sunday'. Local women collected them on that day, and the carrots were supposed to bring fruitfulness to the women who collected them. At the prayer service for the feast of St Michael, handfuls of the carrots were then given to other worshippers as a prized gift. The name 'bird's nest' for wild carrot comes from the fact that, after flowering, the stalks close into themselves in a hollow round form like a bird's nest. The name carrot is believed to be Celtic in origin and means 'red of colour'.

Another important umbellifer in folklore is hogweed (*Heracleum sphondylium*).[3] In Britain hogweed, as its name suggests, was traditionally gathered by country people to use as food for their pigs. In Ireland the hollow stems of hogweed were used by boys like a peashooter to fire rosehips at each other. In Scotland hogweed or 'cow-parsnip' was credited with great ability to break the power of the fairies over a child. Pignut (*Conopodium majus*) is noted for its tasty round tubers, beloved of pigs – hence the name.[4] In Ireland, however, it was also a favourite of schoolboys who used to roast its roots and eat them, calling them 'fairy potatoes'. An alternative name, 'Earth Chestnut', also reflects this habit. In Britain pignuts were similarly dug up by children and eaten. In Ireland pignut was regarded as a fairy plant, and especially for the leprechaun, the fairy shoemaker. Pignut is sometimes called 'St Anthony's Nut' after St Anthony the hermit of Egypt, who came to be looked upon as the patron saint of pigs and swineherds.

In England cow-parsley (*Anthriscus sylvestris*) has a bad reputation in folklore with local names given to it like 'devil's meat' and 'adder's meat'.[5] This reputation may have arisen through a confusion with hemlock. Indeed, umbellifers in general were regarded by many English as being inauspicious plants, probably for the same reason; and in many parts of Britain, all umbellifers are still simply classed under the name hemlock. A widespread English belief was that picking cow parsley and bringing it into the house would lead to the death of one's mother; though perhaps this was to discourage children from bringing the messy flowers indoors. On the other hand, in Ireland cow parsley was sometimes known as 'lady's-lace' and put on the May altars to honour the Virgin Mary.[6]

Shepherd's needle (*Scandix pecten-veneris*) got its name from its distinctive long erect fruits, which recall needles, or the teeth of a comb.[7] Ground elder (*Aegopodium podograria*) was initially introduced into these islands as a pot-herb, to be eaten like spinach, and also as a medicinal plant against gout.[8] The name 'bishop's weed' reflects its origins in ecclesiastical herb gardens. However, once introduced into a plot of land it is very difficult to get rid of, and has now become a pest to farmers in many places, earning it names like 'farmer's plague'.

LEGENDS AND MYTHOLOGY

Like its namesake, hemlock water dropwort (*Oenanthe crocata*) is extremely poisonous, and was feared because it was always possible that someone picking edible waterside plants, like brooklime or watercress, might pick some of it as well – with potentially disasterous results.[9] Reflecting this fear, an Old Irish phrase *athabha i fothlacht* or 'hemlock water dropwort amongst brooklime' meant something bad hidden behind an innocent seeming surface. The phrase appears in a story in the eighth century 'Cormac's Glossary', when the jester Lomna uses it to warn the hero Fionn Mac Cumhaill that his wife is unfaithful. 'Cormac's Glossary' also gives the origin of the Old Irish name *athabae* as deriving from *ath* 'intensive' and *bath* 'death'. The word *athabha* is often incorrectly translated as 'hellebore' or 'deadly nightshade', though sometimes it was apparently used to mean hemlock as well.

PRACTICAL AND HERBAL USES

Hemlock contains the powerful poison coniine, and is famous for being the plant used to poison Socrates in 399 BC after he was found guilty of 'corruption of the young' and 'neglect of the gods' on account of his ideas.[10] Despite its poison, it has been used in Irish folk medicine as a poultice to cure swellings and bad sores of all kinds, and in County Wicklow, hemlock was considered effective in curing rheumatism. In British folk medicine it was often used to cure cancerous tumours of the skin.[11] In Ireland wild carrot was used as a diuretic in Counties Dublin, Cork and Kerry, while the juice was used in a poultice for sores and wounds in County Antrim.[12] The seed of hogweed was burnt under a person's nose to revive them from lethargy or coma in Ireland, and a preparation of the root and the seeds was made into an oil and rubbed into a person's head to relieve them of giddiness, lethargy or restlessness.[13] In Ireland pignut was used in County Donegal to cleanse the blood, and hemlock water dropwort was used as a cure against cancerous tumours of the skin.[14] Shepherd's needle was used in County Tipperary as a cure for toothache.[15] In both Britain and Ireland rock samphire (*Crithmum maritimum*) was collected to be eaten as a salad plant, but collecting it from the steep cliff faces where it grew was a hazardous enterprise.[16] In County Donegal rock samphire was eaten in its raw state to relieve pain in the heart. Umbellifers belong to the carrot family, the *Apiaceae*.

SIMILAR PLANTS

Dwarf Elder – *Tromán* – *Sambucus ebulus*[17]
ALTERNATIVE NAMES: (E) Dane's Blood (Ulster), Danewort, She-elder (Louth), Wallwort. (I) *Lus na nDanar*
Dwarf elder resembles an umbellifer with its flat cap of white flowers, but it is in fact unrelated. A widespread folk belief in Britain and Ireland held that dwarf elder grew where the blood of the Danes (or Vikings) had been shed. However, the name may derive from the fact that it was used in medicine as a purging plant that produced the 'danes' or diarrhoea in Old English. Dwarf elder is a member of the honeysuckle family, the *Caprifoliaceae*.

Common Valerian – *Caorthainn Corraigh* – *Valeriana officinalis*[18]
ALTERNATIVE NAMES: (E) All-heal, Filaera (Ulster), St George's Herb, Valara (Donegal). (I) *Lus na dTrí mBallán, Lus na dTrí mBille*
Valerian's large flat head of pinkish flowers resembles that of an umbellifer, but it is unrelated to them. The roots of valerian have been used since ancient times to produce a tea that acts as a sedative, calms the nerves and prevents hysteria. Animals, and especially cats, seem to be especially attracted to the smell of the bruised leaves and roots of valerian, and in herb gardens will often come and roll around on top of the plants which have been disturbed. Common valerian gives its name to the valerian family, the *Valerianaceae*.

Forget-Me-Not – Ceotharnach

Myosotis

ᙢ   Associated with the zodiac sign Scorpio

SPECIES NAMES:
Water Forget-Me-Not – *Ceotharnach Uisce* – *Myosotis scorpioides*
Field Forget-Me-Not – *Lus Míonla Goirt* – *Myosotis arvensis*

ALTERNATIVE NAMES FOR FORGET-ME-NOT: (I) *Lusán na nÉan*

FOLK BELIEFS AND CUSTOMS
In Europe the striking blue colour and modesty of the flowers have made forget-me-not a symbol of constancy, faithfulness and friendship.[1] In European folklore it is also a symbol of love, and if a person wore some it meant that they were not forgotten by their lover.[2] The name forget-me-not comes from a German legend of a knight who picked a flower of it for his lady as the two of them walked along by the river. The knight fell in, but before he was carried away and drowned, he threw the flowers to his lady crying in (Middle High) German *vergiz min niht* or 'forget me not', which is still the German name for it. In France too, forget-me-not is similarly called *ne m'oubliez pas*. In England forget-me-not went under the older and less romantic name of 'Scorpion grass' because of the way the flowerheads curled over on themselves, until the poet Samuel Coleridge published a love poem in 1802, which included the lines:

> Nor can I find, amid my lonely walk
> By rivulet, or spring, or wet roadside
> That blue and bright-eyed flowerlet of the brook,
> Hope's gentle gem, the sweet forget-me-not!

Coleridge had been inspired by the German legend, and included a footnote explaining what flower was meant by the name, and so forget-me-not quickly caught on as the favourite name. In France forget-me-not is also called *aimez-moi* – 'love me' – and *Les yeux de l'enfant Jesus* – 'the eyes of the baby Jesus'.[3]

PRACTICAL AND HERBAL USES

Forget-me-not features very little in folk medicine, but on the continent it has traditionally been made into a syrup and given for pulmonary complaints. According to tradition a decoction of the juice of forget-me-not has the power to harden steel.[4] Forget-me-not is a member of the borage family, the *Boriginaceae*.

SIMILAR PLANTS

Germander Speedwell – *Anuallach* – *Veronica chamaedrys* [5]
ALTERNATIVE NAMES: (E) Billy Bright-eye, Bird's-eye, Blue-eye (Wicklow), Cat's-eye, Eyebright (Ulster), Fluellin, Jump-up-and-kiss-me (Munster), Speed-well-blue (Kerry). (I) *Lusán Balla, Lus na Banaltran*

Heath Speedwell – *Lus Cré* – *Veronica officinalis*
ALTERNATIVE NAMES: (E) Fluellin, Male Speedwell. (I) *Seamair Chré*
Like forget-me-not, speedwells sport bright, blue flowers, but they are in fact unrelated. In Ireland speedwell was traditionally sewn into the garments of travellers to protect them from accident; but in Munster germander speedwell was known as 'jump-up-and-kiss-me' and anyone wearing it would be greeted with shrieks of laughter. Another name for germander speedwell is 'bird's-eye', and in England children would tell each other that birds would peck out their eyes (or their mother's) if they picked the flower. Speedwell was believed in Ireland to be one of the herbs that nothing natural or supernatural could injure, and in an Irish folk cure, a mixture of yarrow, speedwell and other herbs were boiled together and the water given to cows with calf as a protection against ill luck and the fairies. The Latin name for speedwell, *Veronica*, links the plant to St Veronica, who by tradition wiped Christ's face with a cloth on the way to Calvary. In Ireland, germander speedwell was used by nursing mothers to soothe their sore breasts – hence the name *lus na banaltran* or 'nurses' herb'. It was also extensively used in Ireland as a cure for jaundice, by boiling the leaves and drinking the resulting infusion. Heath speedwell was used in County Donegal as a cure for colds. Speedwells are members of the figwort family, the *Scrophulariaceae*.

Brooklime – *Lochall* – *Veronica beccabunga*[6]
ALTERNATIVE NAMES: (E) Water Pimpernel, Wellink. (I) *Biolar Mhuire, Biolar Uisce, Fochlach(t), Folacht(ain), Foltacht, Fothlacht, Lochall Mothair, Ochall*

The leaves and flowering heads of brooklime have been eaten as a salad plant in northern Europe since the earliest times, and were especially recommended against scurvy. The use of brooklime as food appears several times in Irish legends. In the legend 'The Cattle Raid of Cooley' or *Táin Bó Cúailnge*, the warrior Cuchulainn welcomes his rival Fergus as a guest at one point and offers him a handful of watercress, seaweed and brooklime to eat. In the legend of *Suibhne Geilt* or 'Mad Sweeney', the eponymous Sweeney was a County Antrim king who lost his wits and fled from society to live in the wilderness. Brooklime is mentioned several times as one of the wild plants he ate to survive. In Irish folk medicine brooklime has been used to cure colds and coughs in Counties Wicklow, Limerick and Clare, and as a cure for kidney and urinary troubles in Ulster, and in Counties Wicklow and Clare. Brooklime is a member of the figwort family, the *Scrophulariaceae*.

Great Mullein – Coinnle Muire

Verbascum Thapsus

♄   Ruled by the planet Saturn in traditional herbal medicine

♒   Associated with the zodiac sign Aquarius

SPECIES NAME: As above
Alternative names: (E) Aaron's Rod, Flannelwort, Hag Taper
(Ulster), High Taper (Ulster), Lady's Foxglove, Lungwort (Cow's),
Mary's Candle, Poor Man's Blanket (Donegal), Virgin Mary's
Candle. (I) *Lus Mór*

FOLK BELIEFS AND CUSTOMS
Mullein is one of our most striking native plants, with its tall spires
of bright yellow flowers and silvery furred leaves.[1] In Ireland country people traditionally believed that carrying mullein about preserved the wearer from enchantments and witchcraft. It was also
believed in Ireland that placing some mullein leaves under a churn
would restore the goodness to butter that been stolen by enchantment. In Poitou in France on the Eve of the St John festival, people
passed sprigs of mullein and walnuts across the bonfire flames. The
nuts were supposed to cure toothache, and the mullein was supposed to protect the cattle from sickness and sorcery. In Britain it
was believed that a stalk of mullein gathered when the sun was in
Virgo and the moon in Aries would offer protection against sickness
if it was carried in the pocket. The soft leaves gave rise to such
names as 'flannelwort' and 'poor man's blanket'. The leaves make
excellent timber when dry and were used as wicks in former times.
The name 'hag's taper' derives from the belief that mullein was a
favourite plant for witches to use for wicks in their lamps and candles when casting spells.

LEGENDS AND MYTHOLOGY
In Greek legend the god Mercury gave the hero Ulysses mullein to
defend him from the enchantments of the sorceress Circe.[2]

PRACTICAL AND HERBAL USES

In Roman times mullein was used by women to wash their hair and keep it in good condition, and it was still used for that purpose in Germany until recent times.[3] The bright yellow flowers were rubbed into wet hair to encourage blondness when the hair dried. In Britain and Ireland the stalks of mullein were dipped in tallow and used as torches – hence names like 'Virgin Mary's candle'.[4] The furry leaves of mullein were also put into their shoes by shepherds and wanderers to keep their feet warm.[5] In Ireland mullein was used as a cure for consumption (or tuberculosis). The leaves were boiled in milk and then strained, and the resulting liquid was drunk warm, twice daily. It was widely grown in Irish gardens as a cure for all coughs, colds and bronchitis, and was formerly on sale in even the best chemist shops in Dublin.[6] An Irish cure for asthma and bronchitis was also to dry the leaves of mullein and smoke them like tobacco, making sure to inhale the smoke. The leaves were used to treat bee stings in County Meath and in Westmeath for goitre.[7] Great mullein is a member of the figwort family, the *Scrophulariaceae*.

SIMILAR PLANTS

Agrimony – *Marbhdhraighean* – *Agrimonia eupatoria*[8]
ALTERNATIVE NAMES: (E) Tea-plant (I) *Airgeadán, Géar-bhileach, Méirín na Magh, Tae Fiáin* (Galway)
With its large spike of yellow flowers, agrimony resembles mullein, but it is not related to it. Agrimony has been valued as a herb since ancient times. The Greeks recommended it against snakebites, poor sight, loss of memory and liver complaints. The Anglo-Saxons used it as part of an ointment against evil spirits and poison, and a later English belief held that a man would sleep as though dead if agrimony were put under his pillow, and would not awake until it was removed. In Britain a tea was extensively made from the leaves as a mild tonic and stimulant and to purify the system. In Ireland, the tea was also made in Counties Clare and Galway when real tea was scarce, with a flavour said to be similar to lemon or apricot. Agrimony was also used in County Derry to treat scurvy, jaundice and to heal old ulcers. The flowers of agrimony have also been used to make a yellow dye. Agrimony is a member of the rose family, the *Rosaceae*.

Weld – *Buí Mór* – *Reseda luteola* [9]
Alternative Names: (E) Dyer's Rocket, Yellow Weed
Weld resembles mullein with its large spike of yellow flowers, but it is unrelated. It was one of the ancient trio of dye plants: woad for blue, madder for red, and weld for yellow. In fact, evidence for the use of weld as a dye in Europe goes back as far as the Stone Age. In Ireland, weld was grown extensively in Portmarnock in north County Dubin in order to satisfy the need for yellow dye for Dublin city. Weld is a member of the mignonette family, the *Resedaceae*.

Orchid – Magairlín

Orchis

♀ Ruled by the planet Venus in traditional herbal medicine

♎ Associated with the zodiac sign Libra

SPECIES NAMES:

Early-Purple Orchid – *Magairlín Meidhreach* – *Orchis mascula*
ALTERNATIVE NAMES: (E) Mogolyeen Mire (Dublin), Mogra Myra,
Standergrass. (I) *Cailleach Fhuar, Úrach Bhallach*

Heath Spotted-Orchid – *Na Circíní* – *Dactylorhiza maculata*
ALTERNATIVE NAMES: (I) *Cailleach Bhréagach, Cearc Bhreac*

Common Spotted-Orchid – *Nuacht Bhallach* – *Dactylorhiza fuchsii*
ALTERNATIVE NAMES: (I) *Cailleach Bhréagach*

Early Marsh-Orchid – *Magairlín Mór* – *Dactylorhiza incarnata*
ALTERNATIVE NAMES: (E) Blue Rocket (Donegal), Brush (Donegal),
Cullions (Donegal), Sweet Willie (Donegal). (I) *Magairlín Mór an
Chorraigh*

Common Twayblade – *Dédhuilleog* – *Listera ovata*
ALTERNATIVE NAMES: (E) Wild Tulip (Donegal)

ALTERNATIVE NAMES FOR ORCHID: (E) Dog's-stones, Fool's-stones. (I)
Lus na Magairlí

FOLK BELIEFS AND CUSTOMS

In European folklore the orchid has been seen as a symbol of fertility and an aphrodisiac since the earliest times.[1] Its shape, of an erect
stem rising above two round tubers, resembles the male genitalia,
which was thought to indicate its powers according to the principles of sympathetic magic. As a result of this, the tuberous roots of
orchids, particularly the early purple orchid, were considered very
effective as a love charm in folk beliefs. In Ireland in Counties Cork
and Kerry, young girls would make a powder out of the roots and

give it to the young man of their fancy, so that he would marry them. One orchid tuber is larger than the other, the large one grow-ing stronger for the next year's growth, while the smaller tuber slowly withers as it is used up in the present year. In County Donegal, a girl would choose one of the two tubers to give to a man to eat. If it was the correct tuber (probably the larger one), he would immediately fall deeply in love with her. If it was the wrong one, however, he would go out of his mind. In County Wicklow, early purple orchid, known as *mogra myra*, was also meant to be an effi-cient love potion. Early purple orchid is mentioned in Brian Merriman's poem *The Midnight Court* as one of the love charms resorted to by the women of Ireland in desperation at the lack of romance in Irish men.

In Scotland it was believed that the larger tuber represented the man, and the smaller one the woman, whose affections were to be gained in the love charm. The plant was to be pulled by the roots before sunrise while facing south, and then immediately put into spring water. If the root sank in the water it showed that the person whose love was sought would indeed prove to be the future wife or husband. Alternatively, if the identity of the future wife or husband was not yet known, the roots could be reduced to powder and put under the seeker's pillow to cause dreams of the person to be married. In some parts of northern Scotland it was believed that getting someone of the opposite sex to eat the larger root would produce a strong affection for you in them. However, eating the smaller root would produce in them a strong aversion. For this reason, the early purple orchid was known in the highlands of Scotland as *Gràdh is Fuadh* – 'love and hate'. It was also said that the love gained in this way was quickly dissipated by marriage. In European folklore it was said that witches used the tubers in a similar way, the larger and fresher one being used to promote true love, and the smaller and more withered tuber to check 'wrong passions'.

A very different European legend about the early purple orchid states that the purple spots on its leaves are the marks of Christ's blood from his agony in the garden. Alternatively it was said that the orchid had been growing at the foot of the cross at Calvary, and received the splashes of blood from Our Lord on the cross.[2]

LEGENDS AND MYTHOLOGY
In Roman mythology orchids were said to be the food of the satyrs, and to have excited them to their lecherous excesses.[3] Orchis was said to be the son of a satyr and a nymph, who was killed by the Bacchanalians for his insult to a priestess of Bacchus. His father prayed for him and he was turned into the flower that bears his name as a result. The name orchid in fact derives from the Greek *orkhis* meaning testicle, which is the same meaning as the Irish name *magairlín*, and such English names as 'fool's-stones'.[4]

PRACTICAL AND HERBAL USES
It is difficult to separate any truly medicinal uses for orchids from their magical role.[5] In Classical medicine the herbalist Dioscorides

stated that putting the larger tuber in goat's milk excited desire, while putting in the smaller one restrained it. He also maintained that if men ate the larger tuber, they would produce male children, and if women ate the smaller one they would produce girls. The roots of orchid were also thought to aid conception and strengthen the genitals. Apart from its use in fertility, the roots of orchid were also thought to aid sufferers of tuberculosis, and to relieve diarrhoea.[6] The starchy tubers of orchids have long been considered nutritious and have been used in the Middle East since ancient times to make a refreshing drink called *salep*. *Salep* was widely sold in Britain before the advent of coffee, and is still produced today in countries like Turkey and the Lebanon.[7] It is possible to extract the starch in the same way from native orchids, and Oxfordshire was a centre for the production of a small amount of the *salep* sold in Britain. In the Scottish Highlands twayblade (*Listera ovata*) was used to make *salep* as a folk cure for soothing stomach and bowel irritation. Orchids give their name to the orchid family, the *Orchidaceae*.

SIMILAR PLANTS
Yellow-Rattle – *Gliográn* – *Rhinanthus minor*[8]
ALTERNATIVE NAMES: (E) Bull's-pease (Donegal), Cock's-comb, Pennygrass, Rattlebox, Rattlegrass. (I) *Bodach Gliogair, Bodán na gCloigíní*
Although it resembles a kind of yellow orchid, yellow-rattle is in fact not related. The name rattle refers to the rattling sound the dry seeds make in their pods when shaken by the wind. The name 'cock's-comb' derives from the deeply dented leaves, which were said to resemble the comb of a cockerel. Yellow-rattle is a member of the figwort family, the *Scrophulariaceae*.

Marsh Lousewort – *Milseán Móna* – *Pedicularis palustris*[9]
ALTERNATIVE NAMES: (E) Bog Honeysuckle, Honeycap (Donegal), Red Rattle. (I) *Maothlán Móna, Riabhach, Rianaitín*
Marsh lousewort looks like a kind of orchid, but it is in fact unrelated. Lousewort gets its name from the European idea that cattle that grazed in pastures where it grew became troubled by lice. It was also supposed to give the cattle liver-rot. The name 'red rattle' refers to the rattling sound the dry seeds make in their pods when shaken by the wind. The flowers of marsh lousewort were used in the Scottish Highlands to make a cosmetic. Marsh lousewort is a member of the figwort family, the *Scrophulariaceae*.

Wood Avens – Machall Coille

Geum Urbanum

♃   Ruled by the planet Jupiter in traditional herbal medicine

♓   Associated with the zodiac sign Pisces

SPECIES NAME: As above
ALTERNATIVE NAMES: (E) Colewort, Evans (Cavan), Herb Bennet, Mountain Geum. (I) *Abhcán, Beinidín, Loc Sláinte* (Galway), *Machall Fiáin, Machall Sléibhe*

FOLK BELIEFS AND CUSTOMS
Wood avens, or herb bennet, was considered a powerful herb in European folklore on account of the sweet, spicy smell of its roots, which resembles cloves.[1] It was believed to protect against devils and demons, evil spirits and wild animals. Wood avens was often worn as an amulet, and in fifteenth-century Europe it was hung over doors to ward off evil spirits. A fifteenth-century herbal states that 'where the root is in the house, Satan can do nothing and flies from it, wherefore it is blessed before all other herbs'. The three-lobed leaves were said to represent the Blessed Trinity, and the five petals of the flower represented the five wounds of Christ. The name 'herb bennet' is in fact a corruption of the Latin *Herba benedicta* or 'Blessed Herb'. Wood avens' reputation as a blessed herb led thirteenth-century European architects to use its flower in ornamental carvings on buildings.

LEGENDS AND MYTHOLOGY
Wood avens was also considered an antidote to poisons, and so was linked to the legend of St Benedict, who was saved from death by blessing a poisoned cup. According to the legend, on one occasion a monk presented him with a goblet of poisoned wine. However, as soon as the saint made the sign of the cross over the cup, the poison flew out of it with such force that the glass shattered, thus exposing the monk's attempted crime.[2]

PRACTICAL AND HERBAL USES

The roots of wood avens have a delicate clove-like aroma, and were used as a fly repellent and for flavouring ale.[3] The dried roots were also put amongst stored clothing to protect them from moths.[4] In traditional herbalism wood avens was used as a preservative against plague and poisons, and for complaints like diarrhoea, stomach aches and sore throats. [5] However, it appears to have been used very little in the folk medicine of either Britain or Ireland. Wood avens is a member of the rose family, the *Rosaceae*.

SIMILAR PLANTS

Creeping Cinquefoil – *Cúig Mhéar Mhuire* – *Potentilla reptans*[6]

ALTERNATIVE NAMES: (E) Five Fingers, Five Leaf Grass. (I) *Cúig(id)each, Cúig-bhileach, Cúig-mhéar(ach)*

Throughout Europe, cinquefoil was considered a magical plant because its leaves with five leaflets resemble the five fingers of a hand. In parts of Europe cinquefoil and hawthorn were hung over the door on May Day to keep away witches. However, witches were also supposed to use cinquefoil in their spells, particularly for love potions. In Ireland cinquefoil has been used as a cure for ague in County Cavan. Creeping Cinquefoil is a member of the rose family, the *Rosaceae*.

Tormentil – *Néalfartach* – *Potentilla erecta*[7]

ALTERNATIVE NAMES: (E) Sheep's Knapperty (Ulster), Septfoyl, Tormenting Root (Ulster). (I) *Léanartach, Lus an Chodlata* (Cork), *Neamhain, Neamhnaid, Néanfhartach, Niamhnaid*

In Ireland badgers were said to especially relish the roots of tormentil, while ducks were said to relish its seeds. In traditional medicine the roots of tormentil were boiled in milk and the milk then given to calves and children to cure them of colic. The name 'tormentil' reflects this, as it comes from the Latin *tormentum* which meant both torment and the pains of colic. In Irish folk medicine a mixture of tormentil, wine and milk was recommended for heart complaints, and the roots of tormentil were used to cure diarrhoea and colic. In Ireland tormentil was also traditionally mixed with St John's wort to produce a sleeping draught – the word *néal* is another word for sleep. The roots of tormentil contain a lot of tannin and so were extensively used in Ireland for tanning, especially during the eighteenth century when tree bark had become scarce. The roots

Mallow – Hocas

Malva sylvestris

Ragwort – Buachalán Buí

Senecio jacobaea

Heather (Ling) – Fraoch
Calluna vulgaris

Bilberry (Fraughan) – Fraochán
Vaccinium myrtillus

Dog Rose – Feirdhris
Rosa canina

Bramble – Dris
Rubus fruticosus

Bracken – Raithneach Mhór
Pteridium aquilinum

Ivy – Eidheann
Hedera helix

of tormentil were also used for producing a red dye, while the flowers were used to produce a yellow dye. Tormentil is a member of the rose family, the *Rosaceae*.

Silverweed – *Briosclán* – *Potentilla anserina*[8]

ALTERNATIVE NAMES: (E) Argentina, Blithran, Goose Potentil, Mashcoms (Derry), Mashcorns (from the root), Moors-corn, Wild Tansy. (I) *Blioscán, Blioscarán, Braoscán, Brioscán, Brisceán, Fearbán* (Clare, Dublin)

Silverweed was extensively cultivated for its tuberous roots in Ireland and Scotland before the arrival of the potato. The roots were boiled, roasted or dried and powdered to make bread. This tradition went back a long way, as a twelfth-century Irish text mentions silverweed as one of the wild plants that were eaten in Ireland. Silverweed appears in placenames such as Caherbriscaun (*Cathair Brioscán* – fort of the silverweed), County Galway; Coolnamrisklawn (*Cúil na mBrioslán* – nook of the silverweed), County Kilkenny; and Lugbriscan (*Log Brioscán* – hollow of the silverweed), County Louth. In Ireland silverweed was used in folk medicine in County Derry to staunch diarrhoea or bleeding piles, and in Counties Clare and Galway for heart trouble. In England the leaves of silverweed were used to ease the soreness in travellers' feet. Silverweed is a member of the rose family, the *Rosaceae*.

Wild Strawberry – *Sú Talún Fiáin* – *Fragaria vesca* [9]

ALTERNATIVE NAMES: (I) *Oighreog, Sú Láir, Tlacht-shú*

Wild strawberry was valued as a food in early Ireland. In Irish Law the fruit was classified as *cumra* or 'sweet' as opposed to *fiadain* or 'rough'. An eighth-century poem about the hermit Marbán describes his simple life in the woods. Among the fruits he eats to survive are a patch of wild strawberies, 'good to eat in their plenty'. Another early poem in praise of a glen called Gleann Ghualann mentions wild strawberries as one of the fruits that the warriors of Ireland, the Fianna, ate to sustain themselves. In County Antrim, it was believed that excessive ardour could be cooled with strawberry leaf tea, but that may refer to the garden kind. It was also used in County Cavan to cure red water fever in cattle. Wild strawberry is a member of the rose family, the *Rosaceae*.

Henbane – Gafann

Hyoscyamus Niger

♄   Ruled by the planet Saturn in traditional herbal medicine

SPECIES NAME: As above

ALTERNATIVE NAMES: (I) *Bainne Cíoch na n-Éan, Beann Mhear, Caoch na gCearc, Deodha, Min Mhear*

FOLK BELIEFS AND CUSTOMS

Henbane is one of the most poisonous herbs known to European herbalism and its reputation in folklore reflects this.[1] Although not usually fatal, ingesting it can cause temporary delirium, hallucinations, convulsions and loss of consciousness. These qualities meant that henbane was regarded as a powerful magical plant, used by witches and sorcerers. It was supposed to assist clairvoyance and it was used in evil spells. Its leaves were burnt to invoke the spirits of darkness. The bizarre effects of its poisoning led to the traditional belief that children who had eaten the plant were possessed by evil spirits. In Wales it was believed that if a child fell asleep near henbane, it would never awaken again. Henbane's power was also used in charms. A medieval medical manuscript states that placing henbane on a hareskin and laying it in a field would cause all the hares from the locality to gather around it. Despite its evil reputation, the same manuscript also states that henbane could provide powerful protection against evil spirits. Henbane has been regarded as a magical plant for a very long time: the ancient Assyrians placed it on the outer door and hinges to 'prevent sorcery from approaching a man's house'. The English name 'henbane' and the Irish *Caoch na gcearc* both mean the same, and reflect the fact that henbane can kill poultry if the seeds are eaten by them.

LEGENDS AND MYTHOLOGY

The continental druids were said to have worshipped a god of medicine called Rictenus. The herb 'belinimica' was dedicated to him, and was said to be a species of henbane.[2] In Classical mythology the dead in Hades were crowned with henbane as they wandered along hopelessly by the River Styx.[3]

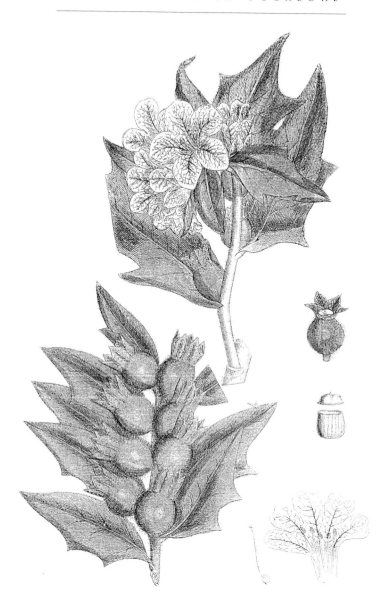

PRACTICAL AND HERBAL USES

Henbane has been used since ancient times as a sedative to provide sleep and alleviate pain, as it is safe to use in small doses.[4] For this reason it has been preferred in traditional medicine for these purposes to deadly nightshade, which shares the same properties in a more virulent form. Since ancient times henbane was also widely used to cure toothache, on account of these sedative qualities. In Britain henbane has also been used in folk medicine as a painkiller, especially for toothache. The only firm record of henbane being used in Irish folk medicine comes from County Cavan, where an infusion of the leaves was given to children with whooping cough, and the juice was drunk as a cure for nervous disorders. However, medieval Irish doctors believed that henbane applied externally was good for relieving the pains of gout and arthritis. In Ireland henbane was also used by poachers to catch fish by poisoning rivers.[5] Henbane is a member of the nightshade family, the *Solanaceae*.

SIMILAR PLANTS
Deadly Nightshade – *Lus na hOíche* – *Atropa bella-donna* [6]
ALTERNATIVE NAMES: (E) Belladonna; (I) *Lus Mór Coilleadh*
In Europe deadly nightshade or belladonna was part of the stock in trade of medieval witches because of its ability to produce hallucinations and whirling sensations. Due to its being so poisonous, deadly nightshade was not used in folk medicine in Britain or Ireland. Deadly nightshade is a member of the nightshade family, the *Solanaceae*.

Bittersweet – *Fuath Gorm* – *Solanum dulcamara*[7]
ALTERNATIVE NAMES: (E) Guinea Goul (Limerick), Woody Nightshade. (I) *Dréimire Gorm, Lus na hOíche, Míog Buí, Miothóg Buí, Míogaide, Searbhóg Milis, Slat Gorm*
Bittersweet derives its name from the fact that the berries taste sweet at first, and then bitter. Bittersweet was believed to have the power to nullify spells and harm. In Britain, a garland of bittersweet was put around the neck of livestock to keep them safe from witches, and people also wore garlands of bittersweet as a remedy for vertigo and dizziness. In Irish folk medicine bittersweet was used as a sedative to counter sleeplessness, and in County Limerick under the name 'guinea goul' to heal cuts that have festered. Bittersweet is a member of the nightshade family, the *Solanaceae*.

Daisy – Nóinín

Bellis/Leucanthemum

♀   Ruled by the planet Venus in traditional herbal medicine

♋   Associated with the zodiac sign Cancer

Species names:
Common Daisy – *Nóinín* – *Bellis perennis*
ALTERNATIVE NAMES: (E) Gowan (Ulster), Noneen, Small Red Daisy.
(I) *Nóinín Beag Dearg, Nóinín Mada*

Ox-Eye Daisy – *Nóinín Mór* – *Leucanthemum vulgare*
ALTERNATIVE NAMES: (E) Ban-daisy (US), Bishop's Posy, Dog Daisy,
Espibawn, Espie-ban (US). (I) *Bán Mór, Bó Dhonn, Bréanán Brothach*
(Donegal), *Bréineán Breothach* (Donegal), *Easpagán, Easpag Bán,*
Easpag Baoch, Easpag Speáin

Chamomile – *Camán Meall* – *Chamaemelum nobile*

Corn Chamomile – *Fíogadán Goirt* – *Anthemis arvensis*
ALTERNATIVE NAMES: (I) *Camán Míonla*

Stinking Chamomile – *Fineál Madra* – *Anthemis cotula*

FOLK BELIEFS AND CUSTOMS
In both Britain and Ireland the common daisy was widely regarded
as a harbinger of spring.[1] In Britain it was believed that spring had
not arrived until either three, nine or twelve daisies could be covered by a person with their foot. On the Aran Islands in County
Galway it was believed that daisies first appeared out of the ground
in the spring on St Brigid's Day. However, in Ireland it was also
believed that if a person stood on the first daisy they saw in the new
year, that they would be 'pushing up the daisies' themselves before
the year was out![2] In Ireland girls clad themselves in wreaths of
daisies, marsh marigolds and buttercups as part of the May Day festivities. Similarly in Bohemia in Europe, the arrival of spring was
heralded on the fourth Sunday in Lent by girls dressed in white and

wearing daisies and violets in their hair, leading a girl dressed as the queen about the village.[3]

In Britain and Ireland a universal custom was for children to make daisy chains by making a slit in the stem of one daisy and inserting the stem of another into the slit.[4] In Ireland they were known as *slabhra sí* – 'fairy chains'. Sometimes in Ireland daisy chains were made by threading the heads of daisies onto a rush, which was then curved around into a chain to be worn. Daisies were also universally used for the children's game of 'he loves me, he loves me not', where the lines were said as the petals were picked. Whichever phrase was said as the last petal was picked was regarded as the truth about the intentions of the beloved. In Britain, a more elaborate version of this was for a girl to pick the petals saying 'rich man, poor man, farmer, ploughman, thief'. Whichever one was said as the last petal was being picked would be the profession of her future husband.[5] In Scotland a female supernatural being called the *glaistig* was said to be very fond of children, and would play games with them by showering them with twigs and daisies.[6] A Scottish name for the daisy is *bairnwort* meaning 'child's flower'.[7]

The other well-known daisy is the ox-eye daisy.[8] It too was used to make daisy chains, at least in Ireland. The ox-eye daisy is associated in European folklore with midsummer and the feast of St John. In Germany it was hung at this time of year upon houses, around the doors, on the roofs and in the haylofts to keep away lightning. In Austria it is called *sunnawendl* – 'solstice flower'. The ox-eye daisy is also devoted to Mary Magdalen in church lore. A widespread alternative name for the ox-eye daisy in Ireland is *easpagán*. This has nothing to do with bishops (*easpag* in Irish), but derives from the word *easpa* meaning an abcess. Ox-eye daisy was used in traditional medicine to cure abcesses, boils and other skin complaints. A common local name for the ox-eye daisy in England is 'moon daisy', on account of its round white flower.

Another member of the daisy family is the aromatic chamomile, well-known on account of its use in making a herbal tea.[9] The cultivated form of chamomile *Anthemis nobilis* is still popular in herb gardens. It was believed to have the power to revive any plant that was wilting when grown nearby, and to have the power to ward off magic spells. It was also thought to bring success, so punters would dip their hands in chamomile-infused water before placing a bet. In North Africa, chamomile, penny-royal and other aromatic plants were burnt on the midsummer fires to give out a purifying smoke.

LEGENDS AND MYTHOLOGY
According to a Scottish story, the ancient Celts believed that every time an infant died a daisy appeared on earth in its stead.[10] The legend states that a Celtic noblewoman called Malvina had lost her infant son and became brooding and inconsolable. Suddenly her attendants arrived in great excitement, with the news that a wondrous new flower had come to earth, white in colour, but tinged

with pink the colour of a baby's flesh at its edge. Malvina understood that this was a miraculous sign meant to console her, and she mourned her son no longer saying: 'this flower will comfort all mothers that have lost their infants.' In Classical mythology the ox-eye daisy was dedicated to Artemis, the goddess of women, while in Germanic and Northern lore it was linked to the youthful sun-god Baldur.[11]

PRACTICAL AND HERBAL USES

Both the common daisy and the ox-eye daisy have been used for a variety of cures in traditional and folk medicine.[12] Both had a great reputation in traditional medicine for curing fresh wounds when applied as an ointment, and for inflammation of the liver when taken as a distilled water. The ox-eye daisy has also been considered since ancient times to be a useful cure for women's complaints, and for bruises, ulcers and abcesses. In Ireland the common daisy was used to cure burns and as an eye lotion. It was also used for skin complaints like whitlows and chilblains in County Meath, and ringworm in County Leitrim. A tea made from ox-eye daisy was used to ward off coughs and colds in Counties Tyrone and Monaghan, while sore eyes were bathed in the cooled boiled juice in Counties Galway and Limerick. Chamomile has always been considered an important herb since ancient times for its calming and sedative properties.[13] Its aromatic scent resembles apples and chamomile was used as a strewing herb in the middle ages to keep rooms fresh. It was also deliberately planted along walks, and in the famous 'chamomile lawn'. The cultivated species was widely used in both Britain and Ireland to make a tea or hot infusion to drink as a relaxant and a painkiller. In Ireland cultivated chamomile was also particularly used to cure swellings and inflammations. Daisies give their name to the daisy family, the *Asteraceae* (or *Compositae*).

SIMILAR PLANTS

Fairy Flax – *Lus na mBan Sí* – *Linum catharticum*[14]

ALTERNATIVE NAMES: (E) Dwarf Flax, Purging Flax. (I) *Bú, Caolach,*

Líon Beag, Líon na mBan Sí, Líon Purgóideach, Míonbhach, Míonsach, Míosach, Míseach, Miúnsach

With its small star-like flowers, fairy flax resembles a small daisy, but it is in fact unrelated. Fairy flax was valued in traditional medicine as a purgative. It was also employed in the Scottish Highlands as a cure for menstrual irregularities, and in Ireland, in County Cavan, as a cure for urinary complaints. Flaxes gives their name to the flax family, the *Linaceae*.

Greater Stitchwort – *Tursarraing Mhór* – *Stellaria holostea*[15]
ALTERNATIVE NAMES: (E) Easter Bell, Lady's-lint, Lady's-white-petticoats, Star-of-Bethlehem (Ulster). (I) *Teanga Éanáin, Toirseach, Tuirseach*
With its star-like white flowers, greater stitchwort looks like a kind of daisy, but it is not. The name 'stitchwort' derives from its use in British and Irish folk medicine for relieving stitches in the side, and other muscular pains, by chewing the flowers. In Britain children feared to pick the flowers in case it provoked thunder and lightning, and in Cornwall the fear was that the picker would become 'pisky-led' (led astray by pixies) or else be bitten by adders. Greater stitchwort is a member of the pink family, the *Caryophyllaceae*.

Corn Spurrey – *Corrán Lín* – *Spergula arvensis*[16]
ALTERNATIVE NAMES: (E) Glengore, Grangore, Granyagh, Yarr (Donegal). (I) *Cabróis, Clamhán, Cluain Lín, Corrán Croipleach*
Corn spurrey was traditionally grown as a fodder in continental Europe, and it was often eaten by humans as well. Spurrey seeds were found in the stomach contents of Tolland man, a prehistoric man found preserved in Tollund bog in Denmark. Corn spurrey is a member of the pink family, the *Caryophyllaceae*.

Eyebright – *Glanrosc* – *Euphrasia officinalis*[17]
ALTERNATIVE NAMES: (E) Euphrasy, Fairy Flax (Donegal), Rock Rue (Donegal). (I) *Caoimín, Glanruisc, Líon Radhairc, Lus an Phápa, Lus na Leac, Radhaircín, Rinnrosc, Roisnín, Rosc, Ruinnrosc, Soilse na Súl*
With its bright white flowers, eyebright looks like it is related to the common daisy, but it is not. In Ireland eyebright was one of the favourite remedies of the fairy doctor for countering the fairy 'stroke' or evil eye, and eyebright was one of the seven herbs that nothing natural or supernatural could injure. Eyebright gets its

Latin name from *Euphrosyne* (meaning gladness), one of the three Greek graces who brought joy and mirth. In both traditional herbal medicine and folk medicine throughout Europe, eyebright has been valued as a cure for eye complaints. The mildly astringent juice was used as a comforting lotion that has been attested medically as being effective in small doses. Eyebright is a member of the figwort family, the *Scrophulariaceae*.

Centaury – Dréimire Mhuire

Centaurium Erythraea

☉   Ruled by the Sun in traditional herbal medicine

SPECIES NAME: As above

ALTERNATIVE NAMES: (E) Dramwe-na-murragh (Donegal). (I) *Céad Duilleach, Crobhán Muire*

FOLK BELIEFS AND CUSTOMS

In Ireland centaury was associated in folklore with the Virgin Mary, perhaps because of its cleansing and purifying properties. For good luck and protection, the belief was that it had to be brought into the house between two feasts linked to the Virgin Mary – the feast of the Annunciation on 15 March (when the angel Gabriel announced to Mary that she was to give birth to Jesus), and the feast of the Assumption on 15 August (when Mary's body upon her death was taken up into heaven along with her soul).[1] However, in County Kerry centaury was believed to be particularly powerful if gathered on May Day.[2] Centaury was also considered good against magic in Irish folklore, and was used in folk medicine as part of a potion to counteract the 'evil eye'.[3] In Irish the name for centaury is *Dreimire Mhuire* or 'Mary's ladder' because the paired leaves around the stem resemble an old fashioned ladder. In light of this, centaury was said in County Mayo to get its powers of protection because it was the ladder that Mary used to get to heaven.[4] In fourteenth-century Europe centaury was similarly known as *Christi Scali* (Christ's ladder) because of the resemblance to an old-style ladder. It was also known by the near identical name of *Christi Schale* (Christ's Cup) in an allusion to the bitter draft offered to Christ on the cross (centaury is noted for its bitter taste).[5] In the Isle of Man centaury was called *Keym Chreest* or 'Christ's Step' because it was said to have sprung from Christ's footprints on his way to Calvary.[6]

LEGENDS AND MYTHOLOGY

In Classical legend centaury is associated with the centaur Chiron, who was famous in Greek mythology for his skill in medicinal herbs.[7] Chiron is supposed to have used centaury to cure himself of

a wound caused by an arrow poisoned by the blood of the hydra. The Latin name *Centaurium* and the English name centaury both derive from this legend.

PRACTICAL AND HERBAL USES

Centaury is noted for its intense bitterness, and was called by the ancients *Fel Terrae* or 'Gall of the Earth' on account of it.[8] It was recommended by them as a wound healer and a large quantity of its charred remains has been excavated from a Roman army hospital on the Rhine.[9] In traditional herbal medicine, centaury was used as a cleansing tonic to purify the blood; for liver, kidney and stomach complaints, and was taken as a tea for muscular rheumatism.[10] In Britain and Ireland centaury was widely used in folk medicine as a tonic; while in many parts of Britain (but only in County Louth in Ireland) it has been used as a remedy for indigestion. In County Wicklow centaury was used to cure liver complaints. Centaury is a member of the gentian family, the *Gentianaceae*.

SIMILAR PLANTS

Field Gentian – *Lus an Chrúbáin* – *Gentianella campestris* [11]
ALTERNATIVE NAMES: (E) Felwort

Autumn Gentian – *Muilcheann* – *Gentianella amarella*
ALTERNATIVE NAMES: (E) Felwort, Pennygrass

Like centaury, the gentians were known for their intense bitterness, and the name 'felwort' derives from the Latin *fel* meaning 'gall'. In northern parts of Britain field gentian was used in folk medicine as a cleansing tonic and for digestive complaints in areas where centaury is absent. In Sweden field gentian was used instead of hops for brewing beer. Gentians give their name to the gentian family, the *Gentianaceae*.

Devil's-Bit Scabious – Odhrach Bhallach

Succisa Pratensis

 Ruled by the planet Mercury in traditional herbal medicine

SPECIES NAME: As above

ALTERNATIVE NAMES: (E) Bitin' Billy (Donegal), Curl-doddy (Ulster), Curly-doddies (US), Lough Shule, Meena Madar (Clare, Galway). (I) *Buarach Bhallach, Caisearbhán Beag, Greim an Deamhain, Greim an Diabhail, Odhrach Mullach, Úrach Bhallach, Úrach Mullaigh*

FOLK BELIEFS AND CUSTOMS

Devil's-bit scabious was considered a powerful plant in folklore.[1] In Ireland it was believed that the milk would be very creamy if the cows ate a lot of it, and that it grew on land that gave good milk. Devil's-bit scabious was an important ingredient in an Irish potion to cure the 'evil eye', and could be used to cure afflictions caused by magic. One story tells of a woman who was cured of a crooked lip caused by enchantment by taking devil's bit scabious. The cure, however, involved drinking an infusion of nine plants boiled in urine! It was also believed that if it was picked before sunrise while saying a charm, devil's-bit scabious could cure a running sore or any evil. Devil's-bit scabious or 'curl-doddy' was used in a children's game in Ireland and Scotland.[2] The game involved twisting the stem around slowly and then seeing if it would turn back to its original shape when let go. While the stem was being twisted the following rhyme was said: 'Curl-doddy on the midden,/Turn around and take my biddin.' In Scotland a similar rhyme was also said to the devil's-bit scabious to try and summon a brownie or imp to clean the house: 'Curl-doddy, do my biddin,/soop my house and hool my midden' (sweep my house and clean out my dungheap). In Cornwall it was believed that picking the devil's bit scabious meant the devil would come to your bedside that night.[3]

LEGENDS AND MYTHOLOGY

The curious name devil's-bit scabious comes from the legend that the devil was jealous of all the healing qualities of the herb, so he bit the end off its root in a fit of spite. Alternatively, it was said that the

devil was acting with such great power by means of the plant, that the Virgin Mary intervened and cut the root short to thwart him.[4] The root of devil's-bit scabious does indeed look foreshortened as if the end part of it has been bitten off.

PRACTICAL AND HERBAL USES

The root of devil's-bit scabious was believed to have great powers in traditional medicine.[5] It was said to be a cure for plague, fever, poison, venomous bites, bruises, falls, blood clots, swellings of the throat, wind, worms, wounds, scurf, dandruff, pimples and freckles. It was also used for coughs, fevers and internal inflammation. A decoction made from the root was used as a wash for skin eruptions, and to clear the head of scurf, dandruff and sores. This emphasis on skin complaints is the origin of the name 'scabious', which derives from the word scabies. In Ireland it was used to cure 'sores such as boils' in County Mayo, and running sores in Counties Clare and Galway. Devil's-bit Scabious is a member of the teasel family, the *Dipsacaceae*.

SIMILAR PLANTS

Field Scabious – *Cab an Ghasáin – Knautia arvensis*[6]
ALTERNATIVE NAMES: (E) Cardies. (I) *Bodach Gorm, Bréanla Gorm*
In Belgium and the west country of England, field scabious was used in love divination. A girl would pick some flowerbuds that were about to open and give each one the name of a suitor. The one that later opened out best gave the name of her husband to be. Like devil's-bit scabious, field scabious was used to cure skin complaints like scabs. Field scabious is a member of the teasel family, the *Dipsacaceae*.

Teasel – *Leadán Úcaire – Dipsacus fullonum*[7]
ALTERNATIVE NAMES: (E) Carde Thistle, Great Shepherd's Rod, Venus Bason. (I) *Leadán Liosta, Lus an Úcadóra, Lus an Úcaire, Lus na Leadán, Taga*
According to the Roman naturalist Pliny, the rainwater or dew collecting in the natural cup between the connate leaves of teasel had healing properties. In Britain this water was thought to be good for

eye complaints, and the heads of teasel were used as a cure for the ague. Teasel gives its name to the teasel family, the *Dipsacaceae*.

Thrift – *Rabhán* – *Armeria maritima*[8]

ALTERNATIVE NAMES: (E) Lady's-cushion, Sea-daisy, Sea-July Flower, Sea-pink. (I) *Caoróg Mhara, Cíob Trá, Murrathach, Nóinín an Chladaigh, Rosc, Tonn an Chladaigh*

With its small drumsticks of pink flowers, thrift looks like a scabious, but it is not in fact related. As a pun, thrift flowers were chosen as an emblem of the threepenny bit of George VI. In the Outer Hebrides of Scotland, a decoction of the roots of thrift was drunk as a cure for tuberculosis. Thrift gives its name to the thrift family, the *Plumbaginaceae*.

Thistle – Feochadán

Cirsium

♃   Ruled by the planet Jupiter in traditional herbal medicine

♐   Associated with the zodiac sign Sagittarius

SPECIES NAMES:
Spear Thistle – *Feochadán Colgach* – *Cirsium vulgare*
ALTERNATIVE NAMES: (E) Buck-thrissle (US), Bull Thistle (Ulster), Scotch Thistle. (I) *Deilgneach, Feochadán Feá*
Creeping Thistle – *Feochadán Reatha* – *Cirsium arvense*
ALTERNATIVE NAMES: (E) Corn Thistle (I) *Feochadán Fireann*
Marsh Thistle – *Feochadán Corraigh* – *Cirsium palustre*

ALTERNATIVE NAMES FOR THISTLE: (E) Thrissle (US); thistle seeds known as Jimmyjoes, Jinny-go-up (Dublin), Jinnyjoes. (I) *Cluarán, Dearcán* (the head), *Faofadán* (Louth), *Feosán* (Aran Is), *Feothann, Fiústán, Fochadán, Fofallán, Fofannán, Foghbhannán, Fothannán, Geosadán, Giúsadán, Omthann*

FOLK BELIEFS AND CUSTOMS
Despite its weedy nature, thistle was regarded in Ireland as being a sign of good land. A folktale tells of a blind man thinking of buying a farm. 'Tie that horse to a thistle,' he said to his son who had accompanied him. 'I don't see any thistles,' said the son. 'Oh,' said the old man, 'we'll go home so, I won't buy this land, it's too poor and bad.'[1] In Ireland the downy seeds of thistle are known as 'jinny-go-ups' or 'jinnyjoes' and a favourite children's game was to catch them. If there was a seed or 'egg' attached to the thistledown, the 'egg' was put in a matchbox. If there was no seed attached, then the down was blown from the palm of the hand saying: 'jinnyjo, jinnyjo, lay me an egg.'[2] Thistle appears in the County Donegal placenames Fofannybane (*Fofannaigh Bhán* – 'white thistle land') and Fofannyreagh (*Fofannaigh Riabhach* – 'striped thistle land').[3]

LEGENDS AND MYTHOLOGY
Thistle appears in some Irish legends.[4] In the legend of the *Táin Bó*

Cuailgne or 'The Cattle Raid of Cooley' the children of Cailidín conjure up an enchanted army of warriors from 'shaggy, sharp, downy thistles, and light-topped puffballs, and fluttering withered leaves of the wood'. In Irish myth, Oisín of the Fianna was said to have eyesight so sharp that he could 'see a thistle thorn on the darkest night'. In the tale, 'The Intoxication of the Ulaid', a strongman of King Conchubhur lifts a heavy stone pillar as if it were 'a wisp of thistle, all fluff and lightness'.

Thistle is best known, however, as being the national emblem of Scotland, and different legends give various explanations for this.[5] One version states that the thistle was first adopted by the eighth-century Scottish king Achaius as his emblem, apparantly in combination with the rue. Achaius supposedly chose the thistle because it will not endure handling, and the rue because it has the power to drive away serpents by its smell and cure their bites. Another widespread legend claims that thistle became the national emblem because it saved the country from being invaded by the Vikings. The story goes that the Scottish army was camped one night on the banks of the River Tay, near Stanley in central Scotland. The Vikings decided to ambush the Scots as they slept, and as they crept up to the unsuspecting Scots they stumbled into a field of thistles. One of the Vikings trod on the sharp spines of the thistle, and his howls of pain woke the Scots and alerted them to the approaching danger. Thus they were able to fight off the Vikings and maintain their freedom, and so adopted the thistle as their emblem in thanks for its role in saving them.

The existence of thistle-like decorations on Norse 'thistle' brooches and pins of the eighth to tenth centuries are sometimes cited as the earliest evidence of the thistle appearing as a Scottish emblem, but this is dismissed by most scholars as the decorations bear only the most superficial resemblance to thistles.[6] Despite the legends, there is no evidence before the fifteenth century of the thistle being used as the Scottish national emblem. It seems that the thistle was first adopted as an emblem of the Stewart kings some time in the late middle ages, probably as a borrowing from their French allies.[7] In fact, an Order of the Thistle was founded in France in 1370 and is depicted in French tapestries of the time. The first Scottish appearance of a thistle is not until 1470 on a silver coin issued by James III, and records show that James III left a coverlet adorned with thistles to his heir, James IV. In addition, the marriage of James IV to Margaret Tudor of England in 1503 was celebrated in a contemporary carol called 'The Thrissle and the Rose'. Later still, accounts of James V mention the king's bonnet being decorated with gold thistles, and a portrait of that king shows him wearing a collar adorned with thistle heads. By the sixteenth century the thistle had become a full national emblem, appearing on coinage and placed by Mary Queen of Scots on the Great Seal of Scotland. However, the thistle's place as a Scottish national emblem was ultimately copperfastened when James VII (James II of England) founded the Order of the Thistle in 1687, with its chapel in the Abbey Church of Holyroodhouse, and the warlike motto *Nemo me impune lacessit* – 'No one provokes me with impunity'. Nowadays the thistle appears on numerous Scottish logos, from the National Trust for Scotland to the Scottish Sports Council.

It is not difficult to see why the thistle was chosen as an emblem by the Stewarts, as it embodies the qualities of toughness, durability, defiance and pride. Its striking shape and bold colour also make it a satisfactory symbol for decoration. Although there is absolute agreement on thistle's place as a national emblem, there is ongoing debate in Scotland as to which species exactly is the 'true' Scottish thistle. For many, it is the cotton thistle (*Onopordum acanthium*), which is still widely known to many as simply 'Scottish' thistle. This is the thistle chosen by Sir Walter Scott to be carried in procession for the visit of George IV to Edinburgh in 1822. It is the largest and most striking thistle to grow in Britain, but it suffers the disadvantage of being very rare north of the border. In fact, it may not be native to Britain at all, but introduced as a garden plant on account of the white cottony down on its leaves and stems, which was used to stuff pillows, cushions and beds.[8] It is more likely that what the Stewarts had in mind was the most striking of the native thistles of Britain and Ireland, the spear thistle (*Cirsium vulgare*) which has always grown freely thoughout the pastures of Scotland.

Practical and Herbal Uses

Thistles have been little used in folk medicine.[9] Spear thistle (*Cirsium vulgare*) was used in County Donegal as a cure for kidney infections, while unspecified species of thistles were used to heal wounds in Counties Dublin and Limerick. In the Scottish Highlands a thistle tea was drunk to dispel depression. The flowers of spear thistle were also said to have the power to curdle milk.

Thistles provide good fodder for cattle and horses once they have been crushed to destroy the spines.[10] In Ireland it was said that donkeys were the one livestock animal that liked to eat thistle uncrushed because their hard tongues had no problem with its spines. In Ireland thistle was also cut up as food for chickens.[11] Thistles are members of the daisy family, the *Asteraceae*.

SIMILAR PLANTS

Common Knapweed – *Mínscoth* – *Centaurea nigra*[12]
ALTERNATIVE NAMES: (E) Bachelor's Buttons, Blackbuttons, Blackheads, Black Knapweed, Buttonweed (Kerry), Drumsticks, Hardhead, Horse-button (Donegal), Horse-knappers, Horse-knob, Ironweed, Mattfellon. (I) *Bodach Dubh, Brealla Gorma, Ceanna Dubha, Cnaipe Dubha, Fonnscoth, Mullach Dubh, Nianscoth, Tobac Capaill*
In Britain the flowerheads of knapweed were used in love divination. The little purple florets were stripped off and the rest of the flowerhead placed in the bosom. It was later withdrawn, and if another floret had emerged (which was likely), then it meant the lover was true. In Ireland a decoction of the roots of knapweed was used in folk medicine as a cure for jaundice and liver trouble, and as a tonic for cleansing the system. Common knapweed is a member of the daisy family, the *Asteraceae*.

Cornflower – *Gormán* – *Centaurea cyanus*[13]
ALTERNATIVE NAMES: (E) Bluebottle, Corn Bluebottle, St Barnaby's Thistle, Sweet Sultan. (I) *Coirce Gorm, Goirmín, Lus Gormáin*
With its deep blue flowers, cornflower used to be a common feature of arable land, but improved agricultural techniques mean that it is now very scarce. The Latin name *cyanus* recalls the nymph Cyane, who was changed into a dark blue spring, or well. In traditional medicine cornflower was used against plague, poison, wounds, fever and inflammations. Cornflower is a member of the daisy family, the *Asteraceae*.

Lesser Burdock – *Cnádán* – *Arctium minus*[14]
ALTERNATIVE NAMES: (E) Clot-bur, Cradan, Credan, Cuckle (Fin). (I) *Cop* (the leaf), *Copóg Thuathail, Crádán, Leadán* (the burr), *Leadán an Úcaire, Leadán Liosta, Meacan Tua(in), Mille-riugail* (the burr), *Min-bhriúgail, Tobha, Tua, Tuabhal, Tuafal*
The burrs or prickly seeds of burdock are covered in tiny hooks

which catch onto hair, fur or clothing, and a favourite children's game is to throw them at each other. In the Scottish town of South Queensferry on the second Friday in August, by tradition a man in a costume covered in burdock burrs called the 'Burry man' goes about the town, walking its boundaries and collecting money, before returning to the town hall. The origin of the custom is unknown, but it takes place the day before a local fair. In Britain and Ireland a decoction of the roots of burdock was extensively used to cleanse the sytem and so to cure boils and other skin complaints. In Ireland it was also used in Counties Meath and Wicklow to cure burns and in County Cavan for cuts, colds and respiratory trouble. In addition it was used to cure convulsions in County Louth and nervousness in County Meath. Lesser burdock is a member of the daisy family, the *Asteraceae*.

Prickly Sow-Thistle – *Bleachtán Colgach* – *Sonchus asper*[15]
Smooth Sow-Thistle – *Bleachtán Mín* – *Sonchus oleraceus*
ALTERNATIVE NAMES FOR SOW-THISTLE: (E) Hare's-lettuce, Milk Thistle, Milkweed, Milkwort, Swine-thistle (Donegal), Swine-thrissle (US). (I) *Bainne Muice, Bleachtán Buí, Bleacht-fheochadán, Fothannán Mín, Leitis Giorria, Sleochtán, Slóchtán*
Sow-thistle gets its name from the idea that it was favoured by sows because it would increase the flow of their milk. The name 'hare's lettuce' derives from an old European legend that sow-thistle gave strength to hares when they were overcome with heat. It was also said that when the hare was under the sow-thistle it believed itself to be quite safe from harm. In both Britain and Ireland the milky sap of sow thistles has been used as a cure for warts. Sow-thistles are members of the daisy family, the *Asteraceae*.

Sea-Holly – *Cuileann Trá* – *Eryngium maritimum*[16]
ALTERNATIVE NAMES: (E) Eryngo, Sandbox. (I) *Cuileann Chapaill, Cuileann Duimhche*
Despite its similar appearance, sea-holly is not related to holly or thistle either. In Britain the long, thick roots of sea-holly were peeled, boiled and cut into slivers, then covered with a strong syrup and sold as a cure for coughs and colds, under the name 'eryngo-root'. In Ireland, the roots were given to children to rid them of worms in the Aran Islands. Sea-holly is a member of the carrot family, the *Apiaceae*.

Plantain – Slánlus

Plantago

♀ Ruled by the planet Venus in traditional herbal medicine

Species names:
Ribwort Plantain – *Slánlus* – *Plantago lanceolata*
Alternative names: (E) Blackheads (Dublin, Donegal), Carl-doddy (Donegal), Cocks, Cocks-and-hens, Curl-doddy (Donegal), Grass Plantain, Ribbonleaf, Ribgrass, St Patrick's Leaf, Soldiers. (I) *Cál Phádraig*, *Ceann-táthair* (flower), *Lus na Saighdiuirí*, *Lusra an tSeanchais*, *Slándus*, *Snárlus*

Greater Plantain – *Cuach Phádraig* – *Plantago major*
Alternative names: (E) Blackheads (Dublin, Donegal), Cowgrass (Ulster), Rat-tails, St Patrick's Leaf(een), Slanlis, Waybread, Wayspread. (I) *Cál Phádraig*, *Copóg Phádraig*

Sea Plantain – *Slánlus Mara* – *Plantago maritima*

Folk Beliefs and Customs
In Irish folklore ribwort plantain or *slánlus* – 'health herb', was believed to have great curative properties.[1] Indeed, it was believed that ribwort plantain was so powerful it could be used to bring back the dead. However, while it could be used to cure many ailments, there was also a danger that if the wind changed while you were collecting it, you would lose your mind. Ribwort plantain was mainly used in folk cures to heal wounds, and so it was popularly believed that ribwort had been put on Our Lord's wounds after the crucifixion to heal them. For example, in west Galway it was said that ribwort plantain was put on the wound in Our Lord's side after the spear had entered it. The name ribwort plantain comes from the five ridges on its leaves which look like ribs, and in County Kerry it was said that the five ridges commemorate the five wounds received by Christ during the crucifixion. Not only humans could avail of ribwort's healing powers. One story tells of a fight between a black beetle and a devil's coach horse (a kind of beetle like a large

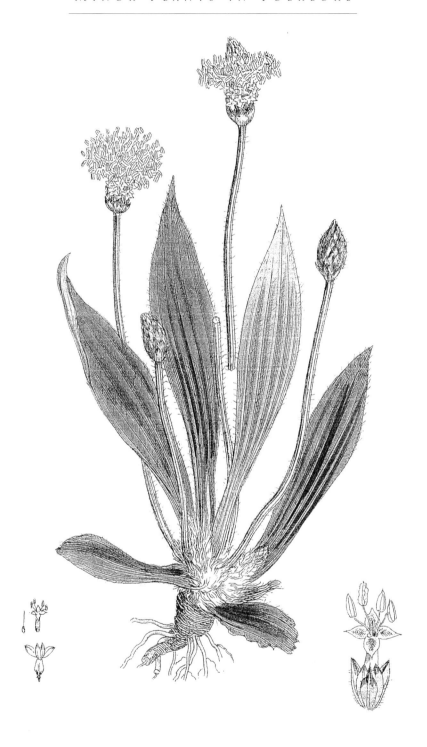

black earwig). The story goes that during the fight, the devil's coach horse injected poison into the beetle from the pincers in its rear and then left, thinking the beetle dead. When it was alone, however, the beetle rose and found a leaf of ribwort plantain and ate some of it, and so was cured on the spot. It was widely believed in Ireland that the devil's coach horse beetle has poison in its pincers, but this has no basis in fact.

In Dublin the flowerheads of ribwort plantain were used by children in a game called 'soldiers'.[2] The children took turns to try and knock the heads of each other's plant with their own flower-head or 'soldier', and the first to succeed won. Another Irish name for the game was 'Fighting Cocks', with the flowerheads called 'cocks' used in the same way. The game of 'soldiers' is also well known in England and Europe and has a long history.[3] A Norman French poem written in England in 1219 refers to a boy using plantain to play *chevaliers* or 'soldiers' with King Stephen (who reigned from 1135 to 1154), while the monarch waited to go into battle.

In Anglo-Saxon medicine greater plantain or 'waybread' (so called because it was found along the ways and roads) was considered a powerful herb because it could survive being trampled on by travellers. An Anglo-Saxon poem praises its strength in withstanding this punishment and calls on its aid:[4]

> And you, waybread, mother of worts,
> Open from eastward, powerful within,
> Over you chariots rolled, over you queens rode,
> Over you brides cried, over you bulls belled;
> All these you withstood, and these you confounded,
> So withstand now the venom that flies through the air,
> And the loathed thing which through the land roves.

Greater plantain in Ireland was traditionally associated with St Patrick, and so was called *copóg Phadraig* or 'St Patrick's dock'.[5]

Plantain traditionally spreads with the arrival of agriculture, and pollen samples of ribwort plantain have been found in Ireland dated from about 4,000 to 3,000 BC, which demonstrate that cultivation was taking place in the country at that time. Similarly, greater plantain followed the first settlers to New England, and became known there as 'white man's foot' as it sprang up wherever the English had travelled.[6]

PRACTICAL AND HERBAL USES

Since ancient times plantain has been valued for its use in stopping bleeding from external wounds, cuts and sores.[7] In Ireland greater plantain or *copog Phádraig* – 'St Patrick's dock' – was used in folk medicine to heal wounds in this way. The leaves were macerated, applied to the wound and then covered with a bandage. It was also said that the rough side of the leaf was to draw out septic matter and the smooth side was to heal. The leaves of ribwort plantain were similarly used to stop bleeding by chewing them into a pulp and applying them to the wound. The leaves of plantain were also used in Ireland to cure lumps and swellings, pimples, chapped hands or legs, corns, warts and headeaches.[8] Plantain juice was also drunk as a cure for a cough in Counties Monaghan, Mayo and Laois, for liver trouble in County Cavan, and for jaundice in County Laois.[9] Plaintains give their name to the plantain family, the *Plantaginaceae*.

Lady's-Mantle – Dearna Mhuire

Alchemilla

♀ Ruled by the planet Venus in traditional herbal medicine

♉ Associated with the zodiac sign Taurus

SPECIES NAMES:
Southern Lady's-Mantle – *Dearna Mhuire Caol* – *Alchemilla filicaulis*
Smooth Lady's-Mantle – *Dearna Mhuire Mhín* – *Alchemilla glabra*
Pale Lady's-Mantle – *Dearna Mhuire Bhuí* – *Alchemilla xanthochlora*

ALTERNATIVE NAMES FOR LADY'S-MANTLE: (E) Dewcup, Lion's-foot (I) *Braitín na Maighdine, Bratóg Mhuire, Cóta Preasach, Crúba Leoin, Cupán Drúchta, Falaing Mhuire, Leamhach, Leamhan Buí, Leathach Buí, Leann, Rodh, Rú, Treascán, Trioscán, Troscán, Turscán.*

FOLK BELIEFS AND CUSTOMS
A characteristic of lady's-mantle is that large drops of dew collect in the base of its leaves, and in folk belief this dew possessed magical properties.[1] In Ireland and Scotland lady's-mantle was used to cure people and animals from fairy bewitchment and the 'evil eye'. For example, in County Antrim a cow was cured of bewitchment in the following fashion: the plant's juice was put into a bucket of water taken from the meeting of three parishes, along with the juice of other plants, a silver coin, a copper coin and a 'fairy flint' or stone age arrowhead. The resulting mixture was then given to the cow to drink. The name lady's-mantle, and the similar Irish names *falaing Mhuire* and *bratóg Mhuire*, derive from the fact that the notched edges of the leaves are reminiscent of the tasselled edges of old style cloaks. The name *dearna Mhuire* means 'Mary's palm' from the hand shaped leaves.

PRACTICAL AND HERBAL USES
The dew from lady's-mantle was also prized by medieval alchemists who collected it at dawn and used it in their experiments to turn base metals into gold.[2] So convinced were the alchemists of its amazing properties that they gave lady's-mantle its Latin name, *Alchemilla*. Lady's mantle also had many virtues in

traditional medicine.[3] It was believed to be good to use on wounds or to stop bleeding, as it dried up the wound and reduced inflammation. It was also used for women's ailments. Women who wished to conceive were recommended to drink a distillation of the juice for twenty days running, and to also sit occasionally in a bath made of a decoction of the herb. In addition lady's-mantle was supposed to have the ability to restore sagging breasts to their former shape and size. In the Scottish Highlands a decoction of lady's-mantle was also supposed to restore beauty after it had faded, and even the dew gathered from its cup-like leaves was believed to have the same effect. In Ireland lady's-mantle was used for kidney trouble in Counties Cavan and Kerry, and for burns and scalds, also in County Cavan.[4] Lady's-mantle is a member of the rose family, the *Rosaceae*.

SIMILAR PLANTS
Round-Leaved Sundew – *Drúichtín Móna* – *Drosera rotundifolia* [5]
ALTERNATIVE NAMES: (I) *Galar na gCat* (Donegal), *Lus na Fearnaighe*, *Rós an tSolais*
Oblong-Leaved Sundew – *Cailís Mhuire* – *Drosera intermedia*

ALTERNATIVE NAMES FOR SUNDEW: (E) Blessed Virgin's Chalice (Limerick), Oilplant (Donegal). (I) *Dealtrua*.
Like lady's-mantle, sundew was esteemed by medieval alchemists because of the dew that forms on its leaves, particularly the fact that the dew did not dry up even in full sunlight – hence the name 'sundew'. The dew in question is in fact a sticky liquid secreted by the leaves to entrap flies and other insects, in order to provide sundew with additional nourishment to the poor bogland in which it grows. The 'dew' was held to be strengthening and nourishing and was distilled with wine and other herbs to make a liquer called *Rosa Solis*, i.e., 'sundew'. Sundew was also said to be effective as a love charm because of its ability to lure and entrap other creatures. For example, in the Isle of Man sundew was called *lus ny graih* – 'herb of love' – and was used by youths to gain the affection of their sweethearts by putting some into their clothes without the girl knowing. In Ireland the leaves of sundew were boiled in milk (that of asses preferably) as a good cure for whooping cough, asthma and jaundice. Despite this, farmers suspected sundew (wrongly) of giving their sheep liver rot. In ancient times sundew was used by Celtic tribes for dyeing their hair. Sundews give their name to the sundew family, the *Droseraceae*.

Poppy – Poipín

Papaver

☽   Ruled by the Moon in traditional herbal medicine

♋   Associated with the zodiac sign Cancer

SPECIES NAMES:
Common Poppy – *Cailleach Dhearg* – *Papaver rhoeas*
Long-Headed Poppy – *Cailleach Fhada* – *Papaver dubium*
Rough Poppy – *Bláth na mBodach* – *Papaver hybridum*

ALTERNATIVE NAMES FOR POPPY: (E) Copprouse (FB), Cop-rose, Corn-rose, Headache. (I) *Barróg Rua*, *Cáithleach Dearg*, *Cocán* (*Dearg*) (the flowerbud), *Poipín Dearg*, *Poipín Rua*.

FOLK BELIEFS AND CUSTOMS
The Irish for the bud of the poppy just before it opens is *cocán*, and the word appears in the phrase *Mar chocán ar chnocán lá gréine* – 'as a poppy on a height on a summer's day', meaning something beautiful.[1] However, in both Ireland and Britain, it was thought that looking at scarlet poppies would cause headaches.[2] In Counties Carlow, Wexford, Wicklow and Waterford, where poppies were once common in the cornfields, they were considered obnoxious to females, particularly young, unmarried women, who had a horror of touching or being touched by them. In England it was also believed by children that staring at the centre of a poppy flower for too long would cause blindness. It seems there is some basis for these beliefs. Veterans of the First World War who recalled long marches through fields of red poppies found that the scarlet colour affected their eyes, making them see red for days. Similarly, in the nineteenth century, military tailors who worked with the bright scarlet of regimental colours were said to go blind more often than other tailors. Another, perhaps related, English belief was that it was unlucky to bring poppies indoors, as they were supposed to cause illness.

In England the poppy is linked to thunder and lightning in popular folklore.[3] For example, it was believed that if a person picked a red poppy and one of the petals fell off, that the person would be struck by lightning. In fact, it was widely thought that the poppy should not be picked at all for fear of provoking thunder storms, and that while they remained unpicked the crops were safe from summer downpours. On the other hand, it was believed that placing poppies among the timbers under the roof warded off lightning. These beliefs are also found in some other European countries. In Belgium poppy is known as *fleur de tonnerre* – the thunder flower. In Irish the poppy is a witch's flower – *cailleach dhearg* – 'red hag', while in Wales it is *llygad y bwgan* – 'goblin's eye'.[4] The Latin name for poppy, *papaver*, is believed to come from a Celtic word *papa* meaning porridge, and to derive from an ancient custom of administering the plant to children in food to make them sleep, on account of its mildy narcotic qualities.[5]

LEGENDS AND MYTHOLOGY

The red poppy had strong associations in the ancient world.[6] To the Egyptians and Assyrians, it was an emblem of growth, blood and new life. The poppy was also the emblem of the Roman crop goddess Ceres, and her statues were adorned with garlands of poppies interwoven with barley or wheat. Ritual offerings of poppy seeds were offered to the goddess to ensure the fertility of the crops. In Greek mythology poppy was sacred to Aphrodite, the goddess of love and vegetation.

Since at least the nineteenth century poppies have been associated with those who have died in war. At Waterloo, the poppies which sprang up from the field after the Duke of Wellington's victory were said to have come from the blood of the troops who fell in battle.[7] However, in the twentieth century the poppy became a symbol of remembrance for those who had died in the First World War and subsequent wars. This arose after a poem by Canadian doctor Colonel John Macrae, and inspired by the second battle of Ypres, was published in *Punch* in December 1915. The poem began with the now famous lines: 'In Flanders fields the poppies blow, / Between the crosses, row on row.'[8]

The poem inspired American, Moina Michael, who took to wearing a poppy to 'keep faith with those who died'. In November 1918 a French woman, Madame Guerin, intrigued by the poppy, enquired of Ms Michael as to its meaning. Madame Guerin decided to get poppies manufactured for sale in France, with the proceeds going to assist those returning to war-devastated areas. Thus, when the British Legion in turn decided to organise the first Poppy Day to sell cloth poppies as lapel badges in order to assist ex-servicemen and their dependants, they were forced to use poppies imported from France. Since then, however, British ex-servicemen (with preference given to the disabled) have been employed making the poppies. In time Poppy Day became the annual Poppy Appeal which is still very popular in Britain with up to 36 million poppies being manufactured each year in recent times. In 1988, for example, the Poppy Appeal raised in excess of £10 million sterling to help ex-service personnel and their dependants.

The poppy remains a mainly British and Commonwealth symbol of remembrance, which has led to objections by some nationalists over its use in Ireland by ex-British servicemen born in Ireland. However, this has not hampered improved efforts in Ireland in recent times to remember the Irish, both Catholic and Protestant, who died in the First and Second World Wars.

PRACTICAL AND HERBAL USES

The common red poppy has slightly narcotic qualities, but it does not contain opium or morphine in any significant amounts.[9] Nevertheless, wild poppies have been used in folk medicine in both Britain and Ireland as painkillers, particularly for curing toothache and earache.[10] In Ireland the poppy has also been used to ease neuralgia and in a syrup to cure coughs in County Wicklow. It is also an ingredient in an eye lotion in Ulster.[11] Poppies give their name to the poppy family, the *Papaveraceae*.

SIMILAR PLANTS

Opium Poppy – *Codlaidín* – *Papaver somniferum*[12]

ALTERNATIVE NAMES: *Cromlus*

Opium poppy, as its name suggests, gives the narcotic and sedative opium, and it has been grown in Britain since at least the Bronze Age for this purpose. In recent centuries commercial crops were abandoned because cheap Asian imports made the trade unprofitable. Despite this, it continued to be used in some parts of England as a folk cure for rheumatism and fever. Incredible as it may seem to us now, it was also widely used to calm babies by macerating the petals into their milk, or dipping the teat on their feeding bottle into the seeds. Poppies give their name to the poppy family, the *Papaveraceae*.

Yellow Horned Poppy – *Caillichín na Trá* – *Glaucium flavum*[13]
Yellow horned poppy exudes a milky latex sap, rather like dandelion or spurge. In the south west of England this was extracted from the roots as a folk cure for bruises. Poppies give their name to the poppy family, the *Papaveraceae*.

Greater Celandine – *Garra Bhuí* – *Chelidonium majus*[14]
ALTERNATIVE NAMES: (E) Sollendine. (I) *Cliathach Buí, Lacha Cheann Rua*
Greater celandine is the true celandine, unlike its namesake lesser celandine (*Ranunculus ficaria*), which shares the name purely due to the perceived likeness of its flowers to those of *Chelidonium*. The name 'celandine' itself is an English version of the Latin *Chelidonium* which derives from the Greek word *chelidon*, meaning a swallow. It was given this name because it comes into flower with the coming of the swallow and fades at their departure. In traditional medicine its acrid sap was believed to be good for removing films and spots from the cornea of the eye. Greater celandine is a member of the poppy family, the *Papaveraceae*.

Corncockle – *Cogal* – *Agrostemma githago*[15]
ALTERNATIVE NAMES: (E) Cockleweed, Pink (Ulster), Popple (Ulster). (I) *Cogal Dearg, Luibh Laoibheach, Roidhléith* (Cork), *Roithléith*
Corncockle used to be a common sight growing among crops like corn and wheat, but more efficient agriculture means that it is now virtually extinct in the wild. Corncockle was traditionally used in Europe as a decoration in harvest wreathes. Corncockle is a member of the pink family, the *Caryophyllaceae*.

Vetch – Peasair

Vicia

☽   Vetch ruled by the Moon in traditional herbal medicine

♊   Vetch associated with the zodiac sign Gemini

♂   Restharrow ruled by the planet Mars in traditional herbal medicine

SPECIES NAMES:
Common Vetch – *Peasair Chapaill* – *Vicia sativa*
ALTERNATIVE NAMES: (E) Chickling, Fitches, Horse-pea, Horse-vetch, Strangle Tare, Vetch Tare. (I) *Pis Capaill, Pis Dubh, Pis Phréacáin, Piseánach Coitianta, Piseánach na mBreas, Siorr(alach)*

Bitter Vetch – *Corra Meille* – *Lathyrus montanus*
ALTERNATIVE NAMES: (E) Cornameliagh (Donegal), Fairies' Corn (Donegal), Heath-pea, Knapperty (Ulster, US), Wood-pea. (I) *Corra Mhilis, Pis Shléibhe, Piseán na nÉan.*

Common Restharrow – *Fréamhacha Tairne* – *Ononis repens*
ALTERNATIVE NAMES: (E) Cammock, Land-whin, Petty-whin, Wild Liquorice-root. (I) *Carrachán, Fan-go-fóill* (?), *Préamh Tharraingthe, Sreang Bogha, Sreang Tharraing, Sreang Thrian*

Kidney Vetch – *Méara Muire* – *Anthyllis vulneraria*
ALTERNATIVE NAMES: (E) Lady's-finger, Stanch. (I) *Cosán, Cúig Mhéar Muire*

Hairy Tare – *Peasair Arbhair* – *Vicia hirsuta*
ALTERNATIVE NAMES: (E) Hairy Vetch, Mouse-pea (Donegal). (I) *Cogal*

Meadow Vetchling – *Peasairín Buí* – *Lathyrus pratensis*
ALTERNATIVE NAMES: (E) Common Yellow Vetch, Meadow-pea, Mouse-pea (Donegal), Yellow Vetchling. (I) *Pis Bhuí, Piseánach na gCapall*

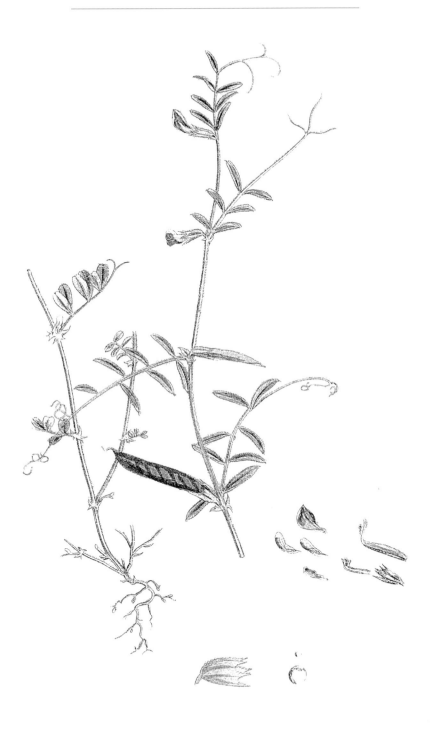

FOLK BELIEFS AND CUSTOMS

Restharrow (*Ononis repens*) was traditionally hated by farmers because its long, tough roots used to make ploughing difficult – its name literally means to 'arrest the harrow'.[1] An Irish folktale reflects this attitude. It tells of a farmer called Lehane, who on his death bed tells his relatives that he willingly forgives everyone and everything who ever caused him harm or injury in this world – everything that is, except the restharrow! Unlike other members of the pea family, restharrow has spines, hence the names 'land-whin' and 'petty-whin' (whin is another name for furze or gorse). In European folklore restharrow was believed to be the plant from which the crown of thorns was woven for Christ's crucifixion. It was also believed that restharrow had the power to repel snakes. Hairy tare (*Vicia hirsuta*) is thought by some authors to be the 'tare' mentioned in the bible in the parable of the tare and the good seed, which explains why sinners are left apparently unpunished in life.[2] In the parable the useless tare is to be left until harvest time so as not to disturb the good crop, but when the harvest is made it is then to be taken and burned while the useful wheat is gathered into the barn. Other authorities, however, maintain that the 'tare' concerned refers to darnel grass. Vetch appears in the placename Pishanagh (*Piseánach* – place of vetches), County Westmeath.[3]

LEGENDS AND MYTHOLOGY

Bitter vetch or 'heath-pea' (*Lathyrus montanus*) appears in the legend *Buile Suibhne* or 'Sweeney Astray'. *Suibhne Geilt* or 'Mad Sweeney' was a County Antrim king who lost his wits and fled from society to live in the wilderness. Sweeney made his way to Gleann Bolcáin, a glen variously located in County Antrim or County Kerry. Among the wild plants mentioned as growing in Gleann Bolcain that Sweeney gathered for food was *melle* or bitter vetch.[4] Similarly, in the eighth-century poem about the hermit Marbán, who also lived alone in the wild, bitter vetch or *melle* appears among the foods which provided him with nourishment.[5]

PRACTICAL AND HERBAL USES

Common vetch (*vicia sativa*) was originally brought to these islands by early farmers as fodder for livestock, and has since naturalised itself everywhere.[6] The tuberous roots of bitter vetch or 'heath-pea' were dried and chewed by Scottish highlanders to give a better relish to their whiskey; and it was believed by them that eating the roots of bitter vetch enabled them to repel hunger and thirst for a long time.[7] Natives of the Scottish island of Mull also used to chew them to prevent drunkenness before a drinking bout. In County Donegal, bitter vetch was used to make a drink for easing stomach ache.[8] The roots of restharrow, despite their toughness, were also widely eaten by country people, and when young have the flavour of liquorice – hence the name liquorice-root.[9] Kidney vetch (*Anthyllis vulneraria*) was known in traditional medicine throughout Europe as a vulnerary – that is, it was used to heal wounds. According to the Irish herbalist Threkeld it was sold for this purpose in eighteenth-century Ireland under the name 'stanch', probably so named for its role in stanching (or staunching) blood flow. In County Wicklow a decoction of the roots of vetch was used as a rub for backache, though the cure does not specify which species of vetch is concerned.[10] Vetches are members of the pea family, the *Fabaceae*.

Similar Plants
Ribbed Melilot – *Crúibín Cait* – *Melilotus officinalis*[11]
ALTERNATIVE NAMES: (E) King's Clover, King's Crown. (I) *Each-sheamair*
Melilot gets its name from *mel* (honey) and *lotus* (meaning honey lotus), on account of its sweet-smelling flowers being a favourite of bees. The names 'king's clover' and 'king's crown' derive from *corona regis*, an older Latin name of medieval apothecaries, because the recemes of yellow bloom suggest the spikes of a king's crown. In traditional medicine it was much recommended for digestive troubles and eye complaints. Ribbed melilot is a member of the pea family, the *Fabaceae*.

Common Bird's Foot Trefoil – *Crobh Éin* – *Lotus corniculatus*[12]
Alternative Names: (E) Claver (Ulster), God-Almighty's-thumb-and-fingers, Lady's-boots, Lady's-shoes-and-stockings, Lady's-slippers, No Blame
Bird's foot trefoil gets its name from its black seed pods which resemble a bird's claws. Other names like 'lady's-boots' and lady's-slippers' refer instead to the yellow, orange and red flowers. In Ireland children called the plant 'no blame' and would gather it on the way to school in the belief that possession of it would save them from punishment. Common bird's foot trefoil is a member of the pea family, the *Fabaceae*.

Common Fumitory – *Camán Searraigh Díge* – *Fumaria officinalis*[13]
Common Ramping-Fumitory – *Camán Searraigh Balla* – *Fumaria muralis*
White Ramping-Fumitory – *Camán Searraigh Bán* – *Fumaria capreolata*
ALTERNATIVE NAMES FOR FUMITORY: (E) Capnos, Earthsmoke, Foal's Favourite. (I) *Deatach Talún, Gidiriam, Giodairiam*
The name fumitory comes from the Latin *fumus terrae,* 'smoke of the earth'. It was called this because the ancient Greeks had earlier called it *kapnos* or 'smoke' in the belief that it caused the eyes to weep as smoke does. There seems to be some basis for this, because the juice of the plant does indeed make the eyes weep, and the roots of fumitory are said to smell strongly of nitric acid when they are first pulled up. The smoke from fumitory was also said by the ancients to have the power to expel evil spirits. In England fumitory was mixed with milk or water and used for clearing the complexion of spots and blemishes. In Ireland in County Cavan it was burnt and the smoke inhaled as a cure for stomach trouble. The name 'foal's favourite' seems to derive from the fact that it was given to foals to cure them of worms. Fumitory gives its name to the fumitory family, the *Fumariaceae.*

Fungi – Fungais

Fungi

☿   Ruled by the planet Mercury in traditional herbal medicine

♈   Associated with the zodiac sign Aries

SPECIES NAMES:
Mushroom – *Beacán* – *Hymenomycetes*
ALTERNATIVE NAMES: (E) Backawn Barragh, Paddocksteel (Ulster), Musheroon (Ulster), Slob (Fin). (I) *Bocán, Bolg Buachaill, Cupán Drúchta, Fás Aon Oíche, Muisiriún*

Field Mushroom – *Beacán Goirt– Agaricus campestris*

Fairy Ring Mushroom – *Beacán Fáinne Sí – Marasmius oreades*
ALTERNATIVE NAME: Fairy Ring Champignon

Jelly Ear – *Cluas Ghlóthaí – Auricularia auricula-judae*
ALTERNATIVE NAMES: Ear Fungus, Jew's Ear

Toadstool – *Beacán Bearaigh – Hymenomycetes*
ALTERNATIVE NAMES: (E) Pookapyle, Pookaun. Ulster names for toad-stool include: Dog's Mushroom, Dogstool, Paddocksteel, Paddy Hat, Puddock (US), Puddocksteel, Puddockstool, Pudyach (US). (I) *Bacán Bearaigh, Púcán Beireach, Púca Peill*

Fly Agaric – *Agairg Cuileoige – Amanita muscaria*

Magic Mushroom – *Muisiriún Mearbhaill – Psilocybe semilanceata*
ALTERNATIVE NAMES: (E) Liberty Cap

Giant Puff-Ball – *Caise an Phúca – Calvatia gigantea*
Puff-Ball – *Bolgan Béice – Lycoperdon*

ALTERNATIVE NAMES FOR PUFFBALLS: (E) Blindball (Meath), Buck Mushroom, Bull-fists, Bull's-fart, Dusty Mushroom, Fuzzball. (I) *Balbhán Béice, Bolg(án) Loscainn, Bolg(án) Séidte, Caochóg, Mún Capaill*

Stinkhorn Fungus – *Adharc an Phúca* – *Phallus impudicus*
ALTERNATIVE NAMES: (E) Witch's Egg (I) *Cosa Púca*

FOLK BELIEFS AND CUSTOMS
Autumn is the time when the majority of fungi are most prominent,
when their fruiting bodies appear above ground or from wood,
mainly in the form of what are commonly called mushrooms and
toadstools. There is no real botanical distinction between toadstools

and mushrooms, as both consist of species of the class *Hymenomycetes* of fungi. In practice, the distinction usually made is that if it is edible, it is a mushroom and if it is poisonous, it is a toadstool. This is useful as far as it goes, but there is no simple way to tell by appearance what is good to eat and what is not, and for the untrained it is impossible. Attempting to eat any wild fungus therefore without the proper knowledge is very unwise. In Britain and Ireland the only wild fungus generally eaten is the field mushroom, (*Agaricus campestris*), and this species is what people in these islands usually have in mind when they think of mushrooms.

In Ireland mushrooms were associated with the fairies, especially the leprechaun or fairy shoemaker.[1] The leprechaun was often said to be glimpsed flitting through woodland, or sitting on a mushroom or toadstool smoking his pipe. One folktale relates how a farmer once saw a leprechaun making a pair of shoes under a huge mushroom in his field. The farmer grabbed the leprechaun and demanded to know where the Danes (or Vikings) had hidden their gold. When it would not tell, he imprisoned the leprechaun in a trunk. Far from it getting him the gold, this act only brought the farmer bad luck, as thieves stole the money that he had himself hidden. In Scotland mushrooms were also linked to the fairies, and they were said to use them as tables for their feasts.[2] Indeed, the Scots Gaelic name for a mushroom, *bocán*, also meant a sprite or hobgoblin. In Ireland a curious belief about mushrooms held that they never grow any further after they have been seen by a person. For example, in County Clare, it was said that if you see a button mushroom you should pick it as 'it will never grow anymore once it is looked at'.[3]

One of the notable features of many fungi is their habit of forming ever larger rings as they grow outwards, rather like the way the trunk of a tree expands every year. The most prominent of these ring-forming mushrooms is the fairy ring mushroom (*Marasmius oreades*), which is noticed more often by people because it grows on close cropped turf or on lawns. *Marasmius* is actually good to eat, but there are a number of very similar look-alikes which are deadly poisonous, so it is best left alone. A widespread belief in Britain and Ireland was that the fairy rings were used by the fairies to dance in, especially in the moonlight.[4] In Ireland it was said that it was safe to walk through them, but unlucky to run or walk around them, as that was the path that the fairies themselves took. In

Scotland it was considered unlucky to sleep in them, or to be found in them after sunset. Indeed, it was considered unlucky to even step into the circle of the ring. In Scotland it was also believed that no one should plough up a fairy ring, or allow livestock to damage or pollute it, on pain of death. In Cornwall it was believed to be bad luck to pick a toadstool from a fairy ring, as to do so would bring death to the person's house. However, in parts of England a fairy ring was considered a lucky place in which to make a wish.

Another very common fungus is the jelly ear (*Auricularia auricula-judae*) which grows in clusters of brown, ear-like folds on dead wood; usually that of elder trees, and sometimes also of beech and sycamore. *Auricularia* is traditionally called 'Jew's ear', because the elder was the tree that Judas was said to have hanged himself on after betraying Jesus, and the fungus was said to have grown on it ever since.[5] Most authorities stick with the traditional name, but others are more conscious of its anti-semitic overtones and use the rather dull 'ear fungus'. As *Auricularia* is a member of a group called the 'jelly fungi', and the description fits its appearance well, the name 'jelly ear' would seem the most appropriate name.

Toadstools feature in one Irish folktale, when a woman enters a fairy fort and is shown various strange sights by the fairy king, including a room full of blindfolded young children sitting on 'pookauns', or toadstools. The king explains that these are the souls of unbaptised infants, who are believed 'to go into naught'.[6] In European folklore the most famous toadstool is undoubtedly the fly agaric (*Amanita muscaria*), with its distinctive red cap flecked with white dots.[7] This is the toadstool depicted in countless children's books and illustrations, usually with an elf, leprechaun (or toad) sitting on top. Fly agaric is notorious for its hallucinogenic properties and related symptoms of sickness and diarrhoea, and for this reason is treated as poisonous by most authorities. However, it is believed to have been used by medieval witches in their potions, and may be the original 'toadstool', as many older European names link it to the toad. It was also used in Siberia for many centuries as an inebriant, where the birch groves that it favours are common. So powerful was it that not only was the toadstool itself consumed, but the urine from a person who had consumed it was also drunk for its inebriating effect! In some languages even today the term for getting drunk literally means 'becoming bemushroomed', and it is said the phrase 'to get pissed' comes from this curious custom.

Another species that has acquired notoriety in recent times is the magic mushroom (*Psilocybe semilanceata*), known for its hallucinogenic properties, which can lead to psychoses, flashbacks and blackouts.[8] Closely related species have been used in Central America among the Aztecs and Mayas since ancient times, but their use seems to have been adopted in Britain and Ireland only since the 1960s. The possession or use of magic mushrooms is illegal in Britain, and has recently also been made illegal in Ireland.

Puffballs and stinkhorns are in another class of fungi to mushrooms and toadstools. Puffballs are so called because they are sphere-shaped and expel their spores from the top in a noticable cloud.[9] The most distinctive of the puffballs is the giant puffball (*Calvatia gigantea*), which can reach a width of 75cm, about the size of a large football. In Scotland it was believed that the spores of puffballs were dirty and could cause blindness. This has some basis in fact, as the tiny, dry spores are very irritating if they get into the eye. A Scottish folktale features one of the smaller species of puffball (*lycoperdon*). The tale relates how a boy called Robin Óg acquired a set of bagpipes from the fairies. When he got home, however, the fairy bagpipe had turned into a puffball and a crumpled fragment of willow reed.

The stinkhorn fungus (*Phallus impudicus*) is one of the most distinctive native fungi of Europe, on account of its phallic shape and smell of sewage (which has the purpose of attracting flies for pollination).[10] In Germany hunters called the stinkhorn *hirschbrunst* – 'deer lust' – because they believed that it grew where stags had rutted, and powdered stinkhorn was used as an aphrodisiac in France and Germany. In Devon in England stinkhorn was called 'snake-comb', in the belief that snakes emerged from it, like bees from a honeycomb. This was said to explain the smell, and children were warned away from it for fear of being 'stung' by the snakes. Before it fully emerges, stinkhorn forms round, white globes known as 'witches' eggs', which were traditionally eaten in many parts of Europe.

Legends and Mythology

It is believed by some scholars that the devotees of Dionysus, the Greek god of wine, consumed fly agaric as part of their orgiastic revelries in his honour. The Greeks believed that all mushrooms and toadstools were engendered by lightning, rather than sprung from seed like plants.[11] In Ireland, puffballs appear several times in myth.[12] In the legend of the *Táin Bó Cuailgne* or 'The Cattle Raid of Cooley', the children of Cailidín conjure up an enchanted army of warriors from 'shaggy, sharp, downy thistles, and light-topped puffballs, and fluttering withered leaves of the wood'. In the tale 'The Intoxication of the Ulaid', a champion of the Ulaid or Ulstermen called Úanchend Arritech dispatches 77 of his enemies, overthrowing them 'as lightly and swiftly as he would have dealt with puffballs'. The eighth-century text 'Cormac's Glossary' also gives the origin of the Irish name for puffball – *bolg belchi* – as coming from *bél cheo* meaning 'mouth vapour', in a reference to the cloud of spores it produces. In the Welsh tale 'Math son of Mathonwy', the magician Gwydyon conjures twelve shields out of toadstools as part of a present for his rival Lord Pryderi, in order to trick him into giving him some valuable pigs that he desired.[13]

PRACTICAL AND HERBAL USES

In both Britain and Ireland the field mushroom is the only fungus that is regularly eaten on a wide scale, and it is safe to eat both cooked and raw. In Ireland the jelly ear fungus was used in the north-western part of the midlands, where it was boiled in milk as a cure for jaundice.[14] The fly agaric gets its name because it was used throughout Europe to kill flies and other insects. The toadstool was steeped in sugar and water to attract the flies, who would then ingest its poison, and so die.[15] Throughout Europe the spores of puffballs have been used in traditional medicine as a very effective way of stopping all but the most profuse forms of bleeding.[16] Country surgeons and many farmers and workmen would stockpile supplies of puffballs in anticipation of accidents. In Ireland the spores of puffball were used in this way and were considered a very suitable emergency dressing. Indeed, puffball spores were also used in Ireland on horses as well as people. The giant puffball was often eaten as a delicacy, and was also sometimes set alight to smoke out bees from their honey.[17] Fungi form a separate 'kingdom' of their own, and in fact are more similar to animals than to true plants in that they must rely on taking in food from an outside source rather than manufacturing it themselves as plants do. Mushrooms and toadstools belong to the class of fungi called *Hymenomycetes*, while puffballs and stinkhorns belong to the class *Gasteromycetes*.

Lords-and-Ladies – Cluas Chaoin

Arum Maculatum

♂ Ruled by the planet Mars in traditional herbal medicine

♈ Associated with the zodiac sign Aries

SPECIES NAME: As above
Alternative names: (E) Adam-and-Eve, Aron, Arum Lily, Arun, Babe-in-a-cradle, Clovas-a-gachir (Laois), Cuckoo Pint, Dog's-spear, Jack-in-the-box (Ulster), Wake Robin. (I) *Bod Gadhair, Bod Géar, Boidín Geimhridh, Cluas an Ghabhair, Cluas Caicín, Gaoicín Cúthaigh, Geathar*

FOLK BELIEFS AND CUSTOMS
Lords-and-ladies, arum lily or cuckoo pint, is one of the most distinctive sights in Irish woodlands in early summer, with its hooded spathe containing the purple spadix within.[1] In European folklore the phallic spadix was taken to be a sign that lords-and-ladies had powers as an aphrodisiac. Thus in an English play *Loves Metamorphosis* written in 1601 by John Lyly, one of the characters remarks: 'They have eaten so much wake robin, that they cannot sleep for love.' In many parts of England it was said that snakes ate the berries of lords-and-ladies, but this story may have been spread to keep children from eating the bright red berries which are poisonous. In north Wales it was said that the spots on the leaves were Christ's blood, which fell on the plant as it grew at the foot of the cross at Calvary.

LEGENDS AND MYTHOLOGY
Lords-and-ladies appears in the legend *Buile Suibhne* or 'Sweeney Astray'.[2] *Suibhne Geilt* or 'Mad Sweeney' was a County Antrim king who lost his wits and fled from society to live in the wilderness. Among the wild plants he praises is lords-and-ladies: '*álainn lí do ghlas ngeadhair/a ghlas uaine fhoithreamhail*' – 'lovely the colour of the green cuckoo pint/ its verdant forest green'. According to the Greek philospher Aristotle, bears coming out of hibernation would restore their strength by eating lords-and-ladies as soon as they emerged.[3]

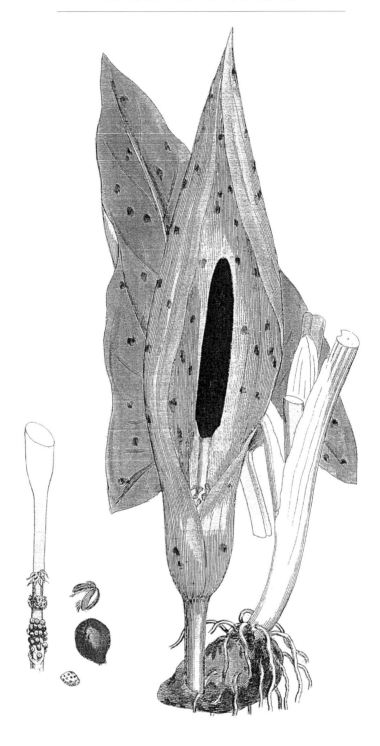

Practical and Herbal Uses

In sixteenth-century England a starch made from lords-and-ladies was used by the aristocracy to keep their elaborate ruffs stiff.[4] The roots of lords-and-ladies have been used as a cure for consumption, and were mixed with cows' milk to provide a remedy for freckles, spots and blemishes of the skin.[5] In Ireland the roots were used in County Offaly to cure children of worms. Lords-and-ladies is a member of the arum family, the *Araceae*.

Spurge – Spuirse

Euphorbia

☿   Ruled by the planet Mercury in traditional herbal medicine

SPECIES NAMES:
Sun Spurge – *Lus na bhFaithní* – *Euphorbia helioscopia*
ALTERNATIVE NAMES: (E) Devil's Churnstaff, Seven Sisters (from the seven branches of the stem), Wartweed. (I) *Lus an Leasaidh*

Irish Spurge – *Bainne Caoin* – *Euphorbia hyberna*
Alternative names: (E) Knot-rooted Spurge, Makinboy, Mountain Spurge, Yellow-root Plant. (I) *Bainne Cian, Bainne Cín Éan, Bainne na nÉan, Bainnicín, Buí na Cian, Buí na nIníon, Buinneacháin, Buinnicín, Glasair Léana, Lasair Léana, Meacan Buí an tSléibhe*

Wood Spurge – *Lus Oilealla* – *Euphorbia amygdaloides*
ALTERNATIVE NAMES: (E) Mare's-tail

ALTERNATIVE NAMES FOR SPURGE: (E) Milkweed. (I) *Buí na mBáb, Spuirse, Spursa*

FOLK BELIEFS AND CUSTOMS
In Irish folk belief sun spurge (*Euphorbia helioscopia*) was said to be good to use when rescuing a woman from fairy abduction. In order for its power to be effective, it was held that sun spurge should be gathered at a particular time of the sun and moon in the month of August.[1]

PRACTICAL AND HERBAL USES
In Britain and Ireland the milky sap from all species of spurges were universally considered a remedy for removing warts and other skin blemishes.[2] The English name 'spurge' derives from the Latin *expurgare* – 'to purge', and the Irish name *buinneachán* (and its variations) has much the same meaning, and all the spurges were considered in traditional medicine to be effective purgatives.[3] For this reason, in Ireland Irish spurge was considered a good cure for diarrhoea. In parts of Counties Cork and Kerry, the sap from Irish spurge was put

into rivers as a quick way to catch fish by poisoning them so they would float up to the surface.[4] Spurges give their name to the spurge family, the *Euphorbiaceae*.

Crane's-Bill – Crobh

Geranium

 Ruled by the planet Venus in traditional herbal medicine

SPECIES NAMES:

Herb-Robert – *Ruithéal Rí* – *Geranium robertianum*[1]
ALTERNATIVE NAMES: (E) Dog's-toe (Donegal), Stinking Crane's-bill, Stinking Robert (Donegal). (I) *Crobh Dearg, Crólus Dearg, Eireaball Rí*

Meadow Crane's-Bill – *Crobh Gorm* – *Geranium pratense*
ALTERNATIVE NAMES: (E) Flower-of-Dunluce (Antrim) (I) *Crólus Gorm*

FOLK BELIEFS AND CUSTOMS

There are several different theories as to how herb-robert got its name. One explanation is that Robert is a corruption of the Latin word *ruber* meaning red, in a reference to its stems and leaves which turn fiery red in autumn. Another explanation is that it is named after St Robert, founder of the Cistercian order of monks, who was said to have used it extensively for medicinal purposes. Yet another theory states that the name is due to a link between herb-robert and the mischevious goblin 'Robin Goodfellow' of English folklore and his German equivalent Knecht Rubrecht (the German name for Herb Robert is *Ruprechtskraut*). Many English local names for herb-robert include the name Robin (which is a dimunitive of Robert), like 'Robin Hood', 'Robin Redbreast' and 'Red Robin', so the plant may also have been linked to the robin, a bird considered powerful in folklore on account of its fiery red breast.

PRACTICAL AND HERBAL USES

In Ireland herb-robert was widely used to staunch bleeding, especially in eastern parts of the country. Herb-robert was also used in Irish folk medicine to cure kidney problems, and to ease sore throats and coughs. In Ireland herb-robert was also extensively used as a cure for a disease of livestock called red-water fever. Crane's-bills give their name to the Crane's-bill family, the *Geraniaceae*.

Butterbur – Gallán Mór

Petasites Hybridus

☉   Ruled by the sun in traditional herbal medicine

SPECIES NAMES: As above[1]
ALTERNATIVE NAMES: (E) Gallon, Pestilence-wort. (I) *Meacan an Phobóil*

LEGENDS AND MYTHOLOGY
The Latin name *Petasites* derives from the Greek word *petasos*, meaning the felt hat worn by Greek shepherds to keep off the sun, which the large leaves of butterbur were said to resemble. Indeed, the leaves themselves were often used for this purpose, and Greek representations of Mercury, the messenger of the gods, show him wearing a hat of butterbur leaves as he went about his business.

PRACTICAL AND HERBAL USES
The name 'butterbur' derives from the habit of using the big leaves to wrap butter in during hot weather before the days of refrigeration. In traditional medicine, the bitter resinous root of butterbur meant it was used to induce sweat, causing it to be used to help 'break' plagues and fevers – hence the name 'pestilence wort'. Butterbur was little used in Irish folk medicine, appearing only in Counties Mayo and Limerick as a treatment for rheumatism. Butterbur is a member of the daisy family, the *Asteraceae*.

Wild Plants and the Zodiac

European herbalism since ancient times has been influenced by astrology, and the linking of herbs and plants to different planets and signs of the zodiac. Despite this, it might be thought by some that astrology was unknown or alien to the Celts, but the evidence is to the contrary.[1] The Roman writer Flavius Magnus Aurelius Cassidorus wrote in the sixth century about a Celtic tribe, the Getae, as knowing 'the course of the twelve signs of the zodiac, and of the planets passing through them and of the whole of astronomy' (there was no distinction between astronomy and astrology until modern science began to take hold). In Ireland the tenth-century Christian prayerbook *Saltair na Rann* or 'Psalter of Quatrains' states clearly that every educated Irish person should know the signs of the zodiac, in their correct order, and the correct month and day when the sun enters each sign. Indeed, St Colmcille is stated in a contemporary reference to have cast a horoscope to determine the best time for his foster son to commence his education! As we have seen, Irish herbalists were always in touch with the European tradition, so there is no doubt that they too would have been familiar with astrology and its link to herbalism.

Nowadays, the main surviving legacy of the tradition of astrological herbalism derives from the work written by the English herbalist Nicholas Culpeper in the early seventeenth century. Culpeper's *Complete Herbal* lists over 300 herbs and plants, and links the vast majority of them with different planets, and even signs of the zodiac. Even though it was written nearly 400 years ago, the book is still popular and in print today. The herbal preserves the precepts of medieval herbalism regarding the properties of each planet, and by extension the plants that were said to be 'ruled' by them. There were seven planets known to ancient astrologers (the sun and moon were included as planets for their purposes); and the different plants that were said to be ruled by them shared their characteristics as follows:

☉ SUN: Plants were said to be ruled by the sun if they were hot and dry, and could strengthen the heart and raise the vital spirits. These plants were thus considered especially useful for heart complaints, and as a cure for melancholy and depression. As the Sun was held to have a brightening and clearing effect, it also ruled plants that were good for curing eye complaints. The Sun is the ruler of the zodiac sign Leo.

☽ MOON: Plants ruled by the moon were believed to be cold and moist in their action. They were particularly used for stomach complaints and restoring digestion, and for cooling inflammation. Plants ruled by the Moon were also believed to be good for curing complaints of the breasts and womb. The Moon is the ruler of the zodiac sign Cancer.

☿ MERCURY: Mercury ruled plants that were believed to be cold and dry in nature, and good for afflictions of the brain, chest and lungs. Such plants were believed to strengthen the brain, and were particularly used for complaints such as giddiness, frenzy and fainting. Plants ruled by Mercury were also thought to be good at cleansing the chest and lungs of unwanted humours, phlegm and wind. Mercury is the ruler of the zodiac signs Gemini and Virgo.

♀ VENUS: Plants that were hot and moist, but also moderating in effect, were said to be ruled by Venus. Such plants were said to be good at cooling inflammations, and providing gentle cleansing action to wounds and ulcers. Sweet smelling and aromatic plants were usually said to be ruled by Venus. Plants ruled by Venus were also said to cure complaints of the kidneys and veins; and any plants that acted as aphrodisiacs. Venus is the ruler of the zodiac signs Taurus and Libra.

♂ MARS: Mars ruled plants that were hot and dry in their action, and also biting and choleric in nature. Usually plants that were peppery or hot in taste, or pungent in some way, were said to be ruled by Mars. Plants ruled by Mars were believed to be particularly good for curing muscular and uro-genital complaints. Mars is the traditional ruler of the zodiac signs Aries and Scorpio.

♃ JUPITER: Plants that were hot and moist and strengthening in effect were said to be ruled by Jupiter. Such plants were believed to be warming and relaxing in action, particularly for liver complaints. Plants ruled by Jupiter were also said to be especially good at cleansing the blood and cooling fevers. Jupiter is the traditional ruler of the zodiac signs Sagittarius and Pisces.

♄ SATURN: Plants that were cool and dry and binding in effect were believed to be ruled by Saturn. Such plants were particularly favoured for complaints involving the gall-bladder, spleen, skin, teeth and bones. Saturn is the traditional ruler of the zodiac signs Capricorn and Aquarius.

Although the idea of linking herbalism with astrology has been shown since Culpeper's day to have no scientific basis, it has left behind a rich legacy which is part of the history and lore of herbalism. For this reason, it would be a pity to ignore this aspect of herbalism simply because it no longer has a place in modern medicine. It is worthwhile therefore to look at ways in which this tradition can bring us to a better appreciation of our native and naturalised wild plants and herbs. Nowadays the main legacy of astrological herbalism is the notion of linking plants and flowers to different signs of the zodiac, based on the planet said to rule both plant and zodiac sign. For example, if foxglove is ruled by the planet Venus, and the zodiac sign Taurus is also ruled by Venus, foxglove can therefore be linked to Taurus as a plant that in some way shares the traits of the Zodiac sign. This idea is popular in astrology today, but a perusal of astrology books will reveal that the plants and flowers they feature are often hopelessly exotic or vague, and that different books frequently contradict each other. It is clear there is no hard and fast tradition, and that many links were probably invented for tenuous reasons.

There is plenty of scope therefore to create a more solid scheme of linking plants with zodiac signs using the principles of medieval herbalism as a basis. What follows is a scheme where each sign of the zodiac has been linked to several native flowers and plants, using Culpeper's herbal as a guide. Occasionally, however, a link has been made for another reason. For example, forget-me-not has been linked to the zodiac sign Scorpio because the old name for the flower was 'Scorpion grass'. There is no requirement to believe in the validity of astrology to accept the scheme, nor is there any attempt to promote it. The rationale is simply to provide emblems for people that help them make an imaginative connection with their native flora, in a way that everyone can identify with, no matter what their background. In an age of ever-increasing alienation from nature, that is surely rationale enough.

ARIES

The assertive, energetic and competitive sign of Aries is linked to the planet Mars. The following plants are also linked to Mars and their attributes give them an affinity to the fire sign Aries: the **Buttercup** family, with their bright yellow flowers and biting, acrid juices reflect the optimism and directness of Aries. The buttercup family includes plants such as marsh marigold and lesser celandine; **Ramsons** or wild garlic is famous for its pungent aroma, strong flavour and healthy nourishing qualities. 'Ram's horns' is a local name for it in parts of England. **Lords-and-Ladies** or cuckoo-pint with its distinctive shape, is a well-known symbol of passionate love and fertility. Unlike the other plants, **Blackberry** is stated by Culpeper as being ruled by Venus in Aries, as it combines the sweetness of blackberries with the prickly thorns of Mars!

TAURUS

The calm, strong and sensuous sign of Taurus is ruled by the planet Venus. The following plants are also linked to Venus and their attributes give them an affinity to the earth sign Taurus: **Primrose**, with its links to May time and the protection of the house and livestock, coincide with the time when the sun is in the sign of Taurus the bull. The association of primrose with love also fits with the solid but passionate romance of Taurus. **Foxglove**, with its strengthening effect on the system, and **Mallow**, with its soothing qualities share these same traits with Taurus. **Lady's Mantle** was also regarded as a calming, gentle, but powerful herb, renowned for its ability to restore female beauty.

GEMINI

The versatile, adaptable and communicative sign of Gemini is ruled by the planet Mercury. The following plants are also linked to Mercury and their attributes give them an affinity to the air sign Gemini: **Clover**, or shamrock was renowned for its ability to bring luck and give its possesser special abilities, like second sight and the power never to be cheated. Trefoil or 'three leaved' is another name for clover, which suits Gemini, the third sign of the zodiac. **Fern** could also give special powers, like invisibility, to the person who collected its seeds, which fits the clever, trickster qualities of Gemini. **Bittersweet**, with its purple and yellow flowers, gets its name from the fact that it tastes first sweet and then bitter. This gives bittersweet a duality which it shares with the sign of Gemini, the twins. **Vetch**, or wild pea, with its pink or purple flowers, is said by Culpeper to be ruled by 'the moon in an airy figure', which includes Gemini as an air sign. The clambering, flexible tendrils and stems of vetch match well with the adaptable and fast-moving Gemini.

CANCER

The protective, nurturing and sensitive sign of Cancer is ruled by the Moon. The following plants are also linked to the Moon and their attributes give them an affinity to Cancer: **Yellow Iris** and **Water-lily** grow in or near rivers and wet places, which suits Cancer, a water sign. They are also both symbols of feminine beauty, like the moon itself. **Poppy** is used in medicine as a narcotic, to bring nurturing sleep and rest from pain to those who need it. **Daisy** is stated by Culpeper as being ruled by Venus in Cancer as it was traditionally used in medicine in soothing ointments for the breasts and other female parts, combining the calming aspects of Venus with lunar complaints. Ox-eye daisy is also known in England as 'moon-daisy' or 'moon-flower' on account of its round, white flowers.

LEO

The charismatic, confident and creative sign of Leo is ruled by the Sun. The following plants are also linked to the Sun and their attributes give them an affinity to the fire sign Leo: the cheerful and brightly coloured flowers, **St. John's Wort** and **Scarlet Pimpernel**, were valued for their medicinal usefulness in dispelling depression and bringing a positive outlook, just as the confident leadership sign of Leo is said to do. The bright yellow, sun-like **Corn Marigold** was considered good at dispelling fevers, and **Eyebright** was valued for removing dimness in eyesight and restoring brightness of vision.

Virgo

♍

The analytical, critical and methodical sign of Virgo is ruled by Mercury. The following plants are also linked to Mercury and their attributes give them an affinity to the earth sign Virgo: **Fairy Flax** with its delicate white flowers and cleansing properties suits the refined and hygienic Virgo. Cultivated flax is also ruled by Mercury. **Valerian** was valued in medicine for providing a tea which calmed nerves and soothed afflictions like palpitations and cramps, good for the highly strung sign of Virgo, while **Marjoram** was noted for its uses in providing a tea which eased indigestion, another health concern of the sign Virgo. **Bluebell** or hyacinth is not linked by Culpeper to any planet, but its beautiful, deep-blue drooping flowers mean that it has often been linked to the modest Virgo. Blue is the colour of the Virgin Mary and bluebells flower in May, the month dedicated to her.

Libra

♎

The charming, diplomatic and idealistic sign of Libra is ruled by the planet Venus. The following plants are also linked to Venus and their attributes give them an affinity to the air sign Libra: **Yarrow** and **Mint** are both aromatic and healing plants, often used in love charms; and the sweet-smelling beautiful **Violet** is itself an ancient symbol of love. **Orchid** too, has been used in folk medicine as a love potion. One tuber was supposed to provoke love, and the other hate, when given to the intended person, which links well with the two sides of the often wavering Libra.

Scorpio

♏

The intense, determined and passionate sign of Scorpio was traditionally ruled by the planet Mars. The following plants are also linked to Mars and their attributes give them an affinity to the water sign Scorpio: **Honeysuckle** with its beautiful flowers and heady fragrance reflects the passion of Scorpio, and the iron grip of the honeysuckle around its chosen host reflects the sign's determination.

Like a scorpion, **Nettle** has a sting, but only for those who do not grasp it firmly. **Gentian**, with its purple flowers, was used as a bitter but cleansing tonic. **Forget-me-not** is not linked by Culpeper to any planet, but its curling flowerheads gave it the older name of 'Scorpion-grass'. The newer name 'forget-me-not' also goes well with the steadfast nature of Scorpio.

SAGITTARIUS

The freedom-loving, broad-minded and optimistic sign of Sagittarius is ruled by the planet Jupiter. The following plants are also linked to Jupiter and their attributes give them an affinity to Sagittarius: **Mistletoe** is a symbol of love, romance and new beginnings, which suits the adventurous Sagittarius. The **Wild-rose**, which is a symbol of beauty and freedom, and the **Dandelion**, with its cheerful, sunny flowers and slightly irregular charm, both fit in with the frankness and devil-may-care attitude of the fire sign of Sagittarius. **Thistle**, with its spiny leaves, is also a suitable symbol of the forthright Sagittarius which will not tolerate any attempt to cramp its style!

CAPRICORN

The responsible, disciplined and ambitious sign of Capricorn is ruled by the planet Saturn. The following plants are also linked to Saturn and their attributes give them an affinity to Capricorn: **Ivy**, with its dark evergreen leaves, is a symbol of sobriety and fidelity, which reflects the attributes of Capricorn. **Hemlock**, although poisonous, is also a powerful drug when used responsibly, and **Tutsan** was famed for its skill at cooling inflammations and healing skin complaints. **Heather** is not linked by Culpeper to any plant, but its qualities of hardiness and resilience, thriving in the poorest soils, make it a suitable plant to link to the earth sign Capricorn.

AQUARIUS

The unconventional, intellectual and innnovative sign of Aquarius was traditionally ruled by the planet Saturn. The following plants are also linked to Saturn and their attributes give them an affinity to Aquarius: **Rushes** are known to grow near water and wells, and so are a suitable symbol for the water carrier Aquarius. **Pansy**, with its quirky flowers and associations of friendship, and **Mullein**, with its unusual furred, silver-grey leaves and tall spikes of yellow flowers, both have an affinity with the open-mindedness and unconventionality of this air sign Aquarius. The bright blue flowers of **Cornflower** match the electric blue colour of Aquarius.

PISCES

♓

The dreamy, idealistic and compassionate sign of Pisces was traditionally ruled by the planet Jupiter. The following plants are also linked to Jupiter and their attributes give them an affinity to Pisces: **Meadowsweet**, with its creamy white flowers and heavy scent, grows near streams and in damp places and was also known as 'Queen-of-the-meadow'. This gives it an affinity with the mysterious and dreamy Pisces, a water sign. **Houseleek**, the protector of hearth and home, and **Wood Avens** or 'Herb Bennet' with its power to repel all evil, reflect the caring, self-sacrificing qualities of Pisces. **Buckbean** or bogbean is not linked by Culpeper to any planet, but its beautiful, delicate white blossoms and habit of growing in bogs and water make it a suitable symbol for the sensitive water sign of Pisces.

Postscript: The Universal Potency of Plants

Throughout this book we have seen how plants are used in every area of our lives. Most of us are never very far from green and growing things, even in urban areas, and our lives would feel much poorer without them. In fact, plants are indispensable to our well being. They feed us and heal (or harm) us, provide us with shelter and clothing, and nourish our souls with their beauty and tranquillity. This is not only true of people in Ireland, of course, or even Europe. Plants are fundamental to all human beings, and around the world, wild plants and flowers are intimately bound up with local folklore and culture. Indeed, one of the striking things about the folklore of plants is how the same themes can be found in very different cultures across the globe.

One universal theme that appears time and again in the traditional uses of plants is the notion of sympathetic magic.[1] For example, among Brazilian Indian tribes at the mouth of the Amazon, a man wishing to increase his fertility would strike himself with the fruit of an aquatic plant called an aninga. This plant was believed to increase fertility because of the phallic shape of its fruit. Similarly, the ancient Egyptians believed that the kidney bean was sacred and should not be eaten, because the shape of the seeds bore a close resemblance to testicles. Plants could also be valued for other properties, like vigour or the colour of their flowers. In the Indonesian island of Celebes, it was thought by certain tribes that the plant Chinese Dragon's Blood (*Dracaena terminalis*) was effective in restoring strength to a person's soul if the affected person was beaten with some of its leaves on the crown of the head. The plant was thought to be potent for this purpose because it grows up again quickly after it has been lopped, and so has a strong soul itself. Among the Aztecs of Mexico the golden yellow sunflower was revered as a powerful symbol of the sun, and in their temples to the sun god, Aztec priestesses wore crowns of sunflowers and carried them about.

Flowers are also used in ceremonies on particular occasions or times of year.[2] For example, the fragrant blossoms of jasmine were

traditionally made by Hindus into neck garlands to welcome honoured guests, and are still used as offerings at ceremonies of the god
Vishnu. Marking the gathering of the first fruits or plants of the season with ceremonies was also very common. To give just one example, the Salish and Tinneh Indians of north-west America celebrated the first appearance of the succulent shoots of wild raspberry
with a solemn ceremony. Each member of the tribe ate a portion of
the shoots from a communal cooking pot after they had been
blessed by the presiding chief, and the spirit of the plants invoked.
Often plants were used in religious rites not out of symbolism but
because of their potent effects as mind-altering drugs. For example,
the mescaline cactus was used in religious ceremonies by Indians in
south-west America on account of the feelings of exaltation it produces in those who eat it.

Quite apart from their magical or tribal uses, plants and flowers
have also appeared as symbols of inspiration in religion and spiri-
tuality. For example, in Hindu philosophy the lotus blossom is used
for meditation on the subject of the awakening consciousness. The
lotus is a potent symbol of this process, growing from its roots
buried deep in the mud, reaching up with its stem through the
water, and finally emerging into the air and the bright light of day
as the beautiful flower. Similarly, in the Old Testament, the psalm
'The Song of Solomon' compares the beauty of flowers to the love of
God: 'I am the rose of Sharon, and the lily of the valleys. As the lily
among thorns, so is my love among the daughters.'

Plants and flowers have also provided inspiration to poets and
artists since the earliest times. One of the most popular themes is the
idea of flowers as emblems of youth's passing beauty. As the poet
Robert Herrick wrote in 'Counsel to Girls': 'Gather ye rose-buds
while ye may,/Old Time is still a-flying:/And this same flower that
smiles today,/To-morrow will be dying.' Many other poets have
been inspired by plants to muse on the mysteries of the universe.
One such was the American poet Walt Whitman, who declared in
his famous poem 'Song of Myself': 'I believe a leaf of grass is no less
than the journey-work of the stars.'

But we do not have to be great poets or botanists to appreciate
the value of wild plants and flowers. Even in this modern age, they
surround us in our parks and gardens, where they refresh us and
lift our spirits. At a fundamental level we all recognise that our lives
depend upon greenery and plants, not just in the mundane sense of

providing for our practical needs, but also in the deeper sense of affirming our connection to nature and other living things. This is the real source of our engagement with plants: the fact that even if we could somehow survive without them, our very souls and our humanity would still be immeasurably diminished.

Notes on Names

The standard English, Irish and Latin names of plants are taken from Scannell and Synnott's *Census Catalogue of the Flora of Ireland* (1987); and An Roinn Oideachas (Department of Education) *Ainmneacha Plandaí agus Ainmhithe* (1978).

Regarding the alternative names, it would be foolish to claim that the lists given in this work are exhaustive. Quite apart from written sources, it is likely that many names have not been recorded in print, and indeed some may never make it to the printed page. However, what can be said is that it is an attempt to provide a comprehensive (and sorely needed) overview of the subject. As such it provides, to the author's knowledge, the largest collection in a single work of plant names in Ireland in both English and Irish. As regards source references, to give a separate one for every individual plant name would be impossibly cumbersome. However, the sources for the vast majority of plant names are as follows:

NAMES IN ENGLISH: The main source by far for names in English is Grigson (1958), which lists an enormous number of local plant names throughout Great Britain and Ireland. The second main source ironically, is Dineen's *Irish-English Dictionary* (1927), which frequently gives a local name in English as the translation from the Irish. I have assumed that this means the English name was extant in Ireland; and this has provided invaluable corroboration for many of the names listed in Grigson, as well as giving an Irish provenance for many others listed by him in relation to Britain only. Other important sources are Scott (K'eogh) (1986), Threkeld (1727), Vickery (1995), Allen and Hatfield (2004) and Tóibín (1955). Other sources include Share (1997), Dolan (1998), Williams (1993), Todd (1990), O'Regan (1997), and Blount (1931). Sources for words in the dialects of Fingal, County Dublin and Forth and Bargy, County Wexford, and for Ulster Scots, are listed below.

Regarding local plant names in English in Ireland, the undeniable point is made that many of them derive from the Irish language. As such, some may object to these names being listed as

English language names. There is no doubt that names such as 'boholawn' (ragwort), or 'pookapyle' (toadstool) are essentially of the same origin as their Irish language counterparts. Other names have been altered by their passage into English, however. 'Espibawn' (Ox-eye Daisy) is derived from the Irish *easpagán*, but it has changed its form. To exclude some names because they are deemed too close to the original Irish, while including others that have undergone change, would be a subjective and inevitably arbitrary exercise. In general, therefore, the rule of thumb followed is that a name is included if it has survived long enough into English to be recorded as a name in its own right. In any case, the very fact that a name has survived in this way is itself worth recording.

NAMES IN IRISH: The main source by far is Dinneen (1927). Also important are Ó Dónaill (1977) and Williams (1993). Some of the plant names Dinneen gives cannot be identified because he gives no specific English name, only a general description. In a few of these cases, where a particular plant seems the most likely candidate, I have included it with a question mark.

LOCATIONS: Locations for the source of a plant name (where known) are given in brackets after the name, and are usually of the county or province concerned. By 'source' is meant only the place where the plant name was collected. There is little doubt that many of the names have a wider usage than what has been recorded. The following abbreviations also occur:

FIN: Fingal in north County Dublin. Names are taken from Archer (1975).

FB: Forth and Bargy in south County Wexford. Names are taken from Dolan and Ó Muirithe (1996).

US: Ulster Scots (chiefly County Antrim). Names are taken from Fenton (1995). Ulster Scots' names have been treated separately from Ulster names in general, though there is no doubt of a large overlap.

TC: Travellers' Cant or Shelta. A few names have been recorded by Macalister (1937).

References

Aspects of Plant Folklore

1. D. Ó hÓgáin, *Myth, Legend and Romance – An Encyclopedia of the Irish Folk Tradition* (New York, 1991), pp. 156-7; Fleetwood, J., *The History of Medicine in Ireland* (Dublin 1983) p. 3; Lady A. Gregory, *Complete Irish Mythology* (London, 1994) pp. 49-50.

2. Fleetwood, op. cit., p. 5.

3. F. Kelly, *Early Irish Farming* (Dublin, 1997) p. 250, p. 259; G. Grigson, *The Englishman's Flora* (Oxford, 1996) p. 95.

4. Fleetwood, op. cit., pp. 12-13.

5. M. Moloney, *Luibh-sheanchus – Irish Ethno-botany* (Dublin, 1919) pp. 58-9; P. Beresford Ellis, *Dictionary of Celtic Mythology* (London 1992) p. 36.

6. W. Wulff, *Rosa Anglica by John of Gaddesden* (London, 1929) p. xii-xv.

7. S. Ó Súilleabháin, *A Handbook of Irish Folklore* (Detroit, 1970) p. 284; P. O'Regan, *Healing Herbs in Ireland* (Dublin, 1997) pp. 6-7.

8. P. O'Farrell, *Irish Folk Cures* (Dublin, 2004) p. 116.

9. Ibid., p. 118, p. 45.

10. F. Kelly, 'The Old Irish Tree List' *Celtica Vol XI* (Dublin, 1976) pp. 107-125.

11. Kelly, op. cit. (1997), p. 250, pp. 257-8, p. 304; Fleetwood, op. cit., p. 8.

12. Kelly, op. cit. (1997), pp. 306-7, p. 309.

13. Ibid (1997), p. 305, p. 264.

14. J.G. Frazer, *The Golden Bough* (London, 1987) pp. 11-12; R. Vickery, *A Dictionary of Plant Lore* (Oxford, 1995) p. 117, p. 407.

15. D. Allen, D. & G. Hatfield, *Medicinal Plants in Folk Tradition* (Oregon, 2004) p. 85; G. Grigson, op. cit., p. 106, p. 156, Lady A. Gregory, *Visions & Beliefs in the West of Ireland* (Toronto, 1970) p. 149; Lady Wilde, *Irish Cures, Mystic Charms and Superstitions* (New York, 1991) p. 99.

16. Allen & Hatfield, op. cit. p. 75.

17. Vickery, op. cit. pp. 109-10.

18. Sir Thomas Innes, *The Scottish Tartans* (Stirling, 1963) pp. 5-6; G. Murphy, *Duanaire Finn Part II* (London, 1933) p. 355; Gregory, op. cit. (1994) p. 184.

19. Vickery, op. cit., p. 288.

20. Ibid, pp. 210-11.

21. D. Flanagan, & L. Flanagan, *Irish Place Names* (Dublin, 1994); N. Williams, *Díolaim Luibheanna* (Dublin, 1993).

Mistletoe

1. Vickery, op. cit., pp. 241-2; I. Opie, & M. Tatum, *A Dictionary of Superstitions* (Oxford, 1989) p. 255; P. Waring, *A Dictionary of Omens and Superstitions* (London, 1978) p. 154; Grigson, op. cit., p. 202.
2. K. Danaher, *The Year in Ireland – Irish Calender Customs* (Cork, 1972) p. 234, 259.
3. Opie & Tatum, op. cit., p. 254; Vickery, op. cit., pp. 242-3; Grigson, op. cit. p. 202.
4. R. Mabey, *Flora Brittanica* (London, 1996) p. 239.
5. Opie & Tatum, op. cit., pp 253-4; Vickery, op. cit., p. 243; Mabey, op. cit., p. 239; Frazer, op. cit., p. 663.
6. M. Grieve, *A Modern Herbal* (London, 1931) p. 547.
7. A. Le Braz, *The Night of Fires & Other Breton Studies* (London, 1912) p. 107.
8. A.W. Wade Evans, *Welsh Medieval Law* (Oxford, 1909) p. 248; Frazer, op. cit., 663.
9. M. McNeill, *The Silver Bough Vol I* (Glasgow, 1957) pp. 77-8.
10. R. Lamont Brown, *A Book of Superstitions* (Devon, 1970) p. 51.
11. T.D. Kendrick, *The Druids* (London, 1927) p. 124.
12. Grigson, op. cit., p. 201.
13. Grieve, op. cit., p. 548; J.A. McCullough, *The Religion of the Ancient Celts* (Edinburgh, 1911) p. 202.
14. Kendrick, op. cit., p. 124.
15. K. Crossley Holland, *The Penguin Book of Norse Myths* (London, 1980) pp. 152-4; Frazer, op. cit., pp. 658-67.
16. R. Graves, *The White Goddess* (London, 1961) p. 125.
17. Allen & Hatfield, op. cit., p. 167.
18. Grieve, op. cit., p. 548.

Rushes

1. Danaher, op. cit. pp. 16-23.
2. Danaher, op. cit., p. 15, p. 37, p. 225; P. O'Farrell, *Irish Customs* (Dublin, 2004) p. 17; Ó Súilleabháin, op. cit. (1970) p. 397.
3. Frazer, op. cit., pp. 134-5.
4. M. Mac Neill, *The Festival of Lughnasa* (Oxford, 1962) p. 353.
5. P.S. Dinneen, *Foclóir Gaedhilge agus Béarla* (Dublin, 1927) p. 678; Vickery, op. cit., pp. 325-6.
6. Ó Súilleabháin, op. cit. (1970) p. 288; W. Wilde, *Irish Popular Superstitions* (Dublin, 1979) p. 213; Gregory, op. cit. (1970) p. 241; Waring, op. cit., p. 193; T. Gwynn Jones, *Welsh Folklore and Custom* (London, 1930) p. 54; D.A. Mackenzie, *Scottish Folklore and Folk Life* (Edinburgh, 1935) p. 137; A.A. McGregor, *The Peat Fire Flame* (Edinburgh, 1937) p. 75.
7. Vickery, op. cit., p. 324.

8. Gregory, op. cit. (1994), p. 441, p. 430, p. 343; J. Gantz, *The Mabinogion* (London, 1976), p. 193.

9. Gregory, op. cit. (1994) p. 221, p. 236, p. 472-3.

10. E. Gwynn, *The Metrical Dindshenchus*, (Dublin, 1903, 1906, 1913, 1924, 1935), pp. 339-47; W. Stokes, *Tripartite Life of St Patrick* (London, 1887) p. 84; W. Stokes, *Lives of the Saints from the Book of Lismore* (Oxford, 1890) p. 330.

11. Wilde, op. cit. (1979) p. 134.

12. Moloney, op. cit., p. 44; R. Mabey, *Plants with a Purpose* (London, 1977) p. 132, 134-5; Ó Súilleabháin, op. cit. (1970) p. 288.

13. Kelly op. cit., (1976) p. 123.

14. Allen & Hatfield, op. cit. p. 332.

15. Ó Súilleabháin, op. cit. (1970) p. 288.

16. Allen & Hatfield, op. cit., p. 325; Innes, op. cit., p. 47, 71; Mabey, op. cit. (1977) p. 129.

17. A. Carmichael, *Carmina Gadelica Vol. II* (Edinburgh, 1928) p. 132; Mabey, op. cit. (1977) p. 128.

18. Ó Súilleabháin, op. cit. (1970) p. 288.

Shamrock/Clover

1. Danaher, op. cit., p. 58.

2. Ibid, p. 64.

3. C. Nelson, *Shamrock: Botany and History of an Irish Myth* (Kilkenny / Aberystwyth, 1991) p. 44.

4. Danaher, op. cit., pp. 64-5.

5. Wilde, op. cit. (1991) p. 55; Ó Súilleabháin, op. cit. (1970) p. 397; S. Ó Cróinín, *Seanchas ó Cairpre* (Dublin, 1985) p. 416.

6. S. O'Sullivan, *Legends from Ireland* (London, 1977), pp. 86-7.

7. McNeill, op. cit., p. 83; Carmichael, op. cit., pp. 106-7; A. Carmichael, *Carmina Gadelica, Vol IV* (Edinburgh, 1941) p. 139.

8. Opie & Tatum, op. cit., pp. 88-9; Vickery, op. cit., p. 71, 73; Gwynn Jones, op. cit., p. 142; Waring, op. cit., p 61.

9. Waring, op. cit., p. 61; Opie & Tatum, op. cit., p. 89.

10. B. Curran, *The Wolfhound Guide to the Shamrock* (Dublin, 1999) p. 16, p. 19, p. 23; J.R. Press, Dr D.A. Sutton & B.R. Tebbs, *Reader's Digest Field Guide to the Wild Flowers of Britain* (London, 1981) p. 116; K. Hawkes, *Cornish Sayings, Superstitions and Remedies* (Penzance, 1973) p. 18; Waring, op. cit., p. 61.

11. Nelson ,op. cit., pp. 153-7.

12. Williams, op. cit., p. 156.

13. Gwynn, op. cit., p. 146, p. 237, p. 307; R.A.S. Macalister, *Lebor Gabála Eirenn Part 3* (Dublin, 1940) p. 145; Stokes, op. cit. (1890) p.177.

14. Gantz, op. cit. (1976) p. 152.

15. Nelson, op. cit., pp. 45-7.
16. Ibid, pp. 130-2.
17. Allen & Hatfield, op. cit., p. 161.
18. Ibid, p. 162.
19. J. Cameron, 'The Gaelic Names of Plants', *Celtic Monthly* (Glasgow, 1900) p. 20.
20. J. G. O'Keeffe, *Buile Suibhne* (Dublin, 1913) p.23, p. 117.
21. Grigson, op. cit. p. 110.
22. Vickery, op. cit., p. 404; Williams, op. cit., p. 160.
23. Mabey, op. cit. (1996) p. 269.
24. Nelson, op. cit., p. 78.
25. Allen & Hatfield, op. cit., p. 174.

Primrose
1. Mackenzie, op. cit., p. 191.
2. Mabey, op. cit., (1996), p. 164.
3. Danaher, op. cit., p. 88, p. 118, Lady Wilde, *Ancient Legends, Mystic Charms and Superstitions of Ireland* (London, 1888) pp. 102-4. M. Uí Chonchubhair, *Flóra Chorca Dhuibhne* (Kerry, 1995) p. 164.
4. M. Killup, *The Folklore of the Isle of Man* (London, 1975) p. 172.
5. Vickery, op. cit., p. 294.
6. Williams, op. cit., p. 154; Vickery, op. cit., pp. 293-4; Opie & Tatum, op. cit., p. 319.
7. Waring, op. cit., p. 183.
8. Vickery, op. cit., p. 294.
9. Waring, op. cit., p. 183.
10. Vickery, op. cit., pp. 296-7.
11. J. Gantz, *Early Irish Myths and Sagas* (London, 1981) p. 55; Gregory, op. cit. (1994) p. 428; Graves, op. cit., p. 41.
12. Allen & Hatfield, op. cit., pp. 124-5; Williams, op. cit., p. 155;. P. Logan, *Irish Country Cures* (Belfast, 1981) p. 161.
13. Ó Súilleabháin, op. cit. (1970) p. 285.
14. D. Blount, *Consider the Lilies of the Fields: Flowers in Sacred Legend and Tradition* (Dublin, 1931) p. 23.
15. Grieve, op. cit., p. 230.
16. Cameron, op. cit., p. 80.
17. Allen & Hatfield, op. cit., p. 126; Uí Chonchubhair, op. cit., p. 165.
18. Allen & Hatfield, op. cit. p. 126; Grigson, op. cit. p. 265.

Marsh Marigold
1. Danaher, op. cit., p. 88, p. 102.
2. Cameron, op. cit., p. 3; Killup, op. cit., p. 173.

3. Grieve, op. cit., p. 519.
4. Wilde, op. cit. (1979) p. 52, 61; Frazer, op. cit., p. 121.
5. Moloney, op. cit., p. 12; S. Ó Súilleabháin, *Irish Folk Custom and Belief* (Dublin, 1967) p. 23; Carmichichael, op. cit. (1928) p. 319.
6. Grieve, op. cit., p. 519.
7. Press, Sutton & Tebbs, op. cit., p. 21.
8. Grieve, p. cit. p. 519.
9. Ibid, p. 519.
10. Allen & Hatfield, op. cit., p. 70.
11. Carmichael, op. cit. (1928) pp. 78-9; Grigson, op. cit., pp. 42-3; Grieve, op. cit., p. 178.
12. Grigson, op. cit., p. 268.

Nettle
1. Danaher, op. cit., p. 120.
2. Vickery, op. cit., p. 256.
3. Danaher, op. cit., p. 120.
4. Williams, op. cit., p. 133.
5. Vickery, op. cit., p. 254.
6. S. Toibín, *Blátha an Bhóithrín* (Dublin, 1955) p. 31.
7. O'Regan, op. cit., p. 106.
8. Waring, op. cit., p. 164.
9. Vickery, op. cit., p. 257.
10. Williams, op. cit., p. 131.
11. Ibid, p. 134.
12. Grieve, op. cit., p. 575.
13. S. Ó Súilleabháin, *Folktales of Ireland* (Chicago, 1966) pp. 134-5.
14. O'Regan, op. cit., p. 2.
15. Grigson, op. cit., pp. 238-9.
16. Waring, op. cit., p. 164.
17. Gregory, op. cit. (1994) p. 111, p. 295.
18. Stokes, op. cit. (1890) p. 302; A.T. Lucas, 'The Sacred Trees of Ireland', *Journal of the Cork Historical and Archaeological Society 68* (Cork, 1963) p. 46.
19. Graves, op. cit., p. 34.
20. Stokes, W., *Cormac's Glossary* (Calcutta, 1868) p. 126.
21. Uí Chonchubhair, op. cit. p. 51; Grigson, op. cit, p. 239; Vickery, op. cit. p. 257.
22. Uí Chonchubhair, op. cit., p. 51.
23. Allen & Hatfield, op. cit., pp. 85-6; M. Scott, *An Irish Herbal: The Botanalogia Universalis by John K'eogh* (Northamptonshire, 1986) p. 110; O'Regan, op. cit., p. 6.
24. Grigson, op. cit., p. 238.

25. Grieve, op. cit., p. 580; Allen & Hatfield, op. cit., p. 216.

26. Grieve, op. cit., p. 580; Allen & Hatfield, op. cit., p 215.

27. Allen & Hatfield, op. cit., p. 214.

Watercress

1. Cameron, op. cit, p. 8; Wilde, op. cit., (1979), p. 55.

2. Williams, op. cit., pp. 18-9; Vickery, op. cit., p. 384.

3. Ó Cróinín, op. cit., p. 397.

4. Vickery, op. cit., p. 384.

5. C. O' Rahilly, *Táin Bo Cúailnge* (Dublin, 1967) p. 182; Gregory, op. cit. (1994), p. 147; Ó hÓgáin, op. cit., pp. 394-5; O'Keeffe, op. cit., p. 83, p. 95.

6. Stokes, op. cit. (1890), p. 286; Gregory, op. cit. (1994) p. 149.

7. Gantz, op. cit. (1981) p. 102; Stokes, op. cit. (1868) p. 19.

8. Kelly, op. cit. (1997) p. 309.

9. Williams, op. cit., p. 19.

10. Allen & Hatfield, op. cit., p. 118; Ó Súilleabháin, op. cit. (1970) p. 313.

11. Uí Chonchubhair, op. cit., p. 87; Vickery, op. cit, p. 384.

12. O'Regan, op. cit, p. 6.

13. Grigson, op. cit., p. 65; Moloney, op. cit., p. 14; O'Keeffe, op. cit., p. 33; Murphy, op. cit. (1933) p. 373; Allen & Hatfield, op. cit., p. 119.

14. Allen & Hatfield, op. cit., p. 117.

15. Allen & Hatfield, op. cit., p. 116; Press, Sutton & Tebbs, op. cit., p. 44.

Bluebell

1. Grigson, op. cit., p. 409.

2. Vickery, op. cit., pp. 40-1.

3. Williams, op. cit., p. 39.

4. Gantz, op. cit. (1981), p. 62, p. 88, p. 90, W. Stokes, *Agallamh na Senórach* (Leipzig, 1900) p. 249.

5. Grieve, op. cit., pp. 116-7.

6. Ibid, p. 40.

7. Allen & Hatfield, op. cit., p. 328; Williams, op. cit., p. 40.

8. Uí Chonchubhair, op. cit., p. 241.

9. Grigson, op. cit., p. 337; Innes, op. cit., p. 102; Blount, op. cit., p. 26.

10. Grigson, op. cit., p. 74; Allen & Hatfield, op. cit. p. 173.

11. Williams, op. cit., p. 47.

12. Opie & Tatum, op. cit., p. 172.

13. O'Keeffe, op. cit., p. 23, p. 117; K. Jackson, *A Celtic Miscellany* (London, 1971) p. 71.

14. Kelly, op. cit. (1997), p. 339, p. 304.

15. Williams, op. cit., p. 47.

16. Allen & Hatfield, op. cit., p. 328.

17. Ibid, p. 329.

Yellow Iris

1. Danaher, op. cit., p. 89.
2. Ibid, p. 89.
3. O'Farrell, op. cit. (*Irish Customs*) p. 112..
4. Danaher, op. cit., p. 131; Williams, op. cit., p. 75.
5. Ó Súilleabháin, op. cit. (1970) p. 287; Williams, op. cit. p. 75.
6. Grigson, op. cit., p. 419; Vickery, op. cit., p. 409.
7. Williams, op. cit., p. 75.
8. Gregory, op. cit. (1994) p. 72, p. 75, p. 120.
9. Grieve, op. cit, p. 434, p. 438.
10. Ibid, p. 438.
11. Ó Súilleabháin, op. cit. (1970) p. 287.
12. Williams, op. cit., p. 77.
13. Grieve, op. cit. p. 438.
14. Allen & Hatfield, op. cit., pp. 331-2.
15. Ibid, pp. 331-2.
16. Logan, op. cit., p. 46.
17. Grigson, op. cit., p. 418; Allen & Hatfield, op. cit., p. 332.
18. Grigson, op. cit., p. 428; Grieve, op. cit., p 726, p. 728.

Bog-myrtle

1. Mabey, op. cit. (1996) p. 70.
2. Dinneen, op. cit., p. 909; Williams, op. cit., p. 145.
3. Innes, op. cit., p. 22; Williams, op. cit., p. 145, Carmichael, op. cit. (1941) p. 137.
4. Dinneen, op. cit., p. 909, p. 931; Ó Súilleabháin, op. cit. (1970) p. 285; S. Tóibín, *Troscán na mBánta* (Dublin, 1967) p. 51; S. Ó hEochaidh, M. Ní Néill, S. Ó Catháin, *Síscéalta ó Tír Chonaill* (Dublin, 1977) p. 327; T.P. Dolan, *A Dictionary of Hiberno-English* (Dublin, 1998) p. 213.
5. Macalister, op. cit., p. 9.
6. Grieve, op. cit., p. 301, p. 306, p. 341; Tóibín op. cit. (1967) p. 51; Grigson, op. cit., p. 243.
7. Kelly, op. cit. (1976) p. 121.
8. D. McManus, 'Irish letter-names & their kennings' *Ériu* 39 (Dublin, 1988) pp. 144-5.
9. Grigson, op. cit., p. 243; Grieve, op. cit., p. 341, Tóibín, op. cit. (1967) p. 51.
10. Toibín, op. cit. (1967) p. 51.
11. Williams, op. cit., p. 143.
12. Dinneen, op. cit., p. 909.
13. Uí Chonchubhair, op. cit., p. 50.
14. Allen & Hatfield, op. cit., p. 87.

Meadowsweet
1. Uí Chonchubhair, op. cit., p. 101.
2. Vickery, op. cit., p. 239.
3. Williams, op. cit., p. 2.
4. Press, Sutton & Tebbs, op. cit., p. 133.
5. Gantz, op. cit. (1976) p. 111.
6. Graves, op. cit. p. 370.
7. M. Seymour, *A Brief History of Thyme* (London, 2002) p. 83.
8. Grigson, op. cit., p. 144.
9. Ibid, p. 144; Seymour, op. cit., p. 83.
10. Grigson, op. cit. p. 144.
11. Williams, op. cit., p. 2.
12. Allen & Hatfield, op. cit., p. 140.
13. Grigson, op. cit., p. 343; Allen & Hatfield, op. cit., p. 352.
14. Grigson, op. cit., p. 340.

Scarlet Pimpernel
1. Ó Súilleabháin, op. cit. (1970) p. 287, p. 397, p. 652; O'Sullivan, op. cit., pp. 86-7.
2. Grieve, op. cit., p. 633.
3. Grigson, op. cit., p. 270; Cameron, op. cit., p. 81; Vickery, op. cit., p. 336.
4. Grigson, op. cit., p. 270.
5. Blunt, op. cit., p. 27.
6. Grieve, op. cit., p. 633.
7. Williams, op. cit., p. 74.
8. Ibid, p. 73; Allen & Hatfield, op. cit., p 128.
9. Williams, op. cit., p. 82; Ó Súilleabháin, op. cit. (1970) p. 286; Fleetwood, op. cit., p. 6; Allen & Hatfield, op. cit., p. 91.

Foxglove
1. O'Farrell, *Irish Folk Cures*, p. 39; Vickery, op. cit., p. 140.
2. Gwynn Jones, op. cit., p. 60.
3. Cameron, op. cit., p. 147.
4. Gregory, op. cit. (1970) p. 138.
5. O'Farrell, op. cit. (*Irish Folk Cures*) p. 68.
6. O' Farrell, op. cit. (*Irish Folk Cures*) p. 69; Danaher, op. cit., p. 148.
7. Gregory, op. cit., (1970), p. 151.
8. Williams, op. cit., p. 106.
9. Gwynn Jones, op. cit., p. 54.
10. McNeill, op. cit., p. 8.
11. Vickery, op. cit., p. 140
12. Uí Chonchubhair, op. cit., p. 194.
13. Grieve, op. cit., p. 323.

14. Vickery, op. cit., p. 140; Ó Súilleabháin, op. cit. (1970) p. 286.
15. Seymour, op. cit., p. 53; Grieve, op. cit., p. 323; Vickery, op. cit., p. 139; Press, Sutton & Tebbs, op. cit., p. 267.
16. Williams, op. cit., p. 103.
17. Gantz, op. cit., (1981), p. 55, p. 62, p. 88, p. 258; Gantz, op. cit. (1976) p. 152; Gwynn Jones, op. cit., p. 210; Gregory, op. cit. (1994) p. 430, p. 148.
18. Grieve, op. cit. p. 326.
19. Gregory, op. cit. (1970) p. 151; Allen & Hatfield, op. cit., p. 254, pp. 256-7.
20. Ó Súilleabháin, op. cit. (1970) p. 286.
21. Moloney, op. cit., p. 35.
22. Tóibín, op. cit. (1955) p. 95; Allen & Hatfield, op. cit., p. 252.
23. Williams, op. cit. p. viii.
24. Allen & Hatfield, op. cit., p. 252.
25. Ibid, p. 252.
26. Grigson, op. cit., p. 298.
27. Grigson, op. cit., p. 198.
28. Allen & Hatfield, op. cit., p. 164; Grieve, op. cit., p. 498; Ó Súilleabháin, op. cit. (1970) p. 287.

Honeysuckle

1. Uí Chonchubhair, op. cit., p. 208; Frazer, op. cit., p. 620; McNeill, op. cit., p. 58, p. 82; Cameron, op. cit., p. 47; Williams, op. cit., p. 80.
2. Grigson, op. cit., p. 356.
3. Tóibín, op. cit. (1967) p. 54.
4. Press, Sutton, & Tebbs, op. cit., p. 315.
5. Vickery, op. cit., p. 188; Danaher, op. cit., p. 89.
6. Vickery, op. cit., p. 188.
7. Grigson, op. cit., p. 356.
8. Vickery, op. cit., p. 189.
9. Grigson, op. cit., p. 355.
10. Williams, op. cit., p. 78.
11. S. O' Grady, *Silva Gadelica* (London, 1892) p. 278; N. MacCoitir, *Irish Trees: Myths, Legends and Folklore* (Cork, 2003) pp. 10-11; Dinneen, op. cit., p. 446; O'Rahilly, op. cit., p. 227, p. 269; J.G. Evan, *The Poems of Taliesin* (Llanbedrog, 1915) p. 31.
12. Ó hÓgáin, op. cit., p. 43.
13. G. Murphy, *Early Irish Lyrics* (Dublin, 1998) pp. 10-19.
14. Kelly, op. cit. (1976) p. 119.
15. McManus, op. cit., pp. 144-5, p. 148-9.
16. Grieve, op. cit., p. 410.
17. Allen & Hatfield, op. cit., p. 273; Williams, op. cit., p. 80; Ó Cróinín, op. cit., p. 417.

18. Tóibín, op. cit. (1967) p. 55.

19. Blount, op. cit., p. 12; Grigson, op. cit., p. 38.

St John's Wort

1. Williams, op. cit., p. 14; Ui Chonchubhair, op. cit., p. 136; Ó Súilleabháin, op. cit. (1970) p. 288; O'Regan, op. cit., p. 116; Wilde, op. cit. (1991) p. 100; O'Farrell, op. cit. (*Irish Folk Cures*) p. 70; O'Farrell, op. cit. (*Irish Customs*) p. 44.

2. Moloney, op. cit., p. 17.

3. Danaher, op. cit., pp. 147-8; Grigson, op. cit., p. 76.

4. Carmichael op. cit. (1928) p. 96; Cameron, op. cit., p. 14.

5. Grigson, op. cit., p. 79.

6. Opie & Tatum, op. cit., p. 336; Press, Sutton & Tebbs, op. cit., p. 68; Vickery, op. cit., p. 331.

7. Opie & Tatum, op. cit., p. 336; T. Owen, *Welsh Folk Custom* (Cardiff, 1959) p. 111.

8. Williams, op. cit., p. 14.

9. Vickery, op. cit., p. 332; V. Vêtvicka, *A Hamlyn Colour Guide to Wildflowers of Field and Woodland* (Prague, 1979) p. 170.; Williams, op. cit., p. 14.

10. Vickery, op. cit., p. 330; Grieve, op. cit., p. 708.

11. Williams, op. cit., p. 14.

12. Grieve, op. cit., p. 708.

13. Allen & Hatfield, op. cit., p. 104.

14. Ibid, p. 106.

15. Moloney, op. cit., p. 18;

16. Ó Súilleabháin, op. cit. (1970) p. 288.

17. Cameron, op. cit., p. 15; Uí Chonchubhair, op. cit., p. 134; Grigson, op. cit., p. 75; Allen & Hatfield, op. cit., p. 103.

18. Grigson, op. cit., p. 268; Grieve, op. cit., p. 498.

19. Grigson, op. cit., p. 398; Grieve, op. cit., p. 72.

Mugwort

1. Grigson, op. cit., p. 382; Frazer, op. cit., p. 623, 626-7.

2. Grigson, op. cit., p. 383; Uí Chonchubhair, op. cit., p. 224.

3. Cameron, op. cit., p. 54.

4. Owen, op. cit., p. 111.

5. Mabey, op. cit. (1996) p. 370.

6. Williams, op. cit., p. 126.

7. Uí Chonchubhair, op. cit., p. 224; Grigson, op. cit., p. 383; Opie & Tatum, op. cit., p. 268.

8. Press, Sutton & Tebbs, op. cit., p. 347.

9. Opie & Tatum, op. cit., p. 268.

10. Grigson, op. cit., p. 383.

11. Williams, op. cit., p. 126.
12. Ibid, p. 127.
13. Allen & Hatfield, op. cit., p. 298.
14. Ibid, p. 297.
15. Grieve, op. cit., p. 557; Allen & Hatfield, op. cit., p. 298.
16. O'Regan, op. cit., p. 102.
17. Grigson, op. cit., p. 384; Grieve, op. cit., p. 556.
18. Seymour, op. cit., p. 125; Cameron, op. cit., p. 55; Allen & Hatfield, op. cit., p. 300.

Yarrow

1. Wilde, op. cit. (1979) p. 53; Cameron, op. cit., p. 60, p. 141; Opie & Tatum, op. cit., p. 453; Ó Súilleabháin, op. cit. (1970) p. 288; Danaher, op. cit., p. 226; Grieve, op. cit., p. 864.
2. Carmichael, op. cit. (1928) pp. 94-6.
3. Opie & Tatum, op. cit., p. 453; Wilde, op. cit. (1991) p. 32; Carmichael, op. cit. (1928) p. 71; Wilde, op. cit. (1979) pp. 68-9.
4. Williams, op. cit., p. 8.
5. Ibid, p. 8.
6. O'Farrell, op. cit., *Irish Folk Cures*, p. 59, p. 70; Ó Súilleabháin, op. cit. (1970) p. 288; Danaher, op. cit., p. 148; Wilde, op. cit. (1991) pp. 99-100; Wilde, op. cit (1888) p. 104, p. 232; Gregory, op. cit. (1970) p. 149.
7. Grieve, op. cit., p. 864.
8. Seymour, op. cit., p. 127.
9. Grieve, op. cit., p. 864.
10. Allen & Hatfield, op. cit., p. 302; Logan, op. cit., p. 108.
11. Allen & Hatfield, op. cit., pp. 300-1; Grigson, op. cit., p. 378.
12. O'Regan, op. cit., p. 9; Allen & Hatfield, op. cit., pp. 295-6; Grigson, op. cit., p. 382.

Vervain

1. Danaher, op. cit., pp. 116-7; Wilde, op. cit. (1991) p. 40; McNeill, op. cit., p. 82, p. 84; Cameron, op. cit., p. 73; Killup, op. cit., p. 135; Opie & Tatum, op. cit., p. 420; Frazer, op. cit., p. 623; Grigson, op. cit., p. 314.
2. Wilde, op. cit. (1888) p. 232; Wilde, op. cit. (1991) p. 100; O'Farrell, op. cit., *Irish Folk Cures*, p. 70; Opie & Tatum, op. cit., p. 420; Press, Sutton & Tebbs, op. cit., p. 282.
3. McCullough, op. cit., p. 206; Wilde, op. cit. (1991) p. 100; Moloney, op. cit., p. 54; Cameron, op. cit., pp. 73-4; Grieve, op. cit., p. 524.
4. Grigson, op. cit., p. 313.
5. C. Threkeld, *Synopsis Stirpium Hibernicarum* (Dublin, 1727); Grieve, op. cit., p. 831.
6. Grieve, op. cit., p. 831.
7. Allen & Hatfield, op. cit., p. 211.

8. Ibid, p. 211.
9. Opie & Tatum, op. cit., p. 420; Threkeld, op. cit.
10. Cameron, op. cit., p. 73.
11. Allen & Hatfield, op. cit., p. 212; Moloney, op. cit., p. 37.
12. Mabey, op. cit., (1996), p. 312.

Mallow
1. Wilde, op. cit. (1991) p. 100; O'Farrell (*Irish Folk Cures*) p. 70; Danaher, op cit., p. 120.
2. Grieve, op. cit., p. 509.
3. Danaher, op. cit., p. 135.
4. Grigson, op. cit., p. 100.
5. Press, Sutton & Tebbs, op. cit., p. 96; Grieve, op. cit., p. 507.
6. Allen & Hatfield, op. cit., pp. 108-9.
7. Ibid, p. 110.
8. Vickery, op. cit., p. 308; Press, Sutton &Tebbs, op. cit., p. 70.
9. Uí Chonchubhair, op. cit., p. 72.
10. Grigson, op. cit., p. 88; Moloney op. cit., p. 16.

Ragwort
1. Uí Chonchubhair, op. cit., p. 227; Ó hÓgáin, op. cit., p. 189; Tóibín, op. cit. (1955) p. 14; Gregory, op. cit.(1970), p. 58; Vickery, op. cit., p. 305.
2. Carmichael, *Carmina Gadelica, Vol III* (Edinburgh, 1940) p. 120;
3. McNeill, op. cit., p. 84.
4. Grigson, op. cit., p. 363.
5. Vickery, op. cit., p. 305.
6. Ibid, p. 253.
7. Ó hEochaidh, Ní Néill, Ó Catháin, op. cit., p. 137, p. 327; Danaher, op. cit., p. 200; Dineen, op. cit. p. 1326.
8. Wilde, op. cit. (1979) p. 13; Williams, op. cit., p. 28.
9. Williams, op. cit., p. 26.
10. Grigson, op. cit., p. 363; Uí Chonchubhair, op. cit., p. 227.
11. Allen & Hatfield, op. cit., p. 307; Logan, op. cit., p. 109.
12. Ó Cróinín, op. cit., p. 411.
13. Williams, op. cit., p. 29.
14. Cameron, op. cit., p. 8; Allen & Hatfield, op. cit., p. 309; Grieve, op. cit., p. 378; Willims, op. cit., p 100.
15. Allen & Hatfield, op. cit. pp. 293-4.
16. Grigson, op. cit., p. 379; Vickery, op. cit., p. 87.

Heather
1. Vickery, op. cit., p. 157; A.T. Lucas, 'Furze: A Survey of its History and Uses in Ireland', *Béaloideas* 26 (1960) p. 186.

2. Blount, op. cit., p. 8.
3. Tóibín, op. cit. (1967) p. 130; Williams, op. cit., p. 84.
4. Opie & Tatum, op. cit., p. 196; Mabey, op. cit. (1996) p. 159; Tóibín, op. cit. (1967) p. 129; Waring, op. cit., p. 256.
5. Waring, op. cit., p. 118.
6. Waring, op. cit., p. 256.
7. Cameron, op. cit., pp.61-2; Dinneen, op. cit., p. 486.
8. Innes, op. cit., pp. 60-3, p. 89, p. 97; Waring, op. cit., p. 118.
9. Mabey, op. cit. (1996) p. 159.
10. Mac Neill, op. cit., p. 183, p. 191.
11. MacGregor, op. cit., p. 1; Gwynn Jones, op. cit., p. 54.
12. Branch Johnson, W., *Folktales of Brittany*, (London, 1972), p. 150.
13. Ó hÓgáin, op. cit., p. 325.
14. Ó hÓgáin, op. cit., p. 234; Gantz, op. cit. (1981) pp. 114-26.
15. Gregory, op. cit. (1994) p. 256; Murphy, op. cit. (1998) pp. 10-19.
16. Mabey, op. cit.,(1977) p. 99.
17. Kelly, op. cit. (1976) p. 121.
18. McManus, op. cit., pp. 146-7.
19. Lucas, op. cit. (1960) p. 12.
20. Ó Súilleabháin, op. cit. (1970) p. 287; Cameron, op. cit., pp. 62-3; Mabey, op. cit. (1996) p. 161; Tóibín, op. cit. (1967) p. 131.
21. Allen & Hatfield, op. cit., pp. 122-3.

Bilberry

1. Grigson, op. cit., p. 262.
2. MacNeill, op. cit., p. 141.
3. Danaher, op. cit., p. 170.
4. Killup, op. cit., p. 176; MacNeill, op. cit., p. 382.
5. MacNeill, op. cit., p. 188, p. 230, p. 237; Danaher, op. cit. p. 168.
6. MacNeill, op. cit., p. 144, 161.
7. Ibid, p. 184, p. 222, p. 254.
8. Innes, op. cit. p. 20, p. 32, p. 77, p. 106; MacGregor, op. cit., p. 307.
9. A. Carmichael, *Carmina Gadelica Vol I* (Edinburgh, 1900) p. 201.
10. Williams, op. cit., p. 87.
11. Murphy, op. cit., (1998), pp. 10-19.
12. MacNeill, op. cit., p. 242.
13. Kelly, op. cit. (1976) p. 121.
14. Kelly, op. cit. (1997) pp. 306-7.
15. Threkeld, op. cit.; Vickery, op. cit., pp. 30-1; Ó Súilleabháin, op. cit. (1970) p. 285; Cameron, op. cit., p. 64.
16. Allen & Hatfield, op. cit., pp. 123-4; Grigson, p. 262.
17. Murphy, op. cit. (1998) pp. 10-19; O'Keeffe, op. cit., p. 95, 117; Cameron, op. cit., p. 65; Innes, op. cit., p. 66.

18. Grigson, op. cit., p. 262.
19. Ibid, p. 259; Innes, op. cit., p. 75.
20. Vickery, op. cit., p. 96.

Dog-rose
1. Press, Sutton & Tebbs, op. cit, p. 145; Vickery, op. cit., p. 314.
2. Waring, op. cit., p. 192; Opie & Tatum, op. cit., p. 122, p. 332.
3. Innes, op. cit., p. 34, p. 95.
4. Vickery, op. cit., p. 110; Tóibín, op. cit. (1967) p. 57; Beecher, S., *A Dictionary of Cork Slang* (Cork, 1983) p.85.
5. Cameron, op. cit., p. 29.
6. Share, B., *Slangauge – A Dictionary of Irish Slang* (Dublin, 1997) p. 153.
7. Fenton, J., *The Hamely Tongue* (Newtownards, 1995) p. 21.
8. Toibín, op. cit. (1955) p. 48.
9. Vickery, op. cit., p. 112.
10. Grieve, op. cit., p. 691; Grigson, op. cit., p. 160.
11. Gregory, op. cit. (1994) p. 289; A. Rees & B. Rees, *Celtic Heritage* (London, 1961) p. 296.
12. Ó Súilleabháin, op. cit. (1966) p. 60.
13. Grieve, op. cit., p. 684.
14. Green, M., *Dictionary of Celtic Myth and Legend* (London, 1992) p. 179.
15. Kelly, op. cit. (1976) p. 121.
16. Kelly, op. cit. (1997) p. 306-7.
17. MacManus, op. cit., pp. 144-5.
18. Vickery, op. cit., p.111-2.
19. Ó Súilleabháin, op. cit. (1970) p. 281.
20. Opie & Tatum, op. cit., p. 32.
21. Ó Súilleabháin, op. cit. (1970) p. 281.
22. Grieve, op. cit., p. 691; Moloney, op. cit., p. 23; Allen & Hatfield, op. cit., p. 151.
23. Grigson, op. cit., p. 162.
24. Grieve, op. cit., p. 691.

Bramble
1. Danaher, op. cit, p. 200, p. 207; Vickery, op. cit., p. 46.
2. Wilde, op. cit. (1979) p. 14; Cameron, op. cit., p. 140; Threkeld, op. cit.
3. Opie & Tatum, op. cit., p. 29; Graves, op. cit., p. 183; Waring, op. cit. p. 35.
4. Cameron, op. cit., p. 140.
5. Graves, op. cit., p. 183.
6. Williams, op. cit., p. 60.
7. Danaher, op. cit., p. 202.
8. Carmichael, op. cit. (1900) p. 201.
9. Cameron, op. cit., p. 29.

10. Grave, op. cit. p. 183.
11. Vickery, op. cit., p. 49; Grieve, op. cit. p. 110.
12. Danaher, op. cit., p. 203; Ó Súilleabháin, op. cit. (1970) p. 397; Opie & Tatum, op. cit., p. 37; Vickery, op. cit., p. 48.
13. O'Farrell, op. cit. (*Irish Customs*) p. 80; Danaher, op. cit., p. 117; Vickery, op. cit., p. 47; MacGregor, op. cit., p. 274; McNeill, op. cit., p. 82; Carmichael, op. cit. (1900) p. 168; Grieve, op. cit. p. 109.
14. Hawkes, op. cit., pp. 18-19, p. 30; Mabey, op. cit. (1996) p. 184.
15. Grigson, op. cit., p. 145.
16. Toibín, op. cit. (1967) p. 46.
17. O'Keeffe, op. cit., pp. 65-8; O'Grady, op. cit., p. 278; Mac Coitir, op. cit., pp. 10-11; Mac Neill, E., *Duanaire Finn Part I* (Dublin, 1908) p. 160; O' Rahilly, op. cit., p. 193; Stokes, op. cit. (1890) p. 204.
18. Kelly., op. cit. (1976) p. 121.
19. Kelly., op. cit. (1997) pp. 306-7.
20. Ibid, p. 307.
21. Murphy, op. cit. (1998) p. 19; Gregory, op. cit. (1994) p. 147; Murphy, op. cit. (1933) p. 375.
22. Mabey, op. cit. (1996) p. 183; Williams, op. cit., p. 60; Ó Súilleabháin, op. cit. (1970) p. 285.
23. Williams, op. cit., pp. 61-2; Grigson, op. cit., p. 145; Ó Súilleabháin, op. cit. (1970) p. 285.
24. Grieve, op. cit. p. 110; Allen & Hatfield, op. cit., p. 142; Grigson, op. cit., p. 145.
25. Innes, op. cit., p. 84.
26. M. Blamey, R. Fitter & A. Fitter, *Wild Flowers of Britain and Ireland* (London, 2003) p. 126.
27. Grigson, op. cit., p. 46; Cameron, op. cit., p. 28.
28. O'Keeffe, op. cit., p. 117; Murphy, op. cit. (1933) p. 375; Allen & Hatfield, op. cit., p. 140.

Bracken

1. Opie & Tatum, op. cit., p. 147; Danaher, op. cit., p. 216.
2. Ó Súilleabháin, op. cit. (1970) p. 397.
3. Frazer, op. cit., pp. 704-5.
4. Cameron, op. cit., p. 125; Vickery, op. cit., p. 44; Lamont Brown, op. cit., p. 53; Blount, op. cit., p. 9.
5. Lamont Brown, op. cit., p. 55.
6. Ó Súilleabháin, op. cit. (1970) p. 286; Vickery, op. cit., p. 157.
7. Dolan, op. cit., p. 170, p. 213; Opie & Tatum, op. cit., p. 147; McNeill, op. cit., p. 84.
8. Carmichael, op. cit. (1928) p. 39; Cameron, op. cit., p. 128; Opie & Tatum, op. cit., p. 147.
9. Hawkes, op. cit., p. 27.

10. Ó Súilleabháin, op. cit. (1970) p. 476; Waring, op. cit., p. 90; Opie & Tatum, op. cit., p. 147.
11. Innes, op. cit., p. 24, 103.
12. Gregory, op. cit. (1994) p. 21; Stokes, op. cit. (1887) p. 167.
13. O'Keeffe, op. cit., p. 65.
14. Gregory, op. cit., p. 428; Rees & Rees, op. cit., p. 339.
15. Kelly, op. cit. (1976) p. 121.
16. McManus, op. cit., pp. 144-5.
17. Macalister, op. cit. (1940) p. 9; Grieve, op. cit., p. 301, p. 306, p. 341; Toibín, op. cit. (1967) p. 51; Grigson, op. cit., p. 243.
18. Ó Súilleabháin, op. cit. (1970) p. 285; Cameron, op. cit., p. 125; Uí Chonchubhair, op. cit., p. 47; Grieve, op. cit., p. 306; Williams, op. cit., p. 149.
19. R.A.S. Macalister, *The Secret Languages of Ireland* (Cambridge, 1937) p. 131.
20. Grieve, op. cit., p. 305.
21. Allen & Hatfield, op. cit., p. 60.
22. Cameron, op. cit., p. 126; Vickery, op. cit., p. 322; Allen & Hatfield, op. cit., p. 57.
23. Allen & Hatfield, op. cit. p. 58; Ó Croinín, op. cit., p. 412.
24. Allen & Hatfield, op. cit., p. 62.
25. Allen & Hatfield, op. cit, p. 62; Grieve, op. cit. p. 303.
26. Allen & Hatfield, op. cit., pp. 60-1.
27. Grieve, op. cit., p. 308; Cameron, op. cit., p. 127.
28. Allen & Hatfield, op. cit., pp. 58-9; Vickery, op. cit., p. 286.

Ivy

1. Danaher, op. cit., p. 234; Vickery, op. cit., p. 202.
2. Danaher, op. cit., p. 244; O'Farrell, op. cit. (*Irish Customs*) p. 70.
3. Opie & Tatum, op. cit., p. 213.
4. Danaher, op. cit., p. 222, p. 259; Owen, op. cit., p. 129; Lamont Brown, op. cit., p. 52; Waring, op. cit., p. 129.
5. Danaher, op. cit., p. 226; Opie & Tatum, op. cit. p. 213.
6. MacGregor, op. cit., p. 274; Carmichael, op. cit. (1928) p. 76; McNeill, op. cit., p. 82, p. 84; Lamont Brown, op. cit., p. 52.
7. Opie & Tatum, op. cit., p. 213; Williams, op. cit., p. 70.
8. Williams, op. cit., p. 70.
9. Lamont Brown, op. cit., p. 52; Ó hÓgáin, op. cit., p. 85; Opie & Tatum, op. cit., p. 213; Logan, op. cit., p. 170; Gregory, op. cit. (1970) p. 158; Ó Súilleabháin, op. cit. (1970) p. 287.
10. Innes, op. cit. p. 39.
11. Mac Neill, op. cit. (1908) p. 133; O'Keeffe, op. cit., p. 39, p. 67, p. 75, p. 133.

12. Jackson, op. cit., p. 98.
13. Kelly, op. cit. (1976) p. 123.
14. McManus, op. cit., pp. 144-7.
15. Grieve, op. cit, p. 441; Graves, op. cit., p. 183.
16. Frazer, op. cit., p. 381, p. 352.
17. Mabey, op. cit. (1996) p. 267.
18. Allen & Hatfield, op. cit., pp. 179-80; Logan, op. cit., p. 69.
19. Allen & Hatfield, op. cit., pp. 179-80.
20. Vickery, op. cit., p. 203.
21. Grigson, op. cit., p. 328; Allen & Hatfield, op. cit. pp. 220-1; Cameron, op. cit., pp. 76-7.
22. Allen & Hatfield, op. cit., p. 200.

Houseleek
1. Wilde, op. cit. (1991) p. 10; Vickery, op. cit., p. 198; Opie & Tatum, op. cit. p. 206; Gwynn Jones, op. cit., p. 177; Grieve, op. cit., p. 422.
2. Grigson, op. cit. p. 183.
3. Ibid, p. 183.
4. Allen & Hatfield, op. cit., pp. 136-7.
5. Logan, op. cit., p. 59.
6. Allen & Hatfield, op. cit., p. 137.
7. Grigson, op. cit., p. 184; Allen & Hatfield, op. cit., pp. 136-7.
8. Grigson, op. cit., pp. 179-80.
9. Ibid, p. 182; Allen & Hatfield, op. cit., pp. 138-9.

Sea Wrack
1. Danaher, op. cit., p14, p. 55, p. 71.
2. H. Becker, *I mBéal na Farraige* (Galway, 1997)
3. Cameron, op. cit., pp. 132-3; Carmichael, op. cit. (1941) p. 33.
4. MacGregor, op. cit., p. 75; Branch Johnson, op. cit., p. 95.
5. Waring, op. cit., p. 202.
6. Hawkes, op. cit., p15; Opie & Tatum, op. cit., p. 346.
7. Opie & Tatum, op. cit., p. 346.
8. O'Keeffe, op. cit., p. 117; O'Rahilly, op. cit., p. 182.
9. Gantz, op. cit. (1976) p. 108.
10. Vickery, op. cit., p. 342.
11. Scott, op. cit., p. 137.
12. Vickery, op. cit., p. 341.
13. Allen & Hatfield, op. cit., pp. 46-7.
14. O'Regan, op. cit., p. 93.
15. Allen & Hatfield, op. cit., p. 44; Tóibin, op. cit., p. 31.
16. Kelly, op. cit. (1997) p. 312; Allen & Hatfield, op. cit., p. 45; Ó C. Coigligh, *Seanchas Inis Meáin* (Dublin) p. 95; Ó Cróinín, op. cit., p. 409.

17. Moloney, op. cit., p. 50; Allen & Hatfield, op. cit., p. 45; Flanagan & Flanagan, op. cit., p. 195.

Grasses
1. Dinneen, op. cit., p. 436; Ó Súilleabháin, op. cit. (1970) p. 287, p. 397; Dolan, op. cit., p. 106; Logan, op. cit., p. 7.
2. Dolan, op. cit., p. 111.
3. Ó Súilleabháin, op. cit. (1970) p. 667; Opie & Tatum, op. cit., p. 179; Vickery, op. cit., p. 29, p. 159.
4. Vickery, op. cit., p. 159.
5. Gerald of Wales, *The History and Topography of Ireland* (London, 1982) p. 53, p. 82, p. 134.
6. Dinneen, op. cit., p. 543; Wilde, op. cit. (1991) p. 86.
7. Moloney, op. cit., p. 47.
8. Ó Súilleabháin, op. cit. (1970) p. 287; Mabey, op. cit. (1977) p. 131; Moloney, op. cit., p. 46.
9. Logan, op. cit., p. 108; Allen & Hatfield, op. cit., p. 324; Logan, op. cit., p. 176; Grieve, op. cit., p. 370.
10. Cameron, op. cit., p. 115; Ó Súilleabháin, op. cit. (1970) p. 288.
11. Grieve, op. cit., p. 457; Grigson, op. cit., p. 230.
12. Williams, op. cit., p. 96; E. Ní Lamhna, *Talking Wild – Wildlife on the Radio* (Dublin, 2002) p. 86; Allen & Hatfield, op. cit., p. 270.

Dandelion
1. Carmichael, op. cit. (1900) p. 171; Ibid, op. cit. (1928) p. 319; Danaher, op. cit., p. 37; McKenzie, op. cit., p. 190.
2. Ó Súilleabháin, op. cit. (1970) p. 286; Vickery, op. cit., p. 103; Opie & Tatum, op. cit., p. 115.
3. Vickery, op. cit., pp. 102-3; Ní Lamhna, op. cit., p. 84.
4. Grigson, op. cit., p. 394.
5. Williams, op. cit., p. 33.
6. Allen & Hatfield, op. cit., p. 287.
7. Ibid, p. 287.
8. Ibid, p. 287.
9. Ibid, p. 288; Logan, op. cit., p. 22.
10. Allen & Hatfield, op. cit., p. 287; Logan, op. cit., p. 59; Fleetwood, op. cit., p. 6.
11. Danaher, op. cit. p. 37; Vickery, op. cit., p. 105.
12. Grieve, op. cit., p. 251.
13. Allen & Hatfield, op. cit., p. 290.
14. Grigson, p. 392.
15. Grigson, op. cit., p. 370; Allen & Hatfield, op. cit., p. 290.
16. Grigson, op. cit., p. 392; Allen & Hatfield, op. cit., p. 285; Cameron, op.

cit., p. 51.

17. Williams, op. cit., pp. 165-7; Grigson, op. cit., p. 367; Allen & Hatfield, op. cit., pp. 309-11.

Buttercup

1. Danaher, op. cit., p. 88.
2. Ó Súilleabháin, op. cit. (1970) p. 285.
3. Wilde, op. cit. (1979) p. 52.
4. Uí Chonchubhair, op. cit., p. 78; Vickery, op. cit., p. 54.
5. Press, Sutton & Tebbs, op. cit., p. 21.
6. Vickery, op. cit., p. 55; Grieve, op. cit., p. 235.
7. Waring, op. cit., p. 45.
8. Williams, op. cit., p. 50.
9. Ibid, p. 50.
10. Rees & Rees, op. cit., p. 74; Gregory, op. cit. (1994) p. 533.
11. Grieve, op. cit., p. 236.
12. Allen & Hatfield, op. cit., p. 72; Logan, op. cit., p. 51
13. Tóibín, op. cit. (1955) p. 16.
14. Allen & Hatfield, op. cit., p. 73.
15. Logan, op. cit., p. 46.
16. Grieve, op. cit., p. 34; Allen & Hatfield, op. cit., p. 71.

Dock

1. Logan, op. cit., p. 68; Tóibín, op. cit. (1955) p. 101; Williams, op. cit., p. 42; Grieve, op. cit., p. 258; Vickery, op. cit., p. 107.
2. Williams, op. cit., p. 42.
3. Ibid, p. 42.
4. Cameron, op. cit., p. 147.
5. Allen & Hatfield, op. cit., pp. 97-9; Williams, op. cit., p. 43.
6. Grieve, op. cit., p. 260; Vickery, op. cit., p. 108.
7. Williams, op. cit., p. 43.
8. O'Keeffe, op. cit., p. 23; Kelly, op. cit. (1997) p. 311, p. 339; Flanagan & Flanagan, op. cit., p. 190, 235; Allen & Hatfield, op. cit. p. 96.
9. Dinneen, op. cit., p. 684; Allen & Hatfield, op. cit., p. 94.
10. Grigson, op. cit., p. 233; Ui Chonchubhair, op. cit., p. 53.
11. Cameron, op. cit., p. 86; Allen & Hatfield, op. cit., p. 94.
12. Grigson, op. cit., p. 96; Kelly, op, cit, (1997), p. 259; Allen & Hatfield, op. cit., p. 90.
13. Grigson, op. cit., p. 95.

Charlock

1. Ó Súilleabháin, op. cit. (1970) p. 285; Ó Croinín, op. cit., p. 412.
2. Scott, op. cit., p. 45; Grigson, op. cit., p. 55.

3. Williams, op. cit., p. 142; Tóibín, op. cit. (1955) p.31; Vickery, op. cit., p. 64.
4. Williams, op. cit., p. 140.
5. Ibid, p. 140; Flanagan & Flanagan, op. cit., p. 259.
6. Logan, op. cit., p. 46.
7. Allen & Hatfield, op. cit., p. 121.
8. O' Daly, M., *Cath Maige Mucrama* (Dublin, 1975) p. 59; Stokes, op. cit. (1890)
   pp. 266-7; Grigson, op. cit., pp. 57-8; Kelly, op. cit. (1997) p. 264.
9. Grieve, op. cit. p. 738; Grigson, op. cit., p. 59; Allen & Hatfield, op. cit., p. 120.

Violet

1. Waring, op. cit., p. 246; Uí Chonchubhair, op. cit., p. 137.
2. Waring, op. cit., p. 95; Uí Chonchubhair, op. cit., p. 137.
3. Blount, op. cit., p. 14.
4. Moloney, op. cit., p. 16; Grigson, op. cit., p. 71.
5. Grigson, op. cit., p. 71.
6. Press, Sutton & Tebbs, op. cit., p. 65.
7. Vêtvicka, op. cit., p. 22; Blount, op. cit., p. 22.
8. Press, Sutton & Tebbs, op. cit., p. 65; Blount, op. cit., p. 26.
9. C. Wickham, *Common Plants as Natural Remedies* (London, 1981) p. 50; Grigson, op. cit., p. 72.
10. Waring, op. cit., p. 174.
11. Gantz, op. cit. (1981) p. 165.
12. Vêtvicka, op. cit., p. 120; Frazer, op. cit., p. 348.
13. Press, Sutton, & Tebbs, op. cit., p. 62.
14. Grieve, op. cit., p. 834.
15. Allen & Hatfield, op. cit., p. 111.
16. Grieve, op. cit., p. 838.
17. Ibid., p 235.
18. Allen & Hatfield, op. cit., p. 112.
19. Ui Chonchubhair, op. cit., p. 137.
20. Vickery, op. cit., p. 56; Mackenzie, op. cit., p. 209; Carmichael, op. cit. (1928) p. 110; Williams, op. cit., p. 20.

Water-lily

1. Press, Sutton & Tebbs, op. cit., p. 28.
2. Cameron, op. cit., p. 147.
3. Press, Sutton, & Tebbs, op. cit., p. 29; Grigson, op. cit., p. 48.
4. Grigson, op. cit., p. 48.
5. Green, op. cit., p. 68.
6. Uí Chonchubhair, op. cit., p. 75.

7. Allen & Hatfield, op. cit., p. 70.

8. Vickery, op. cit., p. 397.

9. Allen & Hatfield, op. cit., p. 70.

10. Gantz, op. cit. (1976) p. 152; Allen & Hatfield, op. cit., p. 201, 203.

11. Allen & Hatfield, op. cit., p. 30.

12. Grigson, op. cit., p. 397.

13. Stokes, op. cit. (1868) p. 141; Allen & Hatfield, op. cit., p. 322.

Mint

1. Wilde, op. cit. (1991) p. 41.

2. Williams, op. cit., p. 118; Wilde, op. cit. (1991) p. 101.

3. Seymour, op. cit., p. 88.

4. Ibid, p. 88.

5. Grieve, op. cit., p. 524.

6. Grigson, op. cit., p. 318.

7. Williams, op. cit., p. 118; Vickery, op. cit., p. 240.

8. Grigson, op. cit., p. 318.

9. Allen & Hatfield, op. cit., p. 238; Williams, op. cit., p. 119.

10. Williams, op. cit., p. 118.

11. Allen & Hatfield, op. cit., p. 238.

12. Williams, op. cit., p. 168; Cameron, op. cit., p. 76; Seymour, op. cit., p. 116; Wickham, op. cit., p. 116; Vickery, op. cit., p. 371; Press, Sutton, & Tebbs, op. cit., p. 287; Grieve, op. cit., p. 814; Allen & Hatfield, op. cit., pp. 236-7.

13. Grigson, op. cit., p. 320; Allen & Hatfield, op. cit., p. 24.

14. Grieve, op. cit., p. 732; Williams, op. cit., pp. 66-7; Allen & Hatfield, op. cit., p. 223.

15. Grigson, op. cit., p. 330. Allen & Hatfield, op. cit., p. 218.

Umbellifers

1. Uí Chonchubhair, op. cit., p. 154; Moloney, op. cit., p. 25; Wilde, op. cit. (1991) p. 41; Lamont Brown, op. cit., p. 54; Grieve, op. cit., p. 392; McNeill, op. cit., p. 84; Cameron, op. cit., p. 147.

2. Uí Chonchubhair, op. cit., p. 159; Carmichael, op. cit. (1900) p. 199, 204; Scott, op. cit., p. 42; Grieve, op. cit., p. 165.

3. Grigson, op. cit., p. 223; Tóibín, op. cit. (1955) p. 48; Cameron, op. cit., p. 147.

4. Moloney, op. cit., p. 26; Scott, op. cit., p. 46; Vickery, op. cit., p. 283; Grigson, op. cit., p. 215; Blount, op. cit., p. 23.

5. Press, Sutton, & Tebbs, op. cit., p. 175; Vickery, op. cit., p. 378, p. 90.

6. Vickery, op. cit., p. 90.

7. Grigson, op. cit., p. 210.

8. Ibid, p. 216.

9. Stokes, op. cit. (1868) p. 10; Williams, op. cit., p. 122.

10. Press, Sutton, & Tebbs, op. cit., p. 180.

11. Allen & Hatfield, op. cit., p. 188.

12. Ibid, op. cit., p. 191.

13. Ui Chonchubhair, op. cit., p. 157.

14. Allen & Hatfield, op. cit., p. 184, p. 186.

15. Ibid, p. 183.

16. Grigson, op. cit., p. 217; Vickery, op. cit., p. 313.

17. Grigson, op. cit., p. 351.

18. Grigson, p. 258; Grieve, op. cit., p. 828.

Forget-me-not

1. Vêtvicka, op. cit., p. 164.

2. Grigson, op. cit., pp. 283-4.

3. Ibid, p. 284; Blount, op. cit., p. 4.

4. Grieve, op. cit., p. 322.

5. Press, Sutton & Tebbs, op. cit., p. 269; Vickery, op. cit., p. 152; Grigson, op. cit., p. 305; Wilde, op. cit. (1991) p. 100; Wilde, op. cit. (1979) p. 69; Moloney, op. cit., p. 36; Allen & Hatfield, op. cit., pp. 258-9.

6. Grigson, op. cit., p. 305; O'Rahilly, op. cit., p. 182; O'Keeffe, op. cit., p. 23, 25, 71, 117; Allen & Hatfield, op. cit., p. 260.

Mullein

1. Scott, op. cit., p. 108; Gregory, op. cit. (1970) p. 247; Frazer, op. cit., p. 629; Seymour, op. cit., p. 92; Grieve, op. cit., p. 564.

2. Scott, op. cit., p. 108.

3. Toibín, op. cit. (1955) p. 23; Seymour, op. cit., p. 91.

4. Seymour, op. cit., p. 91.

5. Ibid, op. cit., p. 92.

6. Allen & Hatfield, op. cit., p. 250; Vickery, op. cit., p. 251.

7. Allen & Hatfield, op. cit., p. 251.

8. Press, Sutton, & Tebbs, op. cit., p. 139; Williams, op. cit., p. 112, p. 114; Allen & Hatfield, op. cit., p. 146, 148.

9. Press, Sutton & Tebbs, op. cit., p. 60; Williams, op. cit., p. 30.

Orchid

1. Williams, op. cit., pp. 110-1; Vickery, op. cit., p. 117; McNeill, op. cit., p. 83; Grieve, op. cit., p. 603.

2. Blount, op. cit., p. 20; Cameron, op. cit., p. 142.

3. Grieve, op. cit., p. 604.

4. Williams, op. cit, p. 108.

5. Grigson, op. cit., p. 426; Scott, op. cit., p. 69.

6. Williams, op. cit., p. 111.

7. Grieve, op. cit., pp. 603-4; Allen & Hatfield, op. cit., p. 334.

8. Grieve, op. cit., p. 673.

9. Grigson, op. cit., p. 306; Allen & Hatfield, op. cit., p. 262.

Wood Avens

1. Grigson, op. cit., p. 153; Uí Chonchubhair, op. cit., p. 107; Grieve, op. cit., p. 73; Press, Sutton & Tebbs, op. cit., p. 140.

2. Grieve, op. cit., p. 73.

3. Press, Sutton & Tebbs, op. cit., p. 140.

4. Grigson, op. cit., p. 153.

5. Grieve, op. cit., p. 74.

6. Grigson, op. cit., p. 151; Grieve, op. cit., p. 316; Allen & Hatfield, op. cit., p. 144.

7. Dineen, op. cit., p. 785; Williams, op. cit., p. 128; Grigson, op. cit., p. 150; Vickery, op. cit., p. 374.

8. Williams, op. cit., pp. 24-5; Kelly, op. cit. (1997) p. 312; Allen & Hatfield, op. cit. pp. 143-4.

9. Kelly, op. cit. (1997) p. 306; Murphy, op. cit. (1998) pp. 10-19; Murphy, op. cit. (1933) p. 375; Allen & Hatfield, op. cit., p. 146, 352.

Henbane

1. Grieve, op. cit., p. 399; Lamont Brown, op. cit., p. 54; Vêtvicka, op. cit., p. 94; Grigson, op. cit., p. 291-2; Williams, op cit., p. 91.

2. Moloney, op. cit., p. 52.

3. Grieve, op. cit., p. 399.

4. Grieve, op. cit., pp. 397-402; Grigson, op. cit., p. 291; Allen & Hatfield, op. cit., p. 198; Williams, op. cit., p. 92.

5. Ó Súilleabháin, op. cit. (1970) p. 287.

6. Vêtvicka, op. cit., p. 188; Allen & Hatfield, op. cit., p. 197.

7. Grigson, op. cit., p. 294; Uí Chonchubhair, op. cit., p. 190; Allen & Hatfield, op. cit., pp. 198-9.

Daisy

1. Mabey, op. cit. (1996) p. 367; Ó Coigligh, op. cit., p. 168.

2. Uí Chonchubhair, op. cit., p. 215.

3. Wilde, op. cit. (1979) p. 52; Frazer, op. cit., p. 131.

4. Dinneen, op. cit., p. 1034; Vickery, op. cit., p. 101.

5. Opie & Tatum, op. cit., p. 115.

6. Mackenzie, op. cit., p. 178.

7. Grieve, op. cit., p. 247.

8. Vickery, op. cit., p. 101; Grigson, op. cit., p. 380; Blount, op. cit., p. 26; Williams, op. cit., p. 135.

9. Seymour, op. cit., p. 15; Frazer, op. cit., p. 631.

10. Cameron, op. cit., p. 58.

11. Grieve, op. cit., p. 248.

12. Grieve, op. cit., pp. 247-8; Allen & Hatfield, op. cit., pp. 294-5, 306.

13. Grieve, op. cit., p. 185; Allen & Hatfield, op. cit., pp. 303-4.

14. Allen & Hatfield, op. cit., p. 172.

15. Allen & Hatfield, op. cit., p. 92; Grigson, op. cit., p. 91.

16. Grigson, op. cit., p. 92.

17. Wilde, op. cit. (1888) p. 232; Wilde, op. cit. (1991) p. 100; Grieve, op. cit., p. 291; Allen & Hatfield, op. cit., p. 260.

Centaury

1. Ó Súilleabháin, op. cit. (1970) p. 327.

2. Uí Chonchubhair, op. cit., p. 173.

3. Williams, op. cit., p. 58.

4. Ibid, p. 57.

5. Cameron, op. cit., p. 68.

6. Williams, op. cit., p. 56.

7. Grieve, op. cit., p. 183.

8. Ibid, p. 183.

9. Allen & Hatfield, op. cit., p. 195.

10. Grieve, op. cit., p. 183; Allen & Hatfield, op. cit., pp. 194-5.

11. Allen & Hatfield, op. cit., p. 195; Grieve, op. cit., p. 350.

Devil's-Bit Scabious

1. Williams, op. cit., p. 137; Gregory, op. cit. (1970) p. 156.

2. Williams, op. cit., p. 137; Grigson, op. cit., p. 362.

3. Grigson, op. cit., p. 362.

4. Ibid, p. 362.

5. Grigson, op. cit., p. 362; Grieve, op. cit., p. 722; Allen & Hatfield, op. cit., p. 278.

6. Grigson, op. cit., p. 361; Press, Sutton & Tebbs, op. cit., p. 322.

7. Allen & Hatfield, op. cit., pp. 275-6.

8. Grigson, op. cit., p. 264; Allen & Hatfield, op. cit., p. 100.

Thistle

1. Vickery, op. cit., p. 369.

2. Share, op. cit., p. 153.

3. Flanagan & Flanagan, op. cit., p. 212.

4. Gregory, op. cit. (1994) p. 211; Jackson, op. cit., p. 46; Gantz, op. cit. (1981) p. 207.

5. Cameron, op. cit., p. 52.

6. Vickery, op. cit., p. 370.

7. Mabey, op. cit. (1996) p. 455.

8. Grigson, op. cit., p. 389.
9. Allen & Hatfield, op. cit., p. 283; Grieve, op. cit., p. 800.
10. Grieve, op. cit., p. 795; Tóibín, op. cit. (1955) p. 61.
11. Williams, op. cit., p. 82.
12. Vickery, op. cit., p. 209; Allen & Hatfield, op. cit., p 284.
13. Vêtvicka, op. cit., p. 58; Grigson, op. cit., p. 390.
14. Vickery, op. cit., p. 53; Allen & Hatfield, op. cit., p. 280, 282.
15. Grigson, op. cit., p. 393; Allen & Hatfield, op. cit., p. 286.
16. Allen & Hatfield, op. cit., p. 182.

Plantain
1. Gregory, op. cit. (1970) p. 148, 150; Uí Chonchubhair, op. cit., p. 207; Williams, op. cit., p. 163; Tóibín, op. cit. (1955) p. 104.
2. O'Regan, op. cit., p. 109; Vickery, op. cit., p. 311.
3. Vickery, op. cit., p. 312.
4. Grigson, op. cit., p. 332.
5. Ibid, p. 332.
6. P. Harbison, *Pre-Christian Ireland* (London, 1988) p. 28; Grieve, op cit., p. 641.
7. Grieve, op. cit., p. 640; Logan, op. cit., p. 87; Vickery, op. cit., p. 161, 312.
8. Allen & Hatfield, op. cit., p. 248.
9. Ibid, p. 248.

Lady's Mantle
1. Williams, op. cit., pp. 51-2.
2. Press, Sutton, & Tebbs, op. cit., p. 141; Wickham, op. cit., p. 58.
3. Grigson, op. cit., p. 158; Press, Sutton, & Tebbs, op. cit., p. 141; Cameron, op. cit., p. 30.
4. Allen & Hatfield, op. cit., p. 150.
5. Press, Sutton, & Tebbs, op. cit., p. 156; Grigson, op. cit., pp. 192-3; Mabey, op. cit (1996) p. 125; Williams, op. cit., p. 64; Allen & Hatfield, op. cit., p. 110; Cameron, op. cit., p. 10.

Poppy
1. Dinneen, op. cit., p. 217.
2. Vickery, op. cit., pp. 286-7; Waring, op. cit., p. 179.
3. Opie & Tatum, op. cit., p. 325; Mabey, op. cit. (1996) p. 51; Grigson, op. cit., p. 50.
4. Grigson, op. cit., p. 50.
5. Vêtvicka, op. cit., p. 164.
6. Mabey, op. cit. (1996) p. 51; Grigson, op. cit., p. 48.
7. Vickery, op. cit., p. 288.
8. Ibid, pp. 288-9.

9. Grieve, op. cit., p. 651.
10. Allen & Hatfield, op. cit., p. 78.
11. Ibid, p. 78.
12. Ibid, p. 77.
13. Ibid, p. 78.
14. Grieve, op. cit., p. 179.
15. Vêtvicka, op. cit., p. 46.

Vetch

1. Toibín, op. cit. (1955) p. 104; Grigson, op. cit., p. 674.
2. Grigson, op. cit., p. 139; Vickery, op. cit., p. 368.
3. Flanagan & Flanagan, op. cit., p. 245.
4. Ó hÓgáin, op. cit., pp. 394-5; O'Keeffe, p. 23, p. 117.
5. Murphy, op. cit. (1998) pp. 10-19.
6. Grigson, op. cit., p. 140.
7. Cameron, op. cit., pp. 22-3.
8. Allen & Hatfield, op. cit., p. 161.
9. Vickery, op. cit., p. 310.
10. Allen & Hatfield, op. cit., p. 161.
11. Grieve, op. cit., p. 526; Grigson, op. cit., p. 132.
12. Vickery, op. cit., p. 33.
13. Grigson, op. cit., pp. 51-2; Cameron, op. cit., p. 5; Allen & Hatfield, op. cit, pp. 80-1; Vickery, op. cit., p. 143.

Fungi

1. Ó hÓgáin, op. cit., p. 270; Ó Súilleabháin, op. cit. (1966) pp. 179-81.
2. Cameron, op. cit., p. 132.
3. Opie & Tatum, op. cit, p. 271.
4. Opie & Tatum, op. cit., p. 146; Vickery, op. cit., p. 130; MacGregor, op. cit., p. 2.
5. P. Harding, T. Lyon, & G. Tomblin, *How to Identify Edible Mushrooms*, (London, 1996), p. 146.
6. Wilde, op. cit. (1979) p. 134.
7. Harding, Lyon & Tomblin, op. cit., p. 34.
8. Ibid, p. 79.
9. Cameron, op. cit., p. 132, Harding, Lyon & Tomblin, op. cit., pp. 68-9; MacGregor, op. cit., p. 33.
10. J. Ramsbottom, *Mushrooms & Toadstools* (Collins, London) pp. 181-2; Vickery, op. cit., p. 361.
11. Graves, op. cit., p. 45.
12. Jackson, op. cit., p. 46; Gantz, op. cit. (1981) p. 207; Stokes, op. cit. (1868) p. 21.
13. Gantz, op. cit. (1976) p. 101.

14. Allen & Hatfield, op. cit., p. 50.
15. Harding, op. cit., p. 34.
16. Allen & Hatfield, op. cit., p. 50; Logan, op. cit., p. 86.
17. Harding, Lyon & Tomblin, op. cit., p. 68.

Lords-and-Ladies
1. Grigson, op. cit., p. 430; Vickery, op. cit., p. 224.
2. Williams, op. cit., p. 35.
3. Grieve, op. cit., p. 237.
4. Vickery, op. cit., p. 225.
5. Williams, op. cit., p. 37.
6. Ibid, p. 38.

Spurge
1. Ó Súilleabháin, op. cit. (1970) p. 474; P.J. Westropp, *Folklore of Clare* (Ennis, 2000) p. 66.
2. Allen & Hatfield, op. cit., p. 170.
3. Williams, op. cit., pp. 10-12; Logan, op. cit., p. 33.
4. Williams, op. cit., p. 202.

Crane's-bill
1. Press, Sutton & Tebbs, op. cit., p. 103; Blount, op. cit., p. 25; Grigson, op. cit., pp. 105-6; Allen & Hatfield, op. cit., pp. 175-6.

Butterbur
1. Grieve, op. cit., p. 148; Allen & Hatfield, op. cit. pp. 311-2.

Wild Plants and the Zodiac
1. P. Beresford Ellis, *Dictionary of Celtic Mythology* (London, 1992) p. 35.

Postscript
1. Frazer, op. cit., p. 581; Grieve, op. cit., p. 88, p. 783.
2. Grieve, op. cit., p. 488, p. 531; Frazer, op. cit., pp. 486-7.

Bibliography

Allen, D. & Hatfield, G. (2004) *Medicinal Plants in Folk Tradition*, Timber Press, Cambridge & Portland, Oregon

An Roinn Oideachais (Department of Education) (1978) *Ainmneacha Plandaí agus Ainmhithe*, Oifig an tSoláthair, Baile Átha Cliath

Archer, P. (1975) *Fair Fingall*, An Taisce, Fingal

Becker, H. (1997) *I mBéal na Farraige: Scéalta agus Seanchas faoi Chursaí Feamainne ó Bhéal na nDaoine*, Cló Iar-Chonnachta, Galway

Beecher, S. (1983) *A Dictionary of Cork Slang*, The Collins Press, Cork

Beresford Ellis, P. (1992) *Dictionary of Celtic Mythology*, Constable & Co., London

Blamey, M., Fitter, R. & Fitter, A. (2003) *Wild Flowers of Britain & Ireland*, A. & C. Black, London

Blount, D. (1931) *Consider the Lilies of the Fields: Flowers in Sacred Legend and Tradition*, Dublin

Branch Johnson, W. (1972) *Folktales of Brittany*, Methuen & Co. Ltd., London

Cameron, J. (1900) 'The Gaelic Names of Plants', *Celtic Monthly*, Glasgow

Carmichael, A. (1900, 1928, 1940, 1941) *Carmina Gadelica Vols 1- 5*, Edinburgh

Challinor, H. (1999) *A Beginner's Guide to Ireland's Seashore*, Sherkin Island

Crossley Holland, K. (1980) *The Penguin Book of Norse Myths*, London

Culpeper, N., *Culpeper's Complete Herbal*, Foulsham & Co. Ltd

Curran, B. (1999) *The Wolfhound Guide to the Shamrock*, Wolfhound Press, Dublin

Curtin, J. (1890) *Myths and Folktales of Ireland*, Dover Publications, (1975) New York

(1894) *Hero Tales of Ireland*, Macmillan Press, London

Danaher, K. (1972) *The Year in Ireland – Irish Calender Customs*, Mercier Press, Cork

Dinneen, P.S. (1927) *Foclóir Gaedhilge agus Béarla*, Irish Texts Society, Dublin

Dolan, T.P. (1998) *A Dictionary of Hiberno-English*, Gill & McMillan Ltd, Dublin

Dolan, T.P. & Ó Muirithe, D. (1996) *The Dialect of Forth & Bargy, County Wexford*, Four Courts Press, Dublin

Evans, J.G. (1915) *The Poems of Taliesin*, Llanbedrog

Fenton, J. (1995) *The Hamely Tongue*, Ulster Scots Academic Press, Newtownards

Flanagan, D. & Flanagan, L. (1994) *Irish Place Names*, Gill and Macmillan, Dublin

Fleetwood, J. (1983) *The History of Medicine in Ireland*, The Skellig Press, Dublin

Frazer, J.G. (1922) *The Golden Bough*, The Macmillan Press Ltd, London (1987)

Gantz, J. (1981) *Early Irish Myths and Sagas*, Penguin Books, London/(1976) *The Mabinogion*, Penguin Books, London

Gerald of Wales (1982) *The History and Topography of Ireland*, Penguin Books, London

Graves, R. (1948) *The White Goddess*, Faber & Faber (1961), London

Green, M. (1992) *Dictionary of Celtic Myth and Legend*, Thames and Hudson, London

Gregory, Lady A., (1902, 1904) *Complete Irish Mythology*, The Slaney Press (1994) London

Gregory, Lady A., (1920) *Visions & Beliefs in the West of Ireland*, Colin Smythe (1970) Toronto

Grieve, M. (1931) *A Modern Herbal*, Jonathan Cape Ltd

Grigson, G. (1958) *The Englishman's Flora*, Helicon Publishing Ltd, Oxford (1996)

Gwynn, E. (1903, 1906, 1913, 1924, 1935) *The Metrical Dindshenchus*, Dublin

Gwynn Jones, T. (1930) *Welsh Folklore and Custom*, Methuen & Co. Ltd., London

Harbison, P. (1988) *Pre-Christian Ireland*, Thames and Hudson, London

Harding, P. (1996) *Collins Gem Mushrooms*, HarperCollins, Glasgow

Harding, P., Lyon, T., Tomblin, G. (1996) *How to Identify Edible Mushrooms*, HarperCollins, London

Hawkes, K. (1973) *Cornish Sayings, Superstitions & Remedies*, Penzance

Innes, Sir Thomas (1963) *The Scottish Tartans*, Johnston and Bacon, Stirling

Jackson, K. (1971) *A Celtic Miscellany*, Penguin Books, London

Kelly F. (1976) 'The Old Irish Tree List' *Celtica Vol XI*, Dublin (1997) *Early Irish Farming*, Dublin Institute for Advanced Studies

Kendrick, T.D. (1927) *The Druids*, Methuen & Co. Ltd, London

Killip, M., (1975) *The Folklore of the Isle of Man*, B.T. Batsford Ltd., London

Lamont Brown, R. (1970) *A Book of Superstitions*, David and Charles Ltd, Devon

Le Braz, A. (1912) *The Night of Fires & Other Breton Studies*, Chapman & Hall Ltd., London

Lippert, W. & Podlech, D. (2001) *Wild Flowers of Britain and Europe*, HarperCollins, London

Logan, P. (1981) *Irish Country Cures*, Appletree Press, Belfast

Lucas, A.T. (1960) 'Furze: A Survey of its History and Uses in Ireland', *Béaloideas* 26, Dublin (1963) 'The Sacred Trees of Ireland', *Journal of the Cork Historical and Archaeological Society* 68, pp. 16-54

Mabey, R. (1977) *Plants with a Purpose*, William Collins Sons & Co. Ltd, London
(1996) *Flora Brittanica*, Sinclair-Stevenson, London
Macalister, R.A.S. (1937) *The Secret Languages of Ireland*, Cambridge University Press
(1940) *Lebor Gabála Eirenn Part 3*, Irish Texts Society, Dublin
Mac Coitir, N. (2003) *Irish Trees: Myths, Legends and Folklore*, The Collins Press, Cork
McCullough, J.A. (1911) *The Religion of the Ancient Celts*, T. & T. Clark, Edinburgh
MacGregor, A.A. (1937) *The Peat Fire Flame*, The Moray Press, Edinburgh
MacKenzie, D.A. (1935) *Scottish Folklore and Folk Life*, Blackie & Sons Ltd., Edinburgh
MacNeill, E. (1908) *Duanaire Finn*, Irish Texts Society, Dubblin
MacNeill, M. (1962) *The Festival of Lughnasa*, Oxford
McManus, D. (1988) 'Irish letter-names and their kennings', *Ériu* 39, pp. 127-168, Dublin
McNeill, M. (1957) *The Silver Bough Vol. 1*, William McLellan, Glasgow
Moloney, M. (1919) *Luibh-Sheanchus – Irish Ethno-botany*, M.H. Gill & Son, Dublin
Murphy, G. (1933) *Duanaire Finn Part II*, Irish Texts Society, London
(1998) *Early Irish Lyrics*, Four Courts Press, Dublin
Nelson, C. (1991) *Shamrock: Botany and History of an Irish Myth*, Boethius Press, Kilkenny & Aberystwyth
Ní Lamhna, E. (2002) *Talking Wild – Wildlife on the Radio*, Townhouse & Countryhouse Ltd, Dublin
Ní Shéaghdha, N. (1967) *Toruigheacht Diarmaid agus Gráinne*, Irish Texts Society, Dublin
Ó Coigligh, C. *Seanchas Inis Meáin*, Coiscéim Press, Dublin
Ó Cróinín, S. (1985) *Seanchas ó Cairbre*, Dublin
O'Daly, M. (1975) *Cath Maige Mucrama*, Irish Texts Society, Dublin
Ó Donaill, N. (1977) *Foclóir Gaeilge – Béarla*, Oifig an tSoláthair, Dublin
O'Farrell, P. (2004) *Irish Customs*, Gill and McMillan, Dublin
O'Farrell, P. (2004) *Irish Folk Cures*, Gill and McMillan, Dublin
O'Grady, S. (1892) *Silva Gadelica*, Williams and Norgate, London
Ó hEochaidh, S., Ní Néill, M., Ó Catháin, S. (1977) *Síscéalta ó Tír Chonaill*, Dublin
Ó hÓgáin, D. (1991) *Myth, Legend and Romance – An Encyclopaedia of the Irish Folk Tradition*, Prentice Hall Press, New York
O'Keefe, J.G. (1913) *Buile Suibhne*, Irish Texts Society, Dublin
O' Rahilly, C. (1967) *Táin Bó Cúalnge*, Irish Texts Society Dublin
O'Regan, P. (1997) *Healing Herbs in Ireland*, Primrose Press, Dublin
Ó Súilleabháin, S. (1966) *Folktales of Ireland*, University of Chicago Press

Ó Súilleabháin, S. (1967) *Irish Folk Custom and Belief*, Cultural Relations Committee of Ireland, Dublin

Ó Súilleabháin, S. (1970) *A Handbook of Irish Folklore*, Singing Tree Press, Detroit

Ó Súilleabháin, S. (1974) *The Folklore of Ireland*, B.T. Batsford Ltd., London

O'Sullivan, S. (1977) *Legends from Ireland*, B.T. Batsford Ltd., London

Opie, I. & Tatum, M. (eds) (1989) *A Dictionary of Superstitions*, Oxford

Owen, T. (1959) *Welsh Folk Customs*, National Museum of Wales

Pilcher, J. & Hall, V. (2001) *Flora Hibernica*, The Collins Press, Cork

Praeger, R.L. (1934) *The Botanist in Ireland*, Hodges Figgis & Co., Dublin

Press, J.R., Sutton, Dr D.A. & Tebbs, B.R. (1981) *Reader's Digest Field Guide to the Wild Flowers of Britain*, London

Ramsbottom, J. *Mushrooms and Toadstools*, Collins New Naturalist Series, London

Rees A. and Rees B. (1961) *Celtic Heritage*, Thames and Hudson, London

Scannell, M. & Synnott, D. (1987) *Census Catalogue of the Flora of Ireland*, Stationary Office, Dublin

Scott, M. (Ed) (1986) *An Irish Herbal: The Botanalogia Universalis by John K'eogh*, Aquarian Press, Northamptonshire

Seymour, M. (2002) *A Brief History of Thyme*, John Murray Ltd., London

Share, B. (1997) *Slanguage – a Dictionary of Irish Slang*, Gill & McMillan Ltd., Dublin

Smyth, D. (1988) *A Guide to Irish Mythology*, Irish Academic Press, Dublin

Stokes, W. (1868) *Cormac's Glossary*, Calcutta

(1887) *Tripartite Life of St Patrick*, London

(1890) *Lives of the Saints from the Book of Lismore*, Clarendon Press, Oxford

(1900) *Agallamh na Senórach*, Irische Texte, Leipzig

Threkeld, C. (1727) *Synopsis Stirpium Hibernicarum*, Dublin

Todd, L. (1990) *Words Apart: A Dictionary of Northern Irish English*, Colin Smythe Ltd, Gerrard's Cross

Tóibín, S. (1955) *Blátha an Bhóithrín*, Oifig an tSoláthair, Baile Átha Cliath

Tóibín, S. (1967) *Troscán na mBánta*, Oifig an tSoláthair, Baile Átha Cliath

Uí Chonchubhair, M. (1995) *Flóra Chorca Dhuibhne*, Oidhreacht Chorca Dhuibhne, Contae Chiarraí

Vêtvicka, V. (1979) *A Hamlyn Colour Guide to Wildflowers of Field and Woodland*, Hamlyn, Prague

Vickery, R. (1995) *A Dictionary of Plant Lore*, Oxford University Press

Wade Evans, A.W. (1909) *Welsh Medieval Law*, Oxford

Waring, P. (1978) *A Dictionary of Omens and Superstitions*, Souvenir Press, London

Webb, D. (1959) *An Irish Flora*, Dundalgan Press, Dundalk

Westropp, P.J. (2000) *Folklore of Clare*, Clasp Press, Ennis

Wickham, C. (1981) *Common Plants as Natural Remedies*, Frederick Muller

Ltd, London

Wilde, Lady (1888) *Ancient Legends, Mystic Charms and Superstitions of Ireland*, Ward & Downey, London
(1991) *Irish Cures, Mystic Charms and Superstitions*, Sterling Publishing, New York

Wilde, W. (1853) *Irish Popular Superstitions*, Irish Academic Press, (1979) Dublin

Williams, N. (1993) *Díolaim Luibheanna*, Sáirséal-Ó Marcaigh Teor. B.Á.C.

Wood Martin, W.G. (1902) *Traces of the Elder Faiths of Ireland*, London

Wulff, W. (ed) (1929) *Rosa Anglica by John of Gaddesden*, Irish Texts Society, London

Index of Plant Names in English

Index of Plant Names in Irish